HARUN FAROCKI

HARUN FAROCKI

Forms of Intelligence

Nora M. Alter

Columbia University Press
New York

Columbia University Press
Publishers Since 1893
New York   Chichester, West Sussex
cup.columbia.edu
Copyright © 2024 Columbia University Press
All rights reserved

Library of Congress Cataloging-in-Publication Data
Names: Alter, Nora M., 1962- author.
Title: Harun Farocki : forms of intelligence / Nora M. Alter.
Description: New York : Columbia University Press, [2024] | Includes bibliographical references and index.
Identifiers: LCCN 2023055074 (print) | LCCN 2023055075 (ebook) |
   ISBN 9780231215497 (hardback) | ISBN 9780231215503 (trade paperback) |
   ISBN 9780231560825 (ebook)
Subjects: LCSH: Farocki, Harun—Criticism and interpretation. |
   Independent filmmakers—Germany—Biography.
Classification: LCC PN1998.3.F365 A58 2024 (print) | LCC PN1998.3.F365 (ebook) |
   DDC 791.4302/33092 [B]—dc23/eng/20240206
LC record available at https://lccn.loc.gov/2023055074
LC ebook record available at https://lccn.loc.gov/2023055075

Cover design: Elliott S. Cairns
Cover image: Courtesy of Andreas Siekmann

For all those past, present, and future who have been touched by Harun Farocki's forms of intelligence

Harun Farocki. Courtesy of Nora M. Alter

For Europe, for ourselves, and for humanity, comrades, we must turn over a new leaf, we must work out new concepts, and try to set afoot a new man.

—Frantz Fanon, *The Wretched of the Earth* (1961),
cited by Harun Farocki in his *The Campaign Volunteer* (1967)

Contents

Acknowledgments xi

Introduction: Farocki Through Time   1

1. Critique and Montage   23
2. Labor   54
3. Critic as Filmmaker   111
4. War   140
5. An Image Lexicon, or Towards a Media Archeology   179

Notes 197

Writings by Harun Farocki 217

Filmography 221

Installations by Harun Farocki 235

Critical Bibliography 241

Index 249

Acknowledgments

Many voices and individuals have contributed to this book on Harun Farocki. Their words, thoughts, and images over the decades have informed the writing of my text. Sadly, some are no longer with us, as is the subject of my text: Harun Farocki. First, my greatest debt goes to Harun—a friend, thinker, and community builder. Farocki thought through and with images. He was modest, undervaluing his influence and impact on an ever growing number of media makers and artists. He was also generous, circulating ideas, teaching, ensuring that his work was readily available, and making connections between people. My book is in gratitude to Farocki as a filmmaker and writer who placed images and texts into new constellations of meaning.

Richard Herskowitz, the director of Cornell Cinema, brought the work of Harun Farocki to my attention while I was a postdoc at Cornell University in the 1990s. He had a videotape distributed by Chris Hoover of Drift Video that he thought might be of interest to me. Indeed, that video, *Bilder der Welt und Inschrift des Krieges* (Images of the World and the Inscription of War, 1988), was unlike any other film I had seen, and it immediately sparked my interest in Farocki's work. Thus began an intellectual journey with Farocki, that extended over the decades. The Goethe Institute supported Farocki through events such as screenings and symposia, and our paths crossed frequently as they did with the growing number of Farocki aficionados. A generous grant from the Max Kade Institute awarded Farocki a visiting professorship at the University of Florida where we team taught for one semester. That experience proved invaluable, for it exposed me to Farocki's pedagogical side and his method of teaching how images work and make arguments. During that semester I also met Farocki's partner

Antje Ehmann. After Harun, my second biggest thanks go to Antje. Without her generosity and support this book would not have been possible. During the last phase of his career, Farocki's most important collaborator was Ehmann, and his installations and artistic practice bear her signature. During my research, Ehmann opened Farocki's personal archives, provided me with full access to his works and materials, and assisted and clarified when necessary. She has done tireless work in organizing his materials, facilitating exhibitions, and continuing their joint project *Eine Einstellung zur Arbeit* (Labour in a Single Shot). In large part, *Harun Farocki: Forms of Intelligence* is dedicated to her.

The thoughts and ideas expressed in this book come out of years of exchange with Farocki and his circle of friends. Many evenings in Berlin were spent conversing around Harun and Antje's kitchen table on Pfaarstrasse. A tight group of interlocutors formed—writers, scholars, artists—whose words circulate through this text. These include Raymond Bellour, Christa Blümlinger, Alice Creischer, Diedrich Diederichsen, Thomas Elsaesser, Anna and Lara Faroqhui, Gertrud Koch, Tom Holert, Volker Pantenburg, Constanze Ruhm, Andreas Sieckmann, Hito Steyerl, and others. Over the years we debated the role of media and its possibilities, and I am thankful to have been part of the conversation.

On both sides of the Atlantic, colleagues and friends have provided me with support for the project in many ways including opportunities to present my research through public lectures, symposia, workshops, fellowships, and early publications. The feedback and conversations have been invaluable. I would like to thank Hakim Abderrezak, Marco Abel, Javier Anguera, Tom Conley, Timothy Corrigan, Okwui Enwezor, Kodwo Eshun, Jaimey Fisher, Florian Fuchs, Anselm Franke, Renée Green, Cassandra Guan, Sir Isaac Julien, Tony Kaes, Lutz Koepnick, Homay King, Kevin B. Lee, Thomas Levin, Aaron Levy, Mark Nash, Bradley Prager, Gerald Prince, Eric Rentschler, D. N. Rodowick, and Kaja Silverman. In Philadelphia, my writing group provided me with crucial feedback on the structure and organization of my ideas: Chris Cagle, Suzanne Gauch, Kathleen Karlyn, Kartik Nair, and Will Schmenner all helped to make this a better book. A special thanks goes to Ron Clark, director of the Whitney Independent Study Program for fifty-five years where both Farocki and I taught. The critically intense nature of the seminars and the international group of artists and scholars that gathered there provided me with an invaluable pedagogical setting to discuss my understanding of Farocki's contributions to global media making.

The impetus to write this book came from Louis Massiah. Shortly after Farocki's death, Louis asked me, what type of films did Farocki make? What was his practice? As I rambled on trying to cover all the facets of Farocki's production, Louis stopped me and asked if there was a comprehensive publication in English that covered Farocki's oeuvre. I stumbled and realized there wasn't. At which point, he told me that I should write one. Thank you, Louis!

Material support for this project has been provided by several institutions. First, I would like to thank Temple University and the Center for the Cinematic and Performing Arts for providing me with research funds and generous leave time. A residential fellowship at the American Academy in Berlin allowed me to complete my research during a restricted time of travel due to Covid. The Academy kept its doors open and the staff made sure that the residents were afforded the best possible stay under the circumstances. Finally, an award of the Andy Warhol Foundation Arts Writer Grant was invaluable and came at a crucial transitional writing moment.

I also want to acknowledge two Berlin-based institutions and express my deepest gratitude to the individuals associated with them. These are the Harun Farocki Institut (HaFI) founded shortly after his death, and the Neue Berliner Kunstverein (n.b.k.). Tom Holert and Volker Pantenburg at HaFI have assisted me in so many ways, from supplying me with rare films, texts, and unpublished materials, to serving as important interlocutors over the years. Marius Babius, director of the n.b.k., is to be commended for his unwavering support in seeing through to the end the publication of the edited volumes of Farocki's collected writings. I would not have been able to write my text without these tomes and they will be an invaluable resource for future researchers. Marius once jokingly asked me why it was taking me so long to write my book. "Because you keep publishing more of Farocki's texts," I quipped back.

I would like to thank Sofia Rabaté for assisting me with compiling the bibliographies and Anna Corrigan for the index. In addition, I bear Kathryn Jorge and the staff of Columbia University Press gratitude, as well as the anonymous readers. I would like to give a special thanks to my editor, Philip Leventhal, who believed in the project and shepherded it through every stage, keeping to a timely and efficient schedule. Since I began working with Philip, I have continuously been impressed by his knowledge of the field, intellectual insights, professional acumen, and patience. I am very grateful he took an interest in this book.

Finally, to those of my most intimate circle who have been part of the journey with Harun: Michelle, who prepared delicious meals for us to enjoy and later provided me with a quiet haven in which to write; my daughters, Arielle and Zoë, who endured many long evenings of conversations and screenings; and Alex Alberro, for whom Harun was a special friend and interlocutor—thank you for your patience and support.

Introduction

Farocki Through Time

Once again, there is an interplay between image and text in the writing of history: texts that should make the images accessible, and images that should make the texts imaginable.

—Harun Farocki, "Reality Would Have to Begin"

When he died unexpectedly at seventy on July 30, 2014, Harun Farocki was one of Germany's most celebrated international contemporary artists. Leading art journals such as *e-flux*, *Artforum*, *October*, *Texte zur Kunst*, and *Trafic* quickly disseminated news of his death. Obituaries and homages proliferated. Writers from around the world described him as an "art star." This status was relatively new, however. For the first two-thirds of his career, Farocki worked in the margins of the culture industry, making independent films and commissions for television, and writing film criticism. He long identified as an experimental filmmaker, despite having made a feature film, and referred to himself as the "best known, unknown filmmaker in Germany."[1]

In the fall of 1973, when visiting New York City for the first time, Farocki was asked what sort of films he made. As he recounts in his posthumously published autobiography *Zehn, zwanzig, dreißig, vierzig* (Ten, Twenty, Thirty, Forty), "Even today the answer [to the question of what sort of films I make] does not come easily because I fear that the person who posed the question does not have a category for the type of films I make. It is uncomfortable for me to make something that practically no one can imagine."[2] Writing some thirty years after he was initially confronted with the question, having made close to a hundred completed films and videos, Farocki still had trouble formulating an adequate response. His inability to locate his filmic production within established genres is a problem this book sets out to address. Broadly speaking, one could argue that Farocki made nonfiction films and within that modality oscillated between documentary and essay films. There is one exception to this taxonomy, though, which is his feature genre film *Betrogen* (Betrayed, (1985). My project seeks to understand Farocki's oeuvre. It tracks developments and shifts in an artistic practice that spanned close to half a century and extended across multiple media, including film, video, television, radio, art, and writing.

Farocki's creative activity culminated in an enormous output comprising over one hundred works of varying length, format, and media, including fifty-five analog films. The years from his first film in 1966 to his last art installation in 2014 saw significant changes in the media employed by independent filmmakers. These ranged from the preferred Super 8 and 16 mm of the 1960s and early 1970s, to videotape in the later 1970s and 1980s, digital formats in the 1990s and early 2000s, and art installations in the twenty-first century. Viewing platforms and venues also evolved from movie theaters to television sets, art galleries to multi-channel screens. Farocki's work changed with these developments. He mastered the novel forms, always mindful of how each new medium came with its own set of possibilities and styles. As he explained in a lecture in 1999, "Even in the days when film reigned, technical advancement always had stylistic implications: one only needed to consider portable cameras, the *blimped* camera, the zoom lens. But today there are technical advances nearly every year, which produce, in turn, stylistic proclivities."[3]

Farocki was largely unknown outside of West Germany prior to the 1990s. Within West Germany, his reputation was that of an outsider. Most found his family name unpronounceable. This awkwardness led him to change it from Harun El Usman Faroqhi to Harun Farocki to facilitate pronunciation and diminish its Muslim connotations.[4] Still, even his new monicker was unusual in a country with strict naming regulations.[5] It inevitably led critics to exoticize his origins and identify him with multiple nationalities, including Egyptian, Persian, Turkish, Indonesian, and Indian. Such myths reinforced Farocki's foreignness and underscored his outsider status. They also mischaracterized an artist who identified as German all his life.

Farocki was born in 1944 in "Neutitschein" (today Nový Jičín) in the Reich-annexed territory of Czechoslovakia. His mother, Lili Draugelattis Faroqhi, had left Berlin in an advanced stage of pregnancy to escape that year's many bombing raids. His father, Abdul Qudus Faroqhi, had immigrated to Germany from India in the 1920s. He was a private physician and follower of Subhas Chandra Bose, the Indian nationalist leader who forged an alliance with the Axis powers in his disdain for British colonialism. Abdul Faroqhi was a willing follower of the Third Reich until its collapse at the war's end. In the aftermath of World War II, the Faroqhi family hurriedly relocated to Indonesia for six years before returning to Bad Godesberg near Bonn in the early 1950s, where the paterfamilias set up a private practice. As Farocki reveals in his autobiography, his father embraced fascist ideals and was highly authoritarian. He was also physically abusive, meting out corporal punishment to maintain order. These personal details position Farocki within a generation of filmmakers, writers, artists, and intellectuals who were born in the context of the Third Reich, came of age in the 1950s during West Germany's reconstruction, and vociferously (and sometimes violently) rejected their parents' values in the 1960s. Farocki's generation sought to radicalize West German society and profoundly change its institutions.[6]

"I should have been born in Berlin," Farocki states in "Written Trailers" (2009).[7] He was, above all else, a Berlin filmmaker, having moved to the city in 1962 from Bad Godesberg at eighteen. He was initially drawn to West Berlin because its precarious geographical and political location had spared it the frenzy of the *Wirtschaftswunder* (economic miracle) that reshaped the rest of the country. The island city's isolation depleted its industrial, economic, and political infrastructure, and yet, its cultural sphere thrived. It received a heavy infusion of resources and energy.[8] Accordingly, the city developed a forlorn rawness, a flourishing bohemia, and a counter-cultural public sphere that attracted hippies, draft dodgers, political activists, and artists of all kinds. Farocki lived in Berlin for over fifty years, getting to know it intimately. The city's importance for the filmmaker/artist is difficult to overestimate. Following reunification, he witnessed the transformation of the divided metropolis into an international hipster capital. Farocki became a celebrated figure in this context. He served as a role model for independent filmmakers and helped train a generation of film and media practitioners. He also developed a remarkable practice. Ironically, despite his enormous impact, his first retrospective exhibition, at Berlin's Hamburger Bahnhof Museum for Contemporary Art, did not occur until February 2014, almost fifty years into his career.

As a physician's child, Farocki's upbringing was solidly petit bourgeois. In Bad Godesberg, his family lived in a former villa divided into several apartments. As he recalls, whereas other residents were "simple people," eating "off of cutting boards in the kitchen..., we were taught to eat even the simplest meals including sandwiches at the dining room table with a plate, knife, and fork."[9] His family strictly followed middleclass conventions against which he struggled his entire life. In his homage to Farocki, Raymond Bellour recalls: "In the last e-mail he sent me in Spring 2014, Harun Farocki wrote: 'In order not to become petit-bourgeois, at the age of eighteen, I resolved to do three things at least once a month: physical work, stealing from a store and hitchhiking.'"[10] In his work, Farocki often addresses the subject of codes of behavior that establish one's place and function in society and that one must learn, imitate, and repeat. Despite his middleclass upbringing, his difference in West Germany was inescapable. Not only his name but also his dark hair, eyes, and complexion coded him as "other"—an identity that followed him throughout his career.[11] Farocki's long-time friend and collaborator filmmaker Christian Petzold recalls an uncomfortable encounter during a trip to a swimming pool in the former East. "Harun is half-Indian, my wife Turkish. When we arrived, they confronted us: what do you want here?"[12] This insider/outsider status gave him a double consciousness that, in turn, contributed to his keen awareness of the architecture of societal codes and norms and the role that media, particularly images, play in these discursive constructions.

Farocki's films often question thematic and formal conventions. However, his provocations were not limited to cinema. In 1978, during the Bundes Film Prize awards ceremony, he staged "Finally: Now You Can Meet Harun Farocki."[13] The circus-like action had Farocki poking his head through a large board and taunting passersby to pelt him with a popular German chocolate-covered marshmallow treat alternately referred to as a *N*g*rkuss* or a *Mohrenkopf*.[14] The police quickly stopped the outrageous event and briefly detained Farocki. The negative optics of a German public pelting a dark man with confections labeled in racist terms broke one too many codes.

FILMIC PRACTICE

Farocki's filmic and artistic practice rigorously investigates the structural underpinnings of visual media. His early critiques of television, and advertising images, in productions such as *Die Ärger mit den Bildern: Eine Telekritik von Harun Farocki* (The Trouble with Images: A Critique of Television, 1973), and more recent projects like *Der Ausdruck der Hände* (The Expression of Hands, 1997), *Arbeiter verlassen die Fabrik in elf Jahrzehnten* (Workers Leaving the Factory in Eleven Decades, 2006), and *Parallel I–IV* (2014), all probe the operation of media. (At the beginning of his career, Farocki titled his works in German, many of which were only posthumously translated, however with the increased internationalization of his practice, Farocki increasingly worked in English.)[15] Farocki openly admired the work of media theorists Vilém Flusser, Friedrich Kittler, and Paul Virilio, and more covertly that of philosopher Martin Heidegger. He sought to understand how the media world he lived in functioned. He regularly organized his investigations of images according to elementary criteria. As he explains, images "don't have to be beautiful and don't have to be unique. Sometimes they can be nearly vulgar. But they must always feature tensions, interesting aspects, or contradictory meanings."[16]

We can divide Farocki's oeuvre into three types of media-making that correspond roughly to three phases of his productive life. First, as a student, he made politically engaged films in Super 8 and 16 mm. These films provided a model for committed filmmakers such as Jill Godmilow and Filipa César to follow.[17] This initial period was followed by his work for television and independent film productions that investigated image creation and subjects of labor. Finally, in the last phase, Farocki recalibrated his film practice to develop an artistic career. However, it should also be noted that Farocki served various roles throughout his career including scriptwriter, dramaturg, and "advisor" to numerous filmmakers, amongst those his two-decade long collaboration with Petzold that resulted in a dozen feature films and ended only with Farocki's death.[18]

The short films he made during his student years (1966–1969) at the Deutsche Film- und Fernsehakademie Berlin (DFFB), the newly inaugurated film and television school in West Berlin, called for direct action. Agit-prop techniques characterize productions such as *Der Wahlhelfer* (The Campaign Volunteer, 1967) and *Die Worte des Vorsitzender* (The Words of the Chairman, 1967). Prior to his marriage to Ursula Lefkes and the birth of his twin daughters (Annabel and Larissa) in 1968, Farocki lived in a commune. He was part of a group of student filmmakers, including Hartmut Bitomsky, Holger Meins, Thomas Mitscherlich, Wolfgang Petersen, and Helke Sanders, who occupied the film school and temporarily renamed it the "Dziga Vertov Academy." Farocki was actively involved in protest actions and demonstrations. According to one anecdote, in 1967, he and Sanders infiltrated a formal press ball. There, they confronted media giant Axel Springer holding a placard that stated: "Axel, this is your final ball."[19] Farocki was also a member of the Socialist Film Cooperative. In 1969, he co-authored "Film in Opposition," which addresses how to make cinema after June 2, 1967, a date that for West Germans came to symbolize what May '68 did for the French left.[20] Besides his organizing activities and political actions, Farocki made several films during this period. Some, such as *Nicht löschbares Feuer* (Inextinguishable Fire, 1969) and *White Christmas* (1968), protest the Vietnam War. Others, like *Anleitung, Polizisten den Helm abzurissen* (How to Remove a Police Helmet, 1969), link to the more general spirit of unrest of the late 1960s.

Many film critics focus primarily on these radical activities of the 1960s when addressing Farocki's career. This tendency leads them to canonize him as a "guerrilla filmmaker."[21] In particular, there has been much speculation about Farocki's acquaintance with Meins and, through that association, with the Red Army Faction (RAF). A former member of the RAF, Meins was arrested in 1972 and died in prison two years later during a hunger strike. In one of the last interviews with Farocki, journalist Philip Goll suggests that a covert pursuit of violence connects his early interest in Marxism–Leninism and his filmic collaboration with Meins. Referring to Lin Bao's dictum cited in Farocki's *The Words of the Chairman* that "words have to become weapons," Goll attempts to get Farocki to admit to participating in terrorist activities or having had a formal relationship with the RAF. At one point, he asks: "Did you ever consider throwing more than just a paper bullet?" Farocki's response to such questions was consistent over the decades: "As a filmmaker, one had to find a deeper justification for oneself . . . I had programmed myself to become a film artist." Upon Goll's further pressing, he elaborates: "To join a terrorist organization was out of the question for me at this time. My daughters were born in 1968, and I had completely different concerns."[22]

To position Farocki only as a committed member of a left-wing direct action organization swerves his half-century of media experimentation in the wrong direction. Farocki was a colleague of Meins, whom he admired. The two occasionally collaborated, as did most of the students at the DFFB. In 1998, Farocki addressed his relationship to Meins in "Risking his Life: Images of Holger Meins." He recalls how disgusting he found the widely circulated image of his friend's dead body, with its flesh wasted away by a hunger strike. Farocki feared that this grotesque image would, in the end, be what people remembered of such a talented and highly ethical individual.²³ To correct this impression, he composed a lengthy essay that details, sequence by sequence and shot by shot, Meins's incomplete film *Oskar Langenfeld* (1966). Through this exacting description of the film, Farocki provided a counter-narrative to the mainstream media's presentation of Meins as a spectacular corpse. Farocki's rearticulation of Meins's film reiterates his friend's filmmaking talents and reminds readers of his admirable commitment to social justice. This gesture of generosity, spurred by the belief that film can resummon fading pasts, rectify wrongs, and improve society, typifies much of Farocki's 1960s and early 1970s production.

Farocki turned to television work during the 1970s mainly for socio-economic reasons. West Germany enacted Film Subsidy Laws that allowed independent filmmakers access to local television networks during those years. Unlike the television industry in the United States, in Europe, television networks were public rather than commercial enterprises. They provided independent artists with an important venue for their work.²⁴ Regional networks such as West Deutsche Rundfunk (WDR) provided Farocki with several decades of steady employment.²⁵ He worked non-stop during these years, producing over fifty television programs. Along the way, he mastered the craft and language of television, becoming adept at its formal and thematic conventions. He experimented with narrative, staging, editing, lighting, and acting techniques. His programs included interviews with intellectual luminaries such as Peter Weiss (*Zur Ansicht: Peter Weiss* [On Display: Peter Weiss], 1979) and Flusser (*Schlagworte-Schlagbilder: Ein Gespräch mit Vilém Flusser* [Catch Phrases-Catch Images: A conversation with Vilém Flusser], 1986); focus pieces on a wide variety of topics, such as *Moderatoren im Fernsehen* (Moderators, 1974) and *Peter Lorre: Das Doppelte Gesicht* (The Double Face of Peter Lorre, 1984); and children's shows. Several of the latter featured his daughters, like *Bedtime Stories* (1976–1977) and *Katzengeschichten* (Stories of Cats, 1978). As he recalls, "Throughout the 1970s, WDR was my port of call. [It] was the richest of all the broadcast channels and founded several new divisions with production possibilities. One of these was the division of 'Media Critique.'"²⁶

Farocki appreciated television's role in the public sphere. He sought to create critical political programs that challenged what the medium typically showed and explained how it made those presentations of reality. Although production managers tightly controlled television, some oversights allowed for subversion. As Farocki recollects, "Publicly-owned television was particularly obliging in terms of its negligence." Luckily, he received commissions from "a department whose boss was so wrapped up in his career machinations" that he granted his staff relative freedom.²⁷ Working for the same boss was a remarkable commissioning editor, Werner Dütsch, with whom Farocki maintained a close and respectful working relationship. Dütsch, a filmmaker and writer in his own right, sought to expand the conventional offerings of public television by supporting alternative programming.²⁸ His efforts enabled Farocki to make fifteen films sponsored by broadcast networks, beginning with *Industrie und Fotographie* (Industry and Photography, 1979) and ending with *Nicht ohne Risiko* (Nothing Ventured, 2004). Often neglected by media critics, Farocki's work for television provided him with crucial media and image production experience and a platform from which to explore new ideas. It also generated a steady source of income for himself and his crew. As he notes in retrospect, "Films for television, which I thought I was producing only to make money, were sometimes better than those [I] thought I was making only for their own sake."²⁹ Film historian Volker Pantenburg astutely sums up Farocki's move from making activist films to developing television productions by paraphrasing Jean-Luc Godard: "This shift could be described as a move from the production of political films to the political production of films."³⁰

WDR's steady support provided Farocki with multiple opportunities to develop televisual production skills and experiment with pushing the boundaries of what he could show on a medium that many viewed as the antithesis of cinema. Farocki practiced his own method of institutional critique, drawing on his knowledge of the inner workings of the television production system. Beginning with a 1973 series of written essays and made-for-television films, he systematically analyzed the burgeoning medium. In particular, his early work for television gave him an intimate knowledge of how images and words are strategically mobilized in nonfiction broadcasts such as news and documentaries to produce narratives and meanings that are often deceptive. Farocki honed in on the genre of documentary television that most closely approximated his mode of production: nonfiction film. In German, these made-for-television documentaries are called "*Fernsehfeatures*."³¹ Farocki explains that this term "covers the majority of television journalism and it may be compared to focus pieces, essays, reports and news stories."³² The *Fernsehfeature* genre, made explicitly for television, is not to be confused with documentary or essay films whose productions are made for theatrical release. Farocki continues: "*Feature* refers to a certain way of mixing the image and sound information. In order to market a subject with a minimum of information depth, a *feature* covers up its message with a barrage of loveless haphazardly selected images."[33] *Features* report on topics the public already knows—their exercise is affirmative. They construct pre-existent theses from images and sounds drawn from a vast televisual archive. The images and sounds illustrate stories with foregone conclusions. The selection of images and sounds occurs after the documentarist fixes the script, subordinating the images and sounds to the thesis. This phenomenon leads Farocki to conclude, "One can understand almost all of these programs without seeing the images."[34] He took this fundamental flaw in production as a challenge to produce television broadcasts in which the images and sounds would be integral.

The result was two distinct modes of nonfiction filmic production: documentaries and essay films. For the former, Farocki followed the tenets of direct or observational cinema that minimized authorial intervention and allowed images and sounds to speak for themselves. Farocki never included a voice-over or commentary in these productions but let the narrative emerge from the material. In contrast to these documentaries, Farocki made essay films. Unlike documentaries that follow strict generic regulations and rules, essay films break with convention and eschew generic categorization.[35] Farocki's essay films are very textual and include a strong determining commentary. Farocki uses the category in his 1988 press release for *Bilder der Welt und Inschrift des Krieges* (Images of the World and the Inscription of War, 1988): "It is an essay film about photography and the *Verwertung* (recycling/recovery) of images."[36] His essayistic practice was recognized early on and in 1991 he participated in one of the first international conferences dedicated to the genre.[37] The development of the essay film has several different paths, with Farocki initially being influenced by the German variant, in particular the writings of Theodor W. Adorno.[38] In response to a question about the relation between Adorno's "The Essay as Form" (1958) and essay films, Farocki responds: "What I liked about Adorno's text is that it offers almost hymnic praises for the essay as form. Adorno was a formative figure for me, and when I was twenty, I tried, as best as I could to imitate his style. . . . his method of ideological critique was well known and applied to film criticism."[39]

While Farocki's documentaries mostly comprise new original footage shot explicitly for each project, his essay films often recycle pre-existent images and film sequences from other films, including his own. This method of filmmaking developed into Farocki's *Verbundsystem* (integrated system). German engineers developed an integrated system to produce steel that emerged in the 1920s. The integrated system redirected and reused the steam generated by the furnaces, ensuring that no material necessary for production would go to waste. The model of the *Verbundsystem* allowed Farocki to experiment with recycling, reassembling, and recombining footage from different projects. "Following the example of the steel industry," he explains, "I try to create a *Verbund* [composite] with my work. The basic research for a project I finance with a radio broadcast, some books I use I review for the book programs, and many of the things I notice during this kind of work end up in my television features."[40] Farocki thus translates a system of industrial economic production into his film and media practice. Nothing is ever wasted. Instead, Farocki recycles material from his television programs, footage from commissioned documentaries, and research from recorded interviews into his non-commissioned work. As the narrator says in *Images of the World and the Inscription of War*, "Why make new images when there are perfectly usable ones already circulating?" Exceptions to this mode of production are Farocki's observational documentaries and his fictional feature *Betrayed*. What began as an outcome of economic necessity became a powerful mode of critique that makes use of media in the manner of Brechtian *Umfunktionierung* (refunctioning) and Situationist *detournement* (rerouting).

During the 1990s, several confluent circumstances significantly affected Farocki's relationship with the institution of television. The most pressing of these was the radical change in European public broadcasting. The television industry homogenized its offerings and radically cut back on the broadcast space and associated economic resources available to directors. The collapse of public funding for experimental filmmaking and its distribution coincided with the widespread shift from analog to digital image technology. These events concurred with the development of new projection equipment that facilitated the installation of large-screen film and video projections in art spaces. These developments opened up new funding sources for the production, exhibition, and distribution of moving-image installations in the art world. The ramifications were considerable. Instead of negotiating with television networks, experimental filmmakers now increasingly looked to galleries, museums, and art festival institutions for production support. The funding source provided by the art world enabled the final phase of Farocki's career as an international media artist. Projects such as *Schnittstelle* (Interface, 1995), *Ich glaubte Gefangene zu sehen* (I Thought I Was Seeing Convicts, 2000), and *Auge/Maschine I–III* (Eye/Machine I–III, 2000–2003), were exceptionally well received when displayed in the contemporary art context.

MONTAGE

Farocki's move from television and cinema to art galleries, museums, and megaexhibitions such as Documenta corresponds to his transition from single- to multichannel work. Beginning in the 1990s, he increasingly experimented with film loops, multiple channel projections, and spatial montages that rely on the spectator's navigation of the installation sites. The shift to multiple screens and images propelled Farocki to develop further his theory of soft montage that went beyond a "strict opposition of equation" produced by the sharp cuts of linear montage to compose a "general relatedness" of images.[41] In soft montage, images are held in place simultaneously within the same spatial field, yielding new configurations. The technique allows for increased flexibility and textual openness; it suggests but does not formally mandate associations. This montage form filmically parallels Adorno's essayistic schema in which "discrete elements set off against one another ... [and] crystallize as a configuration through their motion. The constellation is a force field, just as every intellectual structure is necessarily transformed into a force field under the essay's gaze."[42] Associations are mounted spatially between the moving images but not formally organized in a temporal sequence.[43] In this manner, Farocki moves beyond cinematic montage or defilement of shots, which construct meaning through a linear succession of unfolding images, towards a practice in which discrete units occupy the same visual space. This change in montage is directly related to conceptual transformations facilitated by the shift from analog to digital editing.

In tandem with soft montage, Farocki assimilated the Armenian director Artavazd Peleshyan's "distance montage" theory developed in the early 1970s, which provided an alternative to the Soviet-style dialectical montage of Sergei Eisenstein and expanded on the interval-based montage of Dziga Vertov.[44] Distance montage centers on opening up the "seam" or "interval" between two elements. Instead of "patching" elements together, Peleshyan "ripped them apart" and added more. For him, montage in film should produce a "totality," a "sense of unity," where fragments are free of signification. Shots do not collide, and "only the whole film has meaning."[45] Peleshyan's distance montage also repeats the same images and sounds throughout a given film, a technique Farocki would develop in many of his productions.

In 2002, Farocki elaborated on the effect that three distinct platforms—television broadcasts, film screenings, and art exhibitions—had on his practice.

He notes that although television broadcasts reach a large audience, their "cultural profit is small." For Farocki, the value of "culture" is inextricably bound to class and is a product of myriad forces including education, birthright, professional achievements, and the like.[46] By contrast, film screenings, particularly film premiers, are cultural "events," which increases their value. The event quotient, he adds, only "increases when one exhibit's one's work in museum or gallery exhibitions, where even the end of the show is celebrated." As he puts it, "when a work of mine is shown on television, it is as if I have thrown a message in a bottle into the sea and in order to imagine the viewer I have to invent him/her completely." The constituency of cinemagoers is more defined, though one has to be sensitive to "even the smallest fluctuation in the audience's attention," and to know "how to connect [that fluctuation] to the construction of the film." Farocki considers the impact of projected images in galleries and museums to be altogether different. Spectators walk in and out of these productions, often projected in loops, and construct their own experiences. Unlike television and cinema audiences, "The viewers of showings in art spaces address me more frequently than those at cinema screenings, but I find it more difficult to understand the meaning of their words."[47] The cultural profit of the art-world platform is high and provided Farocki with some of his greatest success. And yet, in line with his keen lifelong awareness of the constructed nature of "culture," Farocki remained skeptical of its value.

WRITINGS

Before he became a filmmaker, Farocki aspired to be a writer and fashioned himself as a wordsmith. He was attentive to how images and words function as sign systems separately and together. In a funding proposal for a never realized essay film, he writes that the production "should produce enough surprising and therefore informative image-image, word-image, or word-word relationships to fill an evening."[48] We should not underestimate the importance of his self-conception as an author. From the beginning of his career, he distinguished himself from his contemporaries as someone who conjoined "*Film-praxis*" with "*Text-praxis*." This conjunction includes not only written essay counterparts to his films but also many reviews and articles on diverse topics ranging from theories of pedagogy and cybernetics to literature, history, media archeology, film analysis, and cultural critique. As media theorist Thomas Elsaesser recalls, he first followed Farocki as a brilliant writer and editor of *Filmkritik* and only later discovered he was a filmmaker as well.

Farocki's written production comprises approximately 220 texts and essays.[49] Starting in 1964, following his completion of the equivalent of high school and gaining his *Abitur* at night school in Berlin, he contributed regular op-eds to the cultural section of the left-leaning *Spandauer Volksblatt*. His first essay, which analyzes the former East German youth initiation ritual *Jugenweihe*, was published under the name "Harun Faroghi." Other early pieces are penned by "Harun Faroquhi" and "Harun Faroqhi." After a trip to Central and South America in the summer of 1967, he wrote four essays on revolutionary politics, including "Revolution der Castro & Co," "Guerilleros ohne Troß" (Guerrillas Without a Troop), and a review of Regis Debray's *Revolution in the Revolution*, under the pseudonym "Franz Putz." He did not settle on the name "Farocki" until 1969.

Many of Farocki's early essays are book reviews of contemporary literature that quickly develop into broader commentaries and social critiques. In one piece, "Unser Schnurre" (Our Schnurre, 1964), he uses the review genre to elaborate on "engaged literature" and the relationship between politics and aesthetics. Dismissing the expressive and highly subjective writing of figures such as Wolfdietrich Schnurre, Farocki champions the work of playwright Bertolt Brecht instead: "Brecht represented the familiar and then set about investigating how the public received what was presented to them."[50] Brecht's theories of cultural production were key for Farocki. They retained seminal importance throughout his career. When they are not reviews, Farocki's early writings investigate a myriad of topics, including old cars, news media, coffee production, and the West's exploitation of the "Third World." In the aptly titled "Manipulierte Wahrheiten" (Manipulated Reality, 1964), Farocki compares the delivery of tabloid news to that of a drug dealer: "Just as the dependency of a morphine addict grows steadily, so must the dose delivered by the Springer company increase daily."[51] As this review indicates, Farocki had a canny insight into how the commercial press and media depend on savvy marketing and advertising strategies to deliver culture or news products. He directly confronts the Springer Publishing Company in his co-directed (with Helke Sander) short *Ihre Zeitungen* (Their Newspapers, 1968), and in *Catch Phrases-Catch Images: A Conversation with Vilém Flusser*, he and Flusser decode the front page of the tabloid *Bild Zeitung*.

Farocki's early writings include a piece that reviewed critic Roland Barthes's newly translated collection of sociological vignettes written between 1954 and 1956 and published under the title *Mythologies* (1957). Written during his more Brechtian phase, Barthes's understanding of how myth and ideology work together in cultural production was to have a sustained impact on Farocki's thought. As Farocki notes in his review, the way Barthes sees the world "also appears in the details of the popular view. The bourgeois, fascist and capitalist ideology is not recognizable today by a label. One has to track it down through its details, in expressions and gestures."[52] To recall, Barthes studies the semiology of myth creation in this volume of collected essays. He unearths historical determinations beneath the pretended "naturalness" of a wide range of contemporary media myths, from professional wrestling and commercial soap powders to jet pilots, Alfred Einstein's brain, and Greta Garbo's face. He subjects a photo of a Black cadet saluting the French flag on the cover of *Paris-Match* to a rigorous semiotic analysis that explains "the mystification that transforms petit-bourgeois culture into a universal nature."[53] Concluding his review, Farocki expresses "hope" that Barthes's volume "will produce a model for ideology critique."

Extending Barthes's semiological method, Farocki translates critique into audiovisual form. Barthes focuses on contemporary myth that rather than "hiding" things or "making them disappear" functions "to distort" them instead.[54] Accordingly, Farocki brings together Frankfurt School critical theory with French structuralist and semiotic thought, with Brecht's teachings serving as the lynchpin. Myths or "culture" appear "natural' and "eternal," and only the astute critic can denaturalize them. Farocki recognizes how much Barthes's critique corresponds with his own observations when the French semiotician critiques the "'naturalness' with which newspapers, art, and common sense constantly dress up a reality which, even though it is the one we live in, is undoubtedly determined by history.... I wanted to track down in the decorative display of *what-goes-without-saying*, the ideological abuse which, in my view, is hidden there."[55]

The contrast Barthes introduces in "Myth Today," in the postscript to *Mythologies*, between "operational language" and "metalanguage" will significantly influence Farocki's theorization of operative images. Barthes writes:

> Here we must go back to the distinction between language-object and metalanguage. If I am a woodcutter and I am led to name the tree, which I am felling, whatever the form of my sentence, I "speak the tree," I do not

speak about it. This means that my language is operational, transitively linked to its object.... But if I am not a woodcutter, I can no longer "speak the tree," I can only speak about it, on it.... Compared to the real language of the woodcutter, the language I create is a second-order language, a metalanguage.[56]

Forty years later, in "War Always Finds a Way" (2005), Farocki refers to "operative images" in a discussion of his *Eye/Machine* series. He explains, "I have called images that are not made to entertain or to inform 'operative images.'" These images don't simply reproduce something; they operate as function. Operative images are those not taken by humans but produced automatically by devices such as surveillance cameras. In his essay, Farocki traces his use of the term "operative" to Barthes's discussion in "Myth Today," and quotes directly from the semiotician's distinction between operational language and meta-language cited above.[57] Thus, already in 1965, Farocki adapts Barthes's theory of a division of language into images.

Farocki's first film review, "Hoffmann ja–Antonioni nein" (Hoffmann Yes–Antonioni No), was published in the journal *Filmkritik*, at the time the most significant critical publication on West German cinema, in 1965. Once he entered film school, Farocki wrote more systematically on film and media theory, publishing in *film*, a popular magazine review for cinema. After regularly contributing review essays and theoretical pieces for *Filmkritik*, he joined the editorial board in 1974. He remained on the board for the next decade.[58] Tracking his first years of writings, one can detect specific themes and interests that will resurface in his films. These interests include theories of media, images, advertising, Marxism, labor, architecture, and pedagogy. Farocki read a wide range of material, processing and integrating it into his writerly and filmic practice. At times, such as in the early 1970s when he began his teaching career, the connection between his writing and filmmaking is more oblique. During this period, he avidly read and reviewed books on radical pedagogy and incorporated some of its strategies into films like *Die Teilung aller Tage* (The Division of All Days, 1970). However, Farocki also published many essays directly linked to his films. This practice begins with *Inextinguishable Fire*. The essays became part of a calculated promotional strategy. He went on to write texts detailing the historical research that went into each of his major films and often published the scenarios. Occasionally, he staged mock interviews about the films with the imaginary interviewer "Rosa Mercedes." This pseudonym appears in the credits of many of his productions, sometimes as editor, sometimes as cinematographer, and sometimes as production manager.[59]

Farocki continued to work as a freelance writer after he resigned from *Filmkritik* in 1984. From 1994 onwards, he was a regular contributor to the French journal *Trafic*, and in 1998 he co-authored a book of critical essays, *Speaking About Godard*, with film theorist Kaja Silverman. Farocki's pace of writing increased in the final decade of his career. He penned pithy catalog essays, contributed to international journals, and edited special volumes. Just before his death, he was working on an autobiography, *Ten, Twenty, Thirty, Forty*, that would address significant events in his life. He divided the autobiography into decades. The manuscript chronicles his trajectory as an independent filmmaker in the fast-changing media environment of the late-twentieth and early-twenty-first centuries. It also provides an exceptional glimpse into everyday life in Berlin during these years.

TEACHINGS

Another facet of Farocki's practice that cannot be overemphasized is its commitment to pedagogy. Beginning in 1968, when he was part of a group of revolutionary students, Farocki sought to develop pedagogical methods to bring together militant politics and exhortation. As early as 1970, he proposed teaching a new type of film course at the DFFB, and throughout his career, he carried out both formal and informal educational projects. In a 1969 interview coinciding with the Berlin premiere of *Inextinguishable Fire*, Farocki emphasizes the film's pedagogical value. "We tried out a variety of theoretical examples in order to find a system for agitation. There wasn't just the approach of learning a theory from seeing it, as in the case of most didactic theories, but also examples from advertisements.... because they are instructional models that are similarly constructed."[60] In "Über das Wannseeheim für Jugendarbeit" (On the Wannseehome for Youth Work, 1971), which focuses on an alternative high school where workers' children learn filmmaking, he stresses the importance of teaching media skills to young people. The text integrates theories of pedagogy, linguistics, film, and information. At one point, it calls, in caps, for workers to "HAVE THE CAMERAS IN THEIR HANDS."[61]

Not surprisingly, given his devotion to Brecht's theories and production techniques, Farocki's early commitment to using film as an instructional device strategically employs theater as a political weapon. Brecht's *Lehrstücke*, or "learning plays," which stage carefully crafted scenarios to draw attention to the inherent socio-political contradictions of everyday life and provoke audiences to question the status quo, provided a model for Farocki's agit-prop films. For example, Farocki and Bitomsky structured *The Division of All Days* into a series of learning plays comprising several skits followed by classroom discussion. Brecht's *Verfremdungstheorie*, or "alienation effect," which calls for making something that has become second nature strange again, is key to these productions. As Farocki and Bitomsky explain, their intention "is to make a walking person think about walking so that he falls down."[62] They believed they could accomplish this through formal strategies, such as the use of gesture (*gestus*), repetition, or highly stilted acting methods that actively work against both on-stage and audience identification. For Brecht, directors should make sure that spectators are aware that they are watching a performance and actively co-producing meaning.

In a short manifesto from 1970, Farocki and Bitomsky claim that film is a political form whose operations a teaching environment can explain. They write:

> Roughly classified, film is there to reproduce the commodity of labour-power (commonly called entertainment). Film is there to convey information (productive force) and to produce information (the science of the productive force). Film is there to lend qualifications. Film shows that these functions, if they are not separated, interfere with and delete each other. We have observed in cinema-like situations that our film pieces are at best met with an aesthetic interest. In teaching situations, that is in schooling, they attracted the full attention of those learning, they were met with a declared desire to learn, and we did not have to bring this desire about surreptitiously or through coercion.[63]

Farocki began to develop his pedagogical strategies in the early militant ad hoc gatherings of his student days. They then developed as he established more extended formal contracts with the DFFB in the 1970s and 1980s and visiting professorships in the United States (at University of California, Berkeley; University of Florida; and California School of the Arts) in the 1990s and 2000s. These "teaching situations" changed throughout Farocki's career. His strict methods evolved as he adapted to the U.S. system's more informal tone that allows for greater student participation.[64] His final professorship was at Vienna's Academy of Fine Arts from 2004–2011. Filmmakers Thomas Arslan, Raoul Peck, and Christian Petzold are only a few of the many who considered Farocki a teacher and mentor. Besides his full-time teaching obligations, Farocki offered numerous seminars and workshops worldwide, many of these supported by the Goethe Institute. Although his teaching philosophy and style changed over the years, his rigorous approach and close reading of film sequences and shots remained constant. As Petzold recollects, "The seminars with Harun were always structured as follows. In the morning, we watched the film in the movie theater, then we walked up to the cutting room and sat around the editing table with 35mm copies of some German motion pictures that were easy to get hold of. . . . And then we went through them take by take; after each take there was a break, where we pondered: why does this take follow that one, what happened there, what kind of decision is that?"[65]

COLLABORATIONS

Farocki's reputation is that of "auteur," a filmmaker who controlled and was responsible for almost every stage of a work from the initial concept, through shooting, editing, and producing. However, the reality is that from the beginning, he collaborated with many colleagues, including Bitomsky, Antje Ehmann, Cathy Lee Crane, Ingemo Engström, Petzold, Silverman, André Ujica, and others. Most of his productions at the DFFB were made with fellow students. For example, Helke Sander served as assistant director on multiple projects, including *Inextinguishable Fire*, and Skip Norman was the cinematographer for many early films. Until the mid-1980s Farocki's most important collaborator was Bitomsky, with whom he made several films, co-authored essays, and was part of the editorial team of *Filmkritik*. Independent filmmaking was, above all, a collective endeavor. As Farocki became more famous, his participation in projects occluded that of his lesser-known colleagues. This was especially true in the art world where, for the most part, the myth of creative genius continues to be ascribed to an individual.[66] Ehmann, who lived and worked with Farocki for almost two decades, remembers how her role in their collaborations was systematically ignored for many reasons, including because she was younger, female, and didn't have a "name." As she explains, "If I sign the work, nobody knows who I am. If we both sign it, nobody knows that 90% of the work was from me."[67] It is important to note that the default establishing of Farocki as the dominant player in joint projects was not something he encouraged. It was generated by the well-oiled machinery of the art world that includes curators, critics, publicists, gallerists, and collectors.

One recent exception to this phenomenon that stands outside of the art world is Farocki's contribution as a screen writer, dramaturg, and consultant to one of Germany's most significant contemporary feature filmmakers: Petzold. While Farocki may have downplayed the extent of his collaboration with the younger director over the years, Petzold has always acknowledged Farocki's impact on his filmic practice. In 2001, he mentions, "I've been collaborating with Harun for years; this goes so smoothly that I do not even try to think about why it is so easy to work with him."[68] Petzold explains his working process with Farocki as an ongoing conversation taking place during walks: "I search for scenes with a strange charge that I then basically build into a house with Harun Farocki on our walks," or in Farocki's kitchen, while smoking and drinking burnt espresso.[69] Petzold recalls that once, when he was having difficulty with a scene in *Barbara* (2012), he visited Farocki to explain the problem, which the two soon resolved: "I could not have managed that with anybody else; he just says one or two things. Kleist calls it 'on the gradual formation of thought in speaking'... One should add to the Kleist quote that the space for articulation matters, too, the social and intellectual or emotional or mental space. And Harun, well, he is precisely such a space for me."[70] Ironically, Farocki died at a swimming pool in Brandenburg that he and Petzold had discovered while filming *Phoenix* (2014).

In sum, Farocki assumed many roles in the productions of artists and filmmakers in his community, including producer, actor, screenwriter, and dramaturg. He worked for decades with a loyal team that included cinematographer Ingo Kratisch, sound designer Klaus Klingler, editor Max Reimann, technical director Jan Ralske, and production assistant Matthias Rajmann. Even the readers of the commentaries are consistent, for example, with the voice of Cynthia Beatt first heard in *Images of the World and the Inscription of War* and later featured in multiple productions.

METHODOLOGY

Farocki's method of close hermeneutic and even deconstructive image analysis remained constant throughout his career. He developed an ability to decode every detail systematically—sequence by sequence, frame by frame. This way of seeing, detecting what is often invisible at first glance, is one of the central characteristics of his practice. It characterizes his examination of aerial surveillance photographs in *Images of the World and the Inscription of War*, his detailed analysis of a scene from *Intolerance* (1916) in *Zur Bauweise des Films bei Griffith* (On Construction in Griffith's Films, 2006), and his close reading of Gaspar Miguel de Berrio's eighteenth-century painting *Descripción del Cerro Rico e Imperial Villa de Potosí* (1758) in *Das Silber und das Kreuz* (The Silver and The Cross, 2010). Many of his productions examine the im/perceptible at the margins of vision or cognition. In a manner that resonates strongly with Walter Benjamin's notion of the "optical unconscious," the eye of the camera records evidence that eludes the human eye.

A recurring theme in Farocki's work is that we see and do not see simultaneously. Often, we only see what we look for. As Allan Sekula argues in "Reading an Archive: Photography Between Labor and Capital," the reader must ask different questions to understand documents differently. The questions posed when mining an archive determine the meaning of its contents.[71] Or, to put it another way, what we see is determined by a shift in perspective. In "Myth Today," Barthes uses the analogy of looking out the window while traveling in a car to explain how myth operates: "I look at the scenery through the window, I can at will focus on the scenery or on the window-pane.... The result of this alternation is constant: the glass is at once present and empty to me, and the landscape unreal and full. The same thing occurs in the mythical signifier: its form is empty but present, its meaning absent but full."[72] A similar process is operative in Farocki's work. Through his focused analyses, he shows that many images function as puzzles embedded in myths, not unlike the picture of a duck that may be that of a rabbit depending on one's perspective. Adorno writes in *Aesthetic Theory*: "Every artwork is a picture puzzle [*Vexierbild*], a puzzle to be solved, but this puzzle is constituted in such a fashion that it remains a vexation.... Artworks are like picture puzzles in that what they hide ... is visible and is, by being visible, hidden."[73] Part of Farocki's project is to reveal both sides of the puzzle. For Adorno, the picture puzzle functions as a metaphor for the operation of ideology because it privileges selected perspectives over others, particularly the transformation in the perception of labor under advanced capitalism. In *Minima Moralia: Reflections from Damaged Life*, the philosopher lamented that workers in societies constructed around an economy of consumption could no longer perceive themselves as individuals. His treatise on the "Picture Puzzle" ends with the "grimly comic riddle" pondered by contemporary sociologists: "Where is the proletariat?"[74] A question many of Farocki's works probe.

Farocki's fascination with film and media images leads directly to a project he never completed: a "cinematographic thesaurus." He set out to produce the project in the 1990s when he realized that a filmic correlative to a dictionary did not yet exist. Farocki's goal was to construct what he described as "an 'illustrated book,' a 'thesaurus' or 'treasure trove of images,' or perhaps even an 'archive of filmic expressions.'"[75] He imagined that the large database, centered on repeating certain scenes, images, and gestures, would span decades, nationalities, and genres. He considered video recording technology, particularly as it enabled the easy copying and reproducing of clips, crucial to constructing such an index.[76] Farocki realized part of this lexicon in projects such as *Arbeiter verlassen die Fabrik* (Workers Leaving the Factory, 1995). This began as a single-channel film that he later expanded into an eleven-channel installation, *Workers Leaving the Factory in Eleven Decades*, with each channel corresponding chronologically to a decade in cinema history. Farocki also developed the project for several multi-screen installations made with Ehmann, such as *Feasting or Flying* (2008) and *War Tropes* (2011). The project culminated in his final installation, *Parallel I–IV*, which tracks video game iconography from the crude graphics of the medium's early years to today's virtual reality manifestations. All along, however, Farocki sought to produce more than an assemblage of canonical scenes from film history commonly cited in textbooks. He aimed to create "knowledge" that included "the obscure and the nameless in cinema history."[77] The lexicon of cinematographic images would reveal changes in film style and editing detected in representations of singular gestures or images.

Yet, the question I noted a critic posed to Farocki upon his first visit to New York City in 1973 remains unanswered: What sort of films did he make? Farocki declared that his production tracked "the industrialization of thought." But this statement does not account for his rich and heterogenous output.[78] The genres that drew his attention over the years were as varied as the media forms in which he worked. Owing to his training at the DFFB, Farocki was familiar with different schools of filmmaking. He began his career making agit-prop films with a solid pedagogical determination. Later, he constructed compilation films, such as *Videogramme einer Revolution* (Videograms of a Revolution, 1992) with Andrei Ujica, and observational documentaries or "Direct Cinema" with little or no commentary (*Leben BRD* [How to Live in the FRG], 1990). He crafted essay films with powerful voice-over narratives (*Wie man Sieht* [As You See], 1986), standard documentaries (*Sarah Schumann malt ein Bild* [Sarah Schumann Paints an Image], 1977), ponderous interviews (*Georg K. Glaser—Schriftsteller und Schmied* [Georg K. Glaser–Writer and Smith], 1988), and a feature film (*Betrayed*). When his work started circulating in the art world, he moved from single-channel productions to multi-screen installations, such as *Parallel I–IV*, that interrogate digital image-making. Over the years, he also wrote film reviews, critiques, meditations on film forms, directors, and techniques such as "shot/countershot" or "soft montage," and reminiscences like "Written Trailers." Additionally, he directed several theater plays, including Heiner Müller's *Die Schlacht* (The Battle, 1974) and *Traktor* (Tractor, 1974), and produced radio broadcasts. His most admired filmmakers included Jean-Luc Godard, Robert Bresson, and Jean-Marie Straub.[79]

This book's challenge is making sense of Farocki's vibrant and diverse practice. How can we account for the multiple platforms and media he used to produce the "forms of intelligence" featured in his large body of work? In what follows, I focus on interconnected constellations of ideas that characterize Farocki's production. I use the categories Labor, Critique, and War to organize these clusters. These themes are loosely interwoven throughout Farocki's oeuvre by a vast network of threads and strands, filaments of thought that merge to produce a dense authorial web. As Farocki reveals in a 2002 discussion of his use of montage, "Imagine three double bonds jumping back and forth between the six carbon atoms of a benzene ring; I envisage the same ambiguity in the relationship of an element in an image track to the one succeeding or accompanying it."[80]

Farocki's practice of placing images and concepts into force fields is key to understanding why he made single-channel versions of most of his later multi-screen projects. Each single-channel production is as carefully crafted and thought out as the multi-channel version. Double projections are diagonally transposed and slightly overlap within one frame. Images in his work do not take the place of other images but supplement, reevaluate, and balance those that precede them. This book analyzes the "double bonds" of Farocki's production and interprets the intricacies of their interrelationship. My goal has been to order the rich plethora of material that comprises Farocki's thought and practice. While I could have taken many routes to accomplish this task, I have opted for one that provides readers with enough ground to continue investigating Farocki's work in their own unique ways.

CHAPTER 1

Critique and Montage

When one doesn't have money for cars, [film] shooting, or nice clothes . . . , when one doesn't have money to make images in which film time and film life flow uninterruptedly, then one has to put one's efforts into intelligently putting together separate elements, one has to produce a montage of ideas (der Montage der Ideen).

—Harun Farocki, Between Two Wars

One image comments on the other. To date, only words, or sometimes music, comment on images. Here images comment on images.

—Harun Farocki, Interface

In 1966, Farocki made the short *Zwei Wege* (Two Paths) (1966) for Sender Freies Berlin television. The film comprises a meticulous examination and analysis of a large poster decorating the office wall of a government building in Kreuzberg. In medieval style, the tableau depicts two paths: one leading to heaven and the other to hell. Farocki's camera tracks the two trajectories as they traverse the plane of representation. The route to heaven meanders across a narrow bridge and passes by a Sunday school on its way to its ultimate destination, where a bible awaits the righteous traveler. The film populates the path to hell with depictions of men drinking, playing cards, gambling, soliciting sex workers, and committing other sins. The camera zooms and pauses over each scene as the commentary, read by Farocki, generates a rhyme that corresponds to the image: "*Ist ihre Beute nicht so mager dann schicht sie doch in Arbeits lager*" (Even if their spoil is not so meager, they will send them to a work camp). The soundtrack features a mix of church and military music and animal noises.

1.1 Harun Farocki, *Two Paths* (1966)

1.2 Harun Farocki, *The Silver and the Cross* (2010)

Forty-four years later, in *The Silver and the Cross* (2010), Farocki repeats this same method of close reading in his examination of an eighteenth-century colonial painting. While much has changed formally and technologically from the moment of the crude three-minute exercise produced for television to the two-screen, seventeen-minute film loop installation designed for an art exhibition, Farocki's close reading method remains the same. He disassembles the text's totality and subjects each of its parts to rigorous examination in his effort to glean meaning and uncover hidden truths.

Farocki's hermeneutic approach to interpretation draws from the German romantic tradition that considers each singular fragment to bear its own particular significance and that too of the whole of which it is part. The whole contains the fragment and vice versa. Following this tradition, observers seeking to understand a visual or literary text study each detail separately before relating it to the systemic whole. Along with the romantic tradition, Barthes's *Mythologies* was fresh on Farocki's mind when he made *Two Paths*. Barthes decodes various systems of signs that produce the image's powerful ideological message. Farocki held Barthes's analytical method in high regard, hoping it would generate "a model for ideology critique."[1]

Another short Farocki made the same year as *Two Paths*, *Jeder ein Berliner Kindl* (Everyone a Berliner Kindl) (1966), examines a display of historical posters advertising the popular beer. Each poster features a man holding a beer bottle in one hand and the tool of his trade in the other: e.g., a fishing rod, a hammer, a musical instrument. The advertisement's message is clear. What unites the men from distinct social classes and different Berlin districts (Wannsee, Moabit, Neukölln, Schöneberg) is their consumption of the same beer: "Berliner Kindl." Beer advertisements forge imaginary communities. (As an aside, one of Farocki's early jobs when he first arrived in Berlin was distributing beer throughout the city, an employment that forced him to learn to map the urban space.)

Farocki's filmic analysis summons the national myths used to build ideologies. Like the subjects Barthes selected from everyday life, Farocki's focus on the vernacular also has its roots in the writings of Walter Benjamin, Siegfried Kracauer, and Georg Simmel. These authors all proposed that everyday life is as revelatory as great works of art, literature, and philosophy. Recall Benjamin's pronouncement that "what in the end makes advertisements superior to criticism? Not what the moving red neon says—but the fiery pool reflecting it in the asphalt."[2] Mining and critiquing everyday-life objects and patterns opens up insight into

1.3 Harun Farocki, *Everyone a Berliner Kindl* (1966)

contemporary social systems. Three decades later, in "Werkstattgespräch mit Harun Farocki" (Studio Conversation with Harun Farocki), Farocki compares Bertolt Brecht's and pop artists' recourse to popular images. Here, he observes that Brecht's and Pop Art's aim was "to avoid naturalizing the image. The difference is that Brecht wants to develop a mode of representation while Pop Art annexes one. Advertising images are disproportionate images and are picked up because there is truth in this distortion."[3]

Farocki's examination of advertising's structure and the seepage of commodity culture into all aspects of everyday life begins with *Everyone a Berliner Kindl*. This analytical interest characterizes many of his films, including *Ein Tag im Leben der Endverbraucher* (A Day in the Life of a Consumer) (1993), *Stilleben* (Still Life) (1997), and the series of observational documentaries that include *Ein Bild* (An Image) (1983) and end with *Sauerbruch Hutton Architects* (2013). In *A Day in the Life of a Consumer*, as well as in the observational documentaries, Farocki unveils, without comment, complex strategies for selling wares, including subject positions, before the camera. In each film, he reveals how commodity culture has thoroughly permeated society and transformed human subjectivity. Understanding commodity culture's operation requires examining its dominant institutions and support structures. It requires, in other words, an analysis of contemporary media.

Farocki's fascination with advertising permeates a 1964 review, "Selbstmord" (Suicide), which analyzes publishing house Suhrkamp's canny marketing strategy.[4] Suhrkamp issued its new edition of Vladimir Mayakovsky's collected poems in a red volume. The design leads Farocki to a broad-ranging discussion about companies that use color to attract consumers. More specifically, he speculates that publishers who release a book series in which each is a different color tease consumers' desire to possess the entire spectrum regardless of the individual volumes' authors or subjects. Farocki's review focuses on Mayakovsky's "An Sergei Jessenin" (To Sergei Jessenin). The poem, about a figure who committed suicide, foreshadows Mayakovsky's death a few years later at the age of thirty-six and in the aforementioned review alludes to Farocki's failed suicide attempt around the same time.[5] Farocki intertwines his discussion of the young poet with biting observations on consumer society. Suhrkamp's publicity, he argues, highlights not, as might be expected, the content of its books but their face value and display potential. With each volume's color distinct, ownership of the entire series makes for an attractive rainbow on the bookshelf. This observation leads Farocki to note how nothing is sacred for consumer capitalism: the economic system turns even literary works into spectacular commodities. He also observes how the Mayakovsky volume's cover conceals the damage the editors inflicted on the book's contents as they willy-nilly pieced together extracts from the author's considerable oeuvre. Farocki describes the editors' curation as violent, concluding with the following question: "When horses are chopped up, songbirds canned, and dogs beaten, help is close at hand, but who helps poor Mayakovsky, who has been beaten, chopped up and turned into a spectre?"[6] Farocki's early derision of this editorial process foreshadows his later condemnation of television editors, whom he refers to as "cutters."

After completing his film training, Farocki quickly moved into the television world. The television industry informed his writings and productions in the 1970s. As he recalls, in 1980, when looking back on this period, "Cinema could still believe that it was fighting against television. Its invisible enemy included everything to do with television. Primarily, this meant the home or apartment where almost all consumer goods are stored. Accordingly, cinema found itself at odds with food producers, appliance manufacturers, the furniture industry, clothes makers, and the like."[7] Farocki learned the particulars of advertising techniques from the television industry and would show this understanding in his work: the industry's relation to advertising is overt and covert, manifested in the commercials aired between programs and the products displayed in broadcasts, the ideologies undergirding programming, and the rules inherent in production. The latter included editing, mise-en-scene, pacing, sequencing, camera angles, lighting, and shooting.

In 1973 and 1974, Farocki made two forty-eight-minute features for WDR 3's "Telekritik," a program that self-reflexively provided a venue where one could discuss television. The features, *The Trouble with Images: A Critique of Television* (1973) and *Die Arbeit mit den Bildern: Eine Telekritik von Harun Farocki* (The Struggle with Images: A Critique of Television) (1974), constitute audiovisual correlatives that expand on topics treated in Farocki's contemporary essays, including "Drückebergerei vor der Wirklichkeit: Das Fernsehfeature/Der Ärger mit den Bildern" (Shirking from Reality: The Television Documentary/The Trouble with Images) (1973), "Bilder aus dem Fernsehen" (Images from Television) (1973), "Über die Arbeit mit Bildern im Fernsehen" (About Working with Images for Television) (1974), "Arbeiten–beim Fernsehen" (Working–In Television) (1975), and "Der

1.4 Harun Farocki, *The Trouble with Images: A Critique of Television* (1973)

Wahnsinn hat Methode, sogar Begriffe" (Irrationality Has a Method, Even Concepts) (1975). Taking the written essays and the audiovisual programs together, one can see how Farocki tests the possibilities and limits of each medium. Though each medium stands independently, we must combine the works to grasp his early media theory in all its complexity.

Farocki's *The Trouble with Images* opens with a crude graphic model of a small television set, with the words "Harun Farocki Kritik," handwritten across the screen. Farocki's use of handwritten intertitles becomes a signature around this time. As he retrospectively remarks, "TV was a highly official affair at the time and using these handwritten scribbled intertitles was a wonderful gesture of rebellion."[8] A voice-over, which uses the same language as Farocki's written essay "Shirking from Reality," defines the techniques of television documentary. Farocki divides the essay into several subsections: "abstraction," "proxy images," "power images," and "idiomatic expressions." For each section, Farocki defines the terms and provides an image. The essay's filmic version operates along the same lines. But now, Farocki splices in various clips from television documentaries. He replays these clips multiple times, meticulously analyzing their structure, function, and strategic employment. He delivers the commentary through the voice of a female narrator. This technique distinguishes Farocki's voice from the male voice-overs in the selected out-takes. (The majority of documentaries—made for television or film and not limited to West Germany—used authoritative male voices to convey their messages.) After several pronouncements on what defines a documentary, the female narrator introduces found footage from a two-minute-and-seventeen-second clip from a program about the condition of the contemporary West German city. This brief sequence is comprised of thirteen different locations and twenty-five statements. The commentator asks rhetorically, "Why so many images and words? In order to make it lively, interesting, dynamic, moving." A photo advertisement of a television set appears with the word "*Dynamik*" scrawled across it. The commentary continues, "... but in order for a whole to be interesting each of its parts must be interesting." Throughout *The Trouble with Images*, between clips, and during transitions, Farocki leaves the screen blank when the production poses a question or offers commentary. Still images of the television set with section markers scrawled across the screen punctuate these moments of visual negation. Three components construct *The Trouble with Images*: found footage from television archives, blank shots, and graphic still images. Thus, the production is a compilation film whose foundations Farocki builds by using prefabricated sources.

Farocki, through the voice of the female narrator, analyzes each of the thirteen shot sequences of the two-minute-and-seventeen-second clip. Sometimes, he replays the shot several times to underscore how it contains multiple layers of meaning. He describes his process as follows: "I begin with the premise that images and words (and their relation to each other) are phrases. In order to make them stand out as phrases, I cite them repeatedly. This separates them from the context in which they have been hidden and allows them to be scrutinized."[9] Different meanings emerge through repetition and replay. The meanings have always been there, but television conventions have obscured them. For example, one sequence features silent images of rushing water, trees blowing in the wind, and clouds in the sky, followed by an urban construction site with added amplified sounds of building. The voice-over from the documentary tells the viewer that, like the cost of living, pollution is on the rise—presumably air, water, and noise pollution. The clip is then muted and replayed. Farocki's narrator states, "One can see air and water, and see and hear machines that make noise. That is concrete. But one can't see inflation." Accordingly, the program combines concrete images with abstract conclusions that do not correspond to the images shown.

Another sequence presents what the broadcast's commentator describes as a "sad" back courtyard. In the replay, Farocki's narrator remarks, "I don't find the courtyard so 'sad,' I have seen worse." A pattern emerges with Farocki's narrator countering, challenging, and revising the clips' commentary. The two disembodied voices engage in a dialogue. The female narrator stresses the power of the documentary's maker, who uses images to illustrate ideas the commentary articulates: "Because the pictures are only there to illustrate thoughts, mostly half thoughts, they also have to be constantly explained and fitted into the context of words."[10] *The Trouble with Images* calls attention to the direct interplay between spoken and audiovisual texts. Breaking apart elements and explicitly questioning narrative authority, Farocki's televisual essay provides a counter-example of what television might be.

From shots of urban blight, the feature then moves to the countryside. The commentary informs us that rural life is not exempt from such problems. Farocki introduces a new section that interrogates the "authority" of who gets to speak in the film, "Wer Kommt zu Wort/Who Is Given Voice." The female narrator critiques television's usual recourse to talking heads who "expertly" make pronouncements that, in effect, manipulate reality. All the while a sequence plays with middle-aged men in suits telling each other how women behave. The voice-over underscores that these figures are predominantly male and rarely bother to include the opinions and perspectives of women. To illustrate this point, Farocki shows how one such broadcast highlighting women's increased independence, voiced by a man, is supported not by interviews with women but by shots of women walking in one direction a decade earlier and another today. In dominant television, Farocki argues, women's voices are silenced and their subject positions are represented visually from a male perspective.

In another sequence, two young men survey a row of communal outhouses and observe that there are still no bathrooms. The camera focuses on the locked door of one outhouse. The female narrator notes that the image makes for a good ending point. The broadcast's commentator announces that people will relocate to overcrowded cities if these impoverished conditions are not improved soon. An image of a large moving truck driving through a small town illustrates the warning. A series of still photographs of children's drawings represent the poor living conditions in cities and the country. For once, the broadcast's commentator is silent. The female narrator observes that the commentator's "silence is there only so that one can read, not so that one can *see* anything." After this brief interlude, the commentator resumes speaking over images of housing developments that he emphasizes need to be "renewed." Farocki's narrator alerts the viewer to the fact that "again there is something more to be heard than to be seen." The broadcaster's voice explains that governments built these complexes in the postwar era to house refugees, the homeless, and other displaced persons. Farocki notes critically that the official subtext is that the postwar period is over, and it is now time for a new direction. Later in the *The Trouble with Images*, Farocki will provide a counter example to this cheery outlook ("*Gast Arbeiter*"/foreign workers) that details the continued presence and poverty of displaced persons in West Germany. Farocki's concern with the "outsider" returns as subject matter in many of his collaborations with Christian Petzold. Films such as *The State I Am In* (2000), *Ghosts* (2005), *Yella* (2007), and *Barbara* (2012) are dominated by marginalized protagonists and individuals who, for myriad reasons, live as ghosts in society.

Farocki shows that the images do not support the broadcaster commentator's argument that the past is over. The end of the clip features an image of the television screen with the word "*Chaos*" scrawled across it. The television screen functions like a blackboard, and Farocki is an instructor. The narrator concludes that although the broadcast's images allegedly relate to its extensive commentary, the connection is highly deceptive. The images function as nodal points for a series of gross, distorting generalizations. The second image of a television screen replaces the first with the word "Order." The narrator explains that this sequence and similar ones that are played every evening generate understanding, but the "quality of understanding" remains in question.

The feature's next segment is from the popular German television real crime series: "Tatort." The narrator notes the poverty of the images featured in the series. She observes that because the foregrounded crimes have already occurred, the best producers can provide are locations. The latter function as tropes: staple images of houses, forests, or parking lots where the deeds may have occurred. They are false traces since the connections between the places they picture and the crimes committed are spurious. The program relies on documentary and news journalism codes to reenact the crimes. But Farocki's narrator emphasizes that these codes are largely fictional, fabricated from an archive of stock images.

Besides stressing these broadcasts' problematic matching of texts and images, Farocki's narrator highlights their formal techniques. She notes how the broadcasts strategically employ pacing to flow smoothly. She also observes their recourse to different editing formulas, such as locating clips with movement, adding music, and cutting rapidly. The narrator stresses the way variations in the broadcast commentary's speed and tone, including, for example, the commentator's whispering, grab the audience's attention. Movement is more essential to television than film because of the size of the images. Whereas images on cinema's large screens immerse spectators, those on television compete for attention with the surrounding environment. The narrator also notes how television programs rely on a large degree of symbolism. For example, a divorce documentary, she explains, begins with an image of a couple sitting at a kitchen table with a child in the middle. A circular saw then cuts through the center of the image, severing the child in two and underscoring divorce's trauma. An image of a traffic light that turns red in the foreground with a steeple in the background conveys the church's position on divorce. The narrator observes how heavy-handed symbolism also characterizes interviews. She remarks that a typical example features a close-up of a man who describes how divorce broke him. As the camera pulls away from the close-up, the scene reveals the rubble of a collapsed building behind him. The allusion is that the man, like the architecture, is destroyed, perhaps beyond repair. Farocki's narrator exposes the tropes—"key words" and "key images"—producers of television documentaries mobilize to build their works.

The extracts selected by Farocki impart well-intentioned liberal messages. As he clarifies, "I only chose examples that had a progressive message. It remains to be seen, which progressive messages go so far as to advocate for better

Critique and Montage 33

1.5 Harun Farocki, *The Trouble with Images: A Critique of Television* (1973)

information programming on television."[11] Farocki's aim is corrective. It seeks to teach media makers how to create progressive works and calls on them to resist the clichéd production formulas they learned in film school. Thus, his imagined public consists not only of viewers who consume images but also of those who make them. As he emphasizes, "I want to show my critique film to those who work in television."[12]

Two sequences in *The Trouble with Images* reveal that alternatives to television's standard order are possible. Both come in the film's final ten minutes, following a passage whispered by the narrator. She tells of the destructive power of sound, which can erase ("cleanse") all emotion and relate ideological opinions from an authorial perspective. The narrator says over a blank screen, "If one really wants to hear someone speaking, then one listens to the material and the thoughts. That can be an adventure." Farocki follows this with a clip from Klaus Wildenhahn's *Der Reifenschneider und seine Frau* (The Tirecutter and his wife, 1968/1969). An anonymous interviewer asks a man who sits with his wife in a domestic setting: "You were a fighter?" The man responds by recounting his experiences in World War II. Although the camera does not move, several cuts indicate that the interview has been stitched together from different segments. The man is filmed slightly in the foreground. His wife listens in the background, leaning forward now and again to contradict or supplement his story. She grows increasingly angry and accuses him of glorifying mass murder. The interview appears unscripted. The couple smokes intermittently while a cat drifts in and out of the frame. A microphone dangles conspicuously in the foreground. As with the cuts, Wildenhahn does not conceal the filmic apparatus. The two-minute clip features no commentary, no Foley sounds, just the couple speaking.

Once the sequence ends, Farocki cuts to a color shot of a city street in the evening. Many windows are illuminated. The words "Using film to make investigations" crawl across the screen. Farocki's narrator explains that filming things and interpreting them with commentary does not satisfy filmmakers like Wildenhahn, who prefers to make his "adventures" by rendering reality purely through camera and sound recordings. Farocki recognizes that the concept of "adventure" in television documentaries is strange since every image and sound has been *pre*-selected to support preconceived notions. The documentaries impose meaning on images and sounds. The graphic "Chaos/Order" appears over the design of a small television model. Farocki's commentary concludes, "The way in which TV documentaries are made is more of a grid for reality (a preconceived plan) than an instrument to discover reality."

Wildenhahn studied "direct cinema" with Richard Leacock, whose films had an observational character. In this style of documentary filmmaking (the French variant was "cinéma verité"), the director records reality without intervening. The productions are purely observational. Meaning emerges from recorded, not manipulated reality. Subjects speak freely and tell their stories in an unscripted manner. Wildenhahn taught at the DFFB from 1968–1972 (some say he helped restore normalcy after its takeover by students). He introduced Farocki to the direct cinema method, greatly impacting the young director. Throughout his career Farocki oscillated between making heavily narrated essay films such as *As You See* (1986) and observational documentaries like *How to Live in the FRG* (1990).

If Wildenhahn offers one model of difference in *The Trouble with Images*, a final clip by Helma Sanders (later Sanders Brahms) *Die industrielle Reservearmee* (The industrial reserve army, 1970/71) provides another. Farocki transitions to her work by returning to the image of the urban street. This time, the written words seem redundant: "Instead: Images + Sounds, Images + Sounds." Paralleling Jean-Luc Godard's meditations on "son + image," the important thing about film is not the components used to make it, but how they are put together.[13] A blank screen holds a silence for several seconds. A woman's voice (not Farocki's narrator) announces the location, "Cologne." The woman then officiously lists a series of days, times, and nationalities: "Tuesday: 9:03 Greeks," "Tuesday: 18:25 Yugoslavians," "Wednesday: 19:38 Turks," and so on. The dark screen gives way to a medium close-up of two women standing with a brick wall in the background. A bar bisects the screen. The blank screen returns, followed by another shot of the two women. This time the shot is taken from slightly further away. We see the dark screen once again and then the women. All the while, the camera gradually tracks back, revealing more people standing on what we now discern is a train platform. It slowly becomes apparent that the camera is filming through a moving train car: the bisected frame is a window, and the dark spaces are parts of the train. The frame/view of the window and the camera merge. The effect resembles an enlarged filmstrip, with each frame containing a slightly different image.

An unobstructed view of the crowded platform comes into focus once the train passes through the station. The people await orders from a man with a bullhorn. Farocki cuts to a color photograph of a film camera/projector with the words: "FREE images and sounds!" The narrator remarks, "Some who make films, like Helma Sanders, clearly show that between things and ideas there is a distance." Filmmakers like Sanders, in other words, do not begin with foregone conclusions. Instead, they show how meaning can emerge and take form. In their productions, images and sounds retain their own agency. Moreover, it is in the connections between images and sounds (montage) that meaning is produced. They are more than merely illustrative.

In one sequence, Sanders films inside a large hall where older women in Red Cross uniforms distribute food. The voice-over in her film states: "The Red Cross helps, the church helps, social organizations help . . . but whom do they help?" Sanders reveals that she recorded this sequence in a distribution center in Cologne's central train station. Foreign workers, organized by their national origin, represent the vast number of laborers that came to West Germany in the 1950s and 1960s in search of employment. An older man's heavily accented voice describes the subhuman conditions of life and work. Other voices gradually add to his, culminating in a disembodied chorus of misery. Sanders's camera slowly tracks the seemingly endless line of people waiting for aid. The personal narratives articulated by the voices in the chorus are interrupted by a female voice that matter-of-factly rattles off statistics on the number of workers brought to West

Germany between 1955–1968. The woman's voice notes that wages have not kept pace with inflation, producing what Karl Marx refers to as "the industrial reserve army" of the working poor. Sanders's vivid depiction of inflation's consequences contrasts with the empty throwaway phrases uttered by the commentary in the initial clip of *The Trouble with Images*. Farocki uses *The Industrial Reserve Army* as a counter-example to tackle complex abstract concepts such as inflation. Sanders's film images human casualties, relates personal stories, and provides official statistics. The viewer is left to make the relations and generate meaning. *The Trouble with Images* ends with Sanders's film. Instead of offering closing words, Farocki leaves the production's viewers to draw their own conclusions.

Reflecting on his methodology in *The Trouble with Images*, Farocki explains: "When I made my critique of television documentaries for Westdeutsches Fernsehen (WDF), I cited from the same excerpts several times. It turned out that they were suddenly no longer so ugly. Because they were now freed from being covered, they could now be perceived for their feelings and thoughts."[14] He explains that his analytical method consists of breaking down individual components to show how they function as parts of a whole. He "frees" the component sounds and images, repeating them to dis-embed them from the montage and restore their uniqueness. In this film, Farocki also turns to Theodor W. Adorno's and Max Horkheimer's critical theory to demonstrate how mass media and television occlude truth and veil reality. However, he emphasizes that, unlike the Frankfurt School philosophers' pessimistic conclusions, his goal, *pace* Alexander Kluge, is to create a counter-public sphere capable of breaking through the prison-house of mass media.[15]

Farocki's *The Trouble with Images* reveals an early instance of his method of thinking through images. He argues here that more than serving as neutral vehicles that transparently convey referents, images have an articulative capacity, signifying in particular ways. Four decades later, in one of his last interviews, he comments on how he has long tried to find ways to shape "cinematography's discourse" not only through words but also through the formal aspects of montage: "It can sound a little bit poetic to say 'having images that think' and 'having films that think,' but it's in this sense one of my ambitions: to find some autonomy in the cinematographic form, in which you don't just repeat things which already exist on paper and try to translate them to film form, but you try to give some autonomy to the cinematic medium."[16] Images and, by extension, films that think relate philosophically to the aesthetic theory of German Romanticism (i.e., Hegel,

Herder, and Schelling), later taken up by Adorno and Benjamin for their concepts of the "*Denkbilder*" or "thought images." "Thought images" are short hybrid texts that combine literature, philosophy, journalism, and art. According to the scholar Gerhard Richter, thought images are inherently political because they offer "a mode of thinking, reading, and writing that allows us to inquire into the history and logic of aesthetic ideologies." He continues that they provide "insight into the often subterranean ways in which seemingly disinterested claims of taste or artistically mediated forms of sensate cognition reinforce an uncritical view of social norms and a tendentious imposition of constructed and contingent worldviews as the expression of alleged political necessity."[17] Thought images have the concept of critique built into them. Adorno described Benjamin's recourse to thought images as "scribbled picture-puzzles, parabolic evocations of something that cannot be said in words. They do not want to stop conceptual thought so much as to shock through their enigmatic form and thereby get thought moving, because thought in its traditional conceptual form seems rigid, conventional, and outmoded."[18] Richter argues that a thought image creates "an image (*Bild*) in words of the ways in which it says what cannot be said. It is a snapshot of the impossibility of its own rhetorical gestures. What it gives us to think (*denken*) is precisely the ways in which it delivers an image (*Bild*)."[19] If thought images produce images out of words for writers, then Farocki folds this concept back onto itself and, through a reversal, creates words and thoughts out of images—*Bilder denken*.

In both filmic and written examples, Farocki relates how media images hide meaning and cover up the truth ("*Vertuschung*"). Paradoxically, television documentary trades in marketing nonfiction. In *The Trouble with Images*, Farocki shows how the different components of this genre, including editing, sound, pacing, commentary, and cinematography, combine to produce what Barthes terms a "referential illusion." According to Barthes, in realism, realistic details do not refer to a deeper meaning but function to signify as markers of reality.[20] As an indexical medium, film is prone to producing a false sense of reality through its manipulation of artificially manufactured appearances and sounds. Farocki laments, "Nothing is sadder than a product that is not aware of its conditions of production. The television documentary, the form of journalistic treatment of the real world on television, is a system of delusions."[21]

Farocki, as a modernist, firmly believed in fixed concepts of truth and reality. Throughout his career, he carefully differentiated between film essays and documentaries, with the latter comprising much of his work. He considered documentary to function as "a magical imitation of reality."[22] He was guided by Brecht's five dictums on telling the truth: "The Courage to Write the Truth," "The Keenness to Recognize the Truth," "The Skill to Manipulate the Truth as Weapon," "The Judgement to Select Those in Whose Hands the Truth Will Be Effective," and "The Cunning to Spread the Truth Among the Many."[23] Importantly, Farocki produced his critique of television self-reflexively through the medium of television. He painstakingly revealed the many falsehoods common to made-for-television programs. As Brecht noted, if one tells the truth, one must expose the lies and those individuals and institutions propagating them: "The truth is belligerent; it strikes out not only against falsehood, but against particular people who spread falsehood." Farocki's own attentiveness to falsehoods explains his often scathing opprobrium against colleagues in the film and media industry. The year following *The Trouble with Images*, he made a second part to this critique: *The Struggle with Images*. Unfortunately, the film is lost, so one can only speculate on its contents based on reviews and Farocki's written descriptions. If *The Trouble with Images* focused primarily on how commentary and voice-over override and obscure meanings in images, *The Struggle with Images* detailed how cinematography, editing, and other aspects of the production process further combine to produce an alternate reality.

Farocki's 1974 essay "About Working with Images for Television" begins with the premise that "stories belong to film, assignments to television."[24] In this essay Farocki compares film and television. He observes that the film medium presents sweeping stories and grand narratives. Television, on the other hand, transmits shorter, smaller topics that avoid more extensive arguments and theses. This difference, in part, corresponds to scale. The latter determines the viewing experience. To see a film is an event. Spectators purchase tickets, visit theaters, and often make an afternoon or evening out of the cinema-going experience. By contrast, to watch television, West German viewers in the 1970s had to subscribe to monthly services that provided them with a predetermined, often highly limited programming. However, television has a much greater potential than film to reach large, diverse audiences. Indeed, *The Trouble with Images* reached thousands of viewers when it first aired. Farocki recognized the broadcast medium's public potential and sought to *refunction* it (in the Brechtian sense, from *Umfunktionierung*) to create programs that demystified its offerings. Although the industry tightly controlled the medium, Farocki discovered some cracks in the industry's governance that enabled him to work from the inside out as a form of "institutional subversion."[25]

In *The Trouble with Images*, Farocki focuses on nonfiction broadcasts, which he distinguishes from nightly news programs. He finds these made-for-television documentaries particularly misleading since they pose as journalism. "The main expression of television is filmed journalism. This language in image and sound and editing surrounds us, a form of expression as decisive and powerful and as directing thought and feeling as written German."[26] Farocki categorizes television production into words, cuts, and images, arguing that the three categories combine to form a mythical whole. He focuses on two interrelated stages in television production: cinematography and editing. He holds the camera operators and editors responsible for manipulating images, forcing the images to fit into a false continuum. Although film too comprises many fragments that together form a whole, Farocki insists that cinematographers and film editors remain aware of the larger concept. By contrast, he asserts that television producers are much more alienated from their labor and remain largely unaware of the industry's overarching agenda. Here, Farocki echoes his scathing rebuke of the Suhrkamp editor of the Mayakovsky volume, who selected material based on the series' formal requirements instead of the book's content. In the written essay "Images from Television," Farocki explains that camera operators and editors, in particular, salvage final products from haphazard heaps of material shot by television directors: "Pretending craftsmanship, the television cameramen and editors have the task of saving what the television directors have not thought about. That is their everyday work. The television directors have only to think about the final product."[27] This leads him to lament that the work of editors is invisible. "Nothing is worse than when someone's work is concealed."[28] In this case, the production process does not just alienate images by tearing them away from their original context. It also alienates the work of editors. It obscures the editors' labor and disregards their artistry and skill. Television editors are cogs in a machine, part of the alienated labor force.

However, Farocki also accuses television producers of sloppiness and even laziness. He disparages the carelessness of many of the cinematographers' shots.[29] This carelessness, he observes, generates images that conform to a generic television house style that is minor compared to cinema's techniques. Television producers take too many shortcuts. Not knowing the role their sequences will play in the final product, they must shoot as many different angles and perspectives as possible. As a result, many of their shots and points of view signify later, when editors make them contribute to the overall meaning. The television cinematographers' viewpoints provide the editors with options to produce smooth, uninterrupted appearances. "To make all the sequences fit together, the lens and camera are constantly moved. The camera operators also record intermediate cuts so that imperceptible cuts can be made later.... The editors, who are supplied with these images, then make sure that everything fits together."[30] The camera operator is not included in the work's conceptual process and therefore does not participate in the co-production of meaning. A strict hierarchy of roles and division of labor organizes production. This division of labor results in disconnected, interchangeable phrases or isolated image fragments that do not coalesce into a contiguous whole. Because the creative process excludes camera operators, they lack control over their shot sequences. As a result, their images are doubly objectified, first by them and then by the editors. The manipulation is even greater if they film without an audio track. Farocki explains, "If you haven't ordered it, it's hard to control what happens in front of the camera. But because there must be control, one prefers to make the images dead and mute. You cover them up with a text instead of working on them until they speak."[31] Silent images can be more easily manipulated since editors can add commentary and Foley sounds to postproduction to shape meaning.

Farocki concludes that "the art of the graduated production of meaning is completely lost in the staged film narrative. There, meaning comes from the presentation and handling of footage. Here one uses what one can get. And the entire text makes detours to take in something else, as in verse from the *rhyming lexicon* [my emphasis]."[32] Industrialization replaces craft and manual techniques. It replaces thought too. Without a rationale behind their employment, camera operators' images become poor copies of cinema's movements, styles, angles, and other characteristics. Farocki continues, "Because the working method destroys the craft, the cinematographers recall the means of expression of the cinema film, in which the camera craft had a fixed value. The apparatus does not permit memory, but only falsification."[33] The production's every aspect is affected, from zooms to cross-cutting, camera movement, lighting, angles, and composition. As a result, television becomes a poor replica of film, an imitation not of life but verisimilitude. The filmed sequences function as hollow phrases and gestures that editors further diminish and degrade.

The next stage in the production of television programs takes place in the studio's editing rooms. The responsibility of cohering a narrative from an array of disconnected images rests with the editors. Farocki describes suites inhabited primarily by female editors (*Cutterinnen*) who work with a panoply of material, including shots of architecture; people kissing, arguing, or trying to kill each other; birds flying; and politicians giving speeches. The editors select images from this vast assortment and order them to conform to the preexistent commentary. They bring together images with no prior connection. The German word for an editor, "*Cutterin*," which appropriates the English word "cut," is instructive here.[34] Remarkably, *Cutterin* draws attention to the violence necessary to reshape the film stock into a new configuration.

The images the editors manipulate exist in a vast repository in the studios. Farocki notes, "In television, we hardly ever work with images that are built up. We almost only work with images that are found. That's why it's hard to decide before shooting and during shooting what should be in the finished film. The films are edited less in the camera and written more at the editing table. Which is not to say that it makes the editor's work better."[35] Editors must make sense of this flood of images stimulated by the director's preconceived ideas. The images are purely illustrative; they do not produce but embellish arguments. Their decorative function obscures the truth because, from the onset, the editors put them together deceptively. This observation leads Farocki to assert that lies underpin the editing process. "The work at the editing table is one of covering up, ironing out, and saving. Because it is devoid of articulation, it reduces the editors to technical assistants who arrange and label the material. The result comprises a heap of *mannerisms* [my emphasis]."[36] The rank of words to images, with the latter subordinate to the former, results in a production hierarchy. Words are the product of a creative director whose status is that of an author. Workers select images that will help produce the composition.[37]

Television production studios resemble factories. Their strict schedules ensure maximum production. During the 1970s, WDR had sixty-five editing rooms and made approximately eighty-five productions a year. Farocki calculates an average of three weeks of editing for each broadcast and notes that this fast-paced production plays havoc with value. The studios assess their editors' success according to categories of quantity and quality. "The two types of work," Farocki observes, distinguishing productivity and craftsmanship, "are separated by payment and status."[38] But despite this scathing critique, Farocki is not entirely dismissive of the profession. His emphasis on how television production has distorted the value of editors seeks to encourage a return to pride in craftwork. He wants to redeem the editors' role and actualize television's potential as a mass medium for education and communication. In this respect, Farocki's take on media echoes Brecht's pronouncements on radio, which underscore that it is not the technology that one should condemn, but the way those in power use it.[39] One should not separate Farocki's critique of television from the industry's production methods and working conditions. However, he adds that although labor disputes in the television industry "are usually about better pay and working conditions, they can also be about better work."[40] What begins as a critique of a specific type of television documentary extends structurally to a critique of the entire production process.

The Trouble with Images and *The Struggle with Images* are compilation films composed of found footage assembled at the editing table. Farocki uses the same editing techniques he critiques to develop his arguments. At first glance, it seems as if he, too, takes images and filmed sequences out of context and arranges them in new constellations to support a preconceived thesis articulated through a voice-over. However, the commentary calls into question the images on display. The narrator's cadence and rhythm are carefully measured, self-reflexively bringing attention to their role. Pauses, blank screens, and repetitions provide spaces for reflection and thought. In another film from the same period, *Moderators* (1974), Farocki further explains how his technique contrasts sharply with those of conventional television. *Moderators* reveals the extent to which television hosts and moderators rely on rhetorical strategies to link disparate stories and images, creating a false sense of an uninterrupted, seamless flow of information.

Farocki quickly corrects the impression that he disapproves of using text in films. As he explains, "I want to avoid the misunderstanding that I have something against many words in films or accompanying films. I'm concerned not about the fact that they're used, but about how they're used, their qualitative use."[41] Farocki conceives words and images as phrases. His edits place sounds and images into constellations of meaning: "The work at the editing table converts colloquial speech into written language.... At the editing table, babble is turned into rhetoric."[42] Farocki repeats images and words, sometimes exactly, sometimes with slight variations, in his films. He follows a schema related to Artavazd Peleshyan's "distance montage" theory, where quoted phrases' repetition pulls them out of previously obscure contexts. As Farocki explains, "There's a simple way to make phrases stand out. One has to remove them from the context in which they want to hide, and to repeat them, expose them to scrutiny."[43]

The fundamental difference between the television productions Farocki critiques and his own is that he serves as both director and editor for the latter. As an auteur he is responsible for and takes part in all aspects of production, constructing his creations from their conceptual beginnings to their ends. He remains involved in each step of the production process and immersed in every detail. As he explains, in 1980, "A director who does his own editing once told me that he could not understand how anyone could translate a text they did not know by heart. That is the work performed at the editing table: getting to know the material so well that the decisions taken as to where to make a cut, which version of a shot to use, or which music to play, follow of their own accord."[44] According to Farocki, skilled editors must scrutinize their material regardless of the predetermined plan or concept. Often, previously undetected elements emerge—elements not visible when shooting or upon first viewing. "At the editing table, one discovers that the shooting has established new subject matter. At the cutting table a second script is created that refers not to intentions but to actual facts."[45] Barthes calls such unplanned details the film's "third meaning," and Benjamin theorizes them as traces of an "optical unconscious." The camera unwittingly captures them. As Chris Marker, whose productions Farocki followed, once remarked: "One never knows what one is filming." The camera person (now with digital technology) puts what they're looking at in focus. But this blinkered gaze commonly leads to oversights, even of blatantly visible details. It is left to the attentive film editor to detect them. Farocki paraphrases Godard, "Don't search, find!"[46]

Farocki first takes up the paradox of the view that does not see in *Bilderkrieg* (Images-War) (1987). In this production, he addresses the then-recent discovery of aerial photographs of the Buna factory adjacent to Auschwitz in Poland. He reflects that, on first viewing, no one saw the camps in the photographs, concluding that they did not see them because they were not looking for them; they were looking for munition factories instead. A camera pictures whatever lies before its viewfinder, regardless of the human intention behind the lens. Farocki takes the documentary power of imaging indiscriminately without subjective intervention one step further when theorizing what he refers to as "operational images." As he explains, the latter are images taken by cameras automatically, beyond the human eye's control. Farocki's later work extensively probes this type of image.

Farocki's editing work was fundamental to his fine art production. Editing entails more than merely assembling images. It involves unearthing what images might hide. "You don't have to search for new, never-before-seen images, but you have to take the images at hand and work on them in such a way that they become new. There are various ways to do this. My way is to look for submerged meaning, clearing away the detritus on the images."[47] The editing table is the site of close reading. The goal of the meticulous analysis of frames is to uncover what images reveal, regardless of what their makers sought to capture. Along the way, editors may also discover production errors or sloppy takes and shortcuts: "At the editing table, with the film winding back and forth, you can experience the autonomy of the image. In the same way as slow-motion scenes from soccer matches have trained the eye to distinguish genuine fouls from faked ones, the editing table teaches one how to tell which fouls in film production are genuine and which fake."[48] For Farocki, as indeed for Godard and Marker, editing was crucial to filmmaking. Many of his productions are editing tour-de forces, assembled almost entirely from found footage.[49] Both aesthetic and economic principles drive this production technique.

Imaging commodities tracks back to capitalism's beginnings. In *Still Life* (1997), Farocki, ventriloquized through Kaja Silverman's voice, analyzes several seventeenth-century Flemish paintings depicting assortments of fruit, vegetables, and luxury items. These things signify their owner's wealth. They also point to colonialism's global trade routes. Farocki intercuts his examination of the Dutch masterworks with three contemporary advertisements that stage objects. One features cheese, another beer, and the third a Cartier watch. Farocki filmed these sequences in an observational mode without commentary. Formally, because there is no commentary, they stand in contrast to his close readings of the Dutch still lifes. Nevertheless, the analogy between the visual fields is striking. The viewer is left to wonder if, in the future, mass media advertisement images will be subject to the same scrutiny as fine art paintings are today.

What differences are innate to each medium—painting vs. photography—and how do they converge? In *Sarah Schumann Paints an Image* (1977), Farocki films over nine weeks in the studio of the eponymous artist as she creates a collage painting. Schumann commences with photographs she has made or cut out of glossy magazines. She places a large photographic portrait of a young woman in the center of her canvas and surrounds it with smaller images sourced from the magazines. Next, Schumann paints over the canvas's remaining white spaces. As the weeks go by, she applies more photographs and paint. Each layer adds meaning, and the resulting composite work oscillates between photography and painting. The two media blend, blurring boundaries. Schumann explains, "The surroundings should penetrate into the photo and the photo into the surroundings." The film unfolds in silence, with intertitles showing the date and number of hours worked marking the days. When Schumann has almost finished the collage painting, Farocki asks her to speak about her process. The artist faces the camera.

Directly behind Schumann is a large mirror that reflects Farocki and his film equipment. The resulting mise-en-scène draws attention to the cinematic apparatus. It breaks the fourth wall and juxtaposes two types of image-making within one frame. The scene also recalls Emile D'Antonio's interview with Andy Warhol in the documentary *Painters Painting* (1973). Farocki wears headphones and is surrounded by recording equipment, including booms, cameras, tripods, and cables. By contrast, Schumann stands with her artwork. When Farocki asks why she altered all the photographs affixed to the canvas except for the initial portrait, she responds, "I know her so I didn't change her—it is the rest, the environment, the structure that changes." Schumann continues with the claim that "the

1.6 Harun Farocki, *Sarah Schumann Paints an Image* (1977)

person's authenticity results from the photograph," which affirms the myth that technology approximates the "real" better than the human hand. The interplay and tension between the "real," as replicated by photography's indexicality, and the "imaginary," produced by painting, is at stake.

Several of Farocki's productions are preoccupied with the relationship between different types of images. These works contrast manually produced sketches, drawings, and paintings with mechanically reproduced photographs and films. The different media co-exist often within the same pictorial frame. For example, in *Über "Song of Ceylon" von Basil Wright* (About *Song of Ceylon* by Basil Wright) (1975), Farocki intersperses Basil Wright's 1934 footage with watercolors. Likewise, during an interview with Vilém Flusser, Farocki suggests that perhaps a hand-drawn sketch would be better for certain subjects. And, the act of drawing repeats several times in *Images of the World and the Inscription of War* (1988).

In *Stadtbild* (View of the City) (1981), Farocki further investigates the ontology of photographic images and their function as indexical signs. He films historical photographs, doubling their indexicality. Farocki displays them against a dark backdrop framed by a thin white border as if in an album. The pictures come from previously published collections. They bear witness to the time when they were first made and the time when Farocki reshot them.[50] The commentator draws attention to the nesting of one medium in another: "Although we are speaking about photographs, the material used is 16mm. The negative is about as big as a fingernail. Under these circumstances I can't replicate the photograph completely, only impart something of its impression. For that reason, I keep a distance from the images and respect that the format of photographs is different than that of TV screens."

Farocki divides *View of the City* into chapters, each marked by an index card upon which he writes the title, author, and year of publication. Index cards aid researchers in accessing archives. Before the invention of digital archives, these shorthand files referenced larger stores of information. Archivists designed their uniform format to be easily accessible to the user. Each card is a condensed record of knowledge; it functions synecdochically, pointing to a greater whole. By contrast, analog photography and celluloid film indexically record what lies before the camera. They encode witnessing, documenting, and preservation. As a bibliophile who loved playing with the etymology of words, Farocki toys with the multiple meanings of "index."

Farocki's dual interest in architecture and filmmaking surfaces in *View of the City*. The project developed from an earlier planned but never realized episode for Sesame Street, *Häuser 1–2* (Buildings 1-2), that compared destroyed houses to intact ones. Farocki explores several themes, including the tension between still photographs and moving images, modernization processes, and using images to tell stories and make arguments. Each section focuses on a photography book. An interview with the person who assembled the pictures and, when possible, the photographer follows. It begins with images of Berlin by photographers Willi Saeger and Friedrich Seidenstücker, taken during the immediate aftermath of World War II. The allied armies' bombing raids and artillery rounds reduced the city to rubble. Photographs of the former bustling urban center reveal vast expanses of open space where once there were buildings. One photo depicts haystacks in front of the former Reichstag. Farocki observes that the city's destruction was so extensive that its former condition seems like "a distant memory": "the time before the war has become an antiquity."

Some photographs featured in *View of the City* impart a sense of restored normalcy, such as one of two students chatting in a bombed-out doorway while clutching their school satchels or another of young people in conversation sitting on collapsed columns in a courtyard. But most picture only the city's destruction. Over a photo of the Siegesallee in ruins, Farocki repeats the line: "the time before the war has become an antiquity."[51] The opening of *View of the City* recalls Roberto Rossellini's *Germany Year Zero* (1948), with its extensive filmed-on-location shots of a bombed-out Berlin. The photographs also evoke Albert Speer's theory of "ruin value," derived from nineteenth-century Romanticism.[52] Speer proposed that the Third Reich construct buildings and monuments with fault lines to ensure they would retain their aesthetic value if destroyed. There is a questionable aesthetic veneration in both the photos and the nostalgic tone of Farocki's analysis. Farocki does not mention why such devastation occurred. Perhaps he considered this historical detail too obvious.

In the next section, Farocki turns to the pre-war period that he fears people might forget. He examines Janos Frecot's *Berlin and Potsdam Architecture Photos: 1872–1875* (1980). Frecot assembled an impressive number of vintage prints of imperial-era houses and buildings. Through meticulous research, he identifies each edifice and provides information about its construction and ownership. Unfortunately, many of the buildings no longer exist. Farocki observes that photographers staged their "portraits of houses" in isolation at the time of their imaging. He likens the open spaces in front of the buildings to the broad exposure of necks and chests in portraits of women that highlight their "décolletage." These majestic houses appear impervious to damage. They stand in sharp contrast to contemporary housing structures.

Farocki imparts that when he was a child, such architecture signified an oppressive past, whereas new construction was full of optimism. He notes that his discovery of Elisabeth Niggemeyer and Wolf Jobst Siedler's photobook *Die gemordete Stadt* (The Murdered City) (1964) changed his perspective in the 1960s. Niggemeyer and Siedler compare ornate details and facades from pre-war buildings to the postwar period's uniformly flat, unadorned surfaces. Niggemeyer, who took the photos, explains that those details reveal a history of the city's "liveliness." Modern structures, she insists, are sterile and comfortless. They prompt a romantic nostalgia for the old buildings. However, Farocki is primarily interested in the design layout of *The Murdered City*, which juxtaposes past and present photos. Farocki examines a first edition of the photo essay, because, as he notes, subsequent editions have changed the format of the images, because the horizontal axis of the page has been shortened thereby not permitting multiple images to be displayed and juxtaposed in the same visual field. In his words, the original layout allows "the book to make arguments with images and imagery." Later, in *View of the City*, Farocki peruses an exhibition by Bazon Brock that explores the rebuilding of Germany after the war by placing contrasting images next to each other. Again, this examination leads him to ask how images think and argue. Spatial composition and montage's connection to rhetorical structures are crucial to his analysis.

Farocki anticipates, by a couple of years, Flusser's theories on the layout of images and their positioning vis-à-vis each other as a mode of communication. Flusser maintains that photographs produce non-linear compositions and readings because they encourage viewers to scan them. By contrast, a film, like a book, is organized linearly. Just as sentences follow in texts and pages, images follow in films. Montage, including dialectical montage based on the collision of opposites, adheres to this linear regime. However, in the visual arts, assemblage, montage, and collage will perform differently according to media distinctions. A picture's surface may feature multiple static images, but the images rush by in a time-based medium like film. Montage can juxtapose pictures and words within a single visual frame: Schumann does this with works that employ printed pictures and paint.

Farocki is intrigued by the rhetorical possibilities enabled by the simultaneous presentation of two discrete image sets. Can two images placed next to each other communicate dialogically? This sort of strategic positioning is fundamental to curatorial and exhibition practices. Meaning depends on the particular makeup of constellations; the building blocks of all signifying practices generate sense based on a relational differentiation process.

Farocki's next step is to apply these principles to moving images. He experimented with running two separate sequences simultaneously within the same frame already in *Eine Sache, die sich versteht (15x)* (Something Self-Explanatory [15x]) (1971). His interest in Ann-Marie Miéville and Godard's *Here and Elsewhere* (1974) and *Numéro Deux* (1975) was primarily due to their split-screen technologies. Although Farocki was thinking about the creative potential of employing multiple screens at that time, it was not until the mid-1990s that two factors coalesced that enabled him to accomplish this feat. First, technological developments in editing systems: from linear analog to digital scanning. Second, he moved from presenting his work on television and film platforms to art exhibition venues.

1.7 Hartmut Bitomsky and Harun Farocki, *Something Self-Explanatory (15x)* (1971)

1.8 Harun Farocki, *Interface* (1995)

Farocki's first two-monitor installation project, *Interface* (1995), explicates and exposes the implications of this dual shift.[53]

Interface begins with footage on the left-hand screen of Farocki writing by hand in a lined notebook. A monitor features on the right-hand screen, on which silent images play from Farocki's co-directed film, with Andrei Ujica, *Videograms of a Revolution* (1992). Farocki then delivers a voice-over commentary that creates a sound bridge between the two screens. He says he "can hardly write a word these days if there isn't an image on the screen at the same time, actually on both screens." The next shot on the left-hand screen reveals him at a desk with two monitors and an editing machine. The same images from *Videograms of a Revolution* continue to play on the right.

The transition from analog to digital editing systems profoundly affected Farocki's production. In a retrospective conversation with Rembert Hüser, Farocki recalls that the effects of the change on his production were both formal and conceptual:

Touching the reel was pleasantly reassuring—like when you open a book and know immediately where you are in the book.... There was always the idea that future projection would turn the caterpillar into a butterfly—you don't get that with electronic images. There, you are dealing with two images! On the right is the edited image; on the left is the next image to be added on. The right image makes a demand, but is also being criticized by the left one, sometimes even condemned. This made me experiment with double projection works.... One image doesn't take the place of the previous one but supplements it, re-evaluates it, and balances it.[54]

Interface's focus is on editing. The film's opening words, spoken by Farocki, articulate his inability to think through a new film if he is not at the editing station. He says, "I write into the images and then read something out of them." He updates his earlier meditations as the film progresses. At one point, he describes editing as an intimate experience, "which I would never be able to share with anyone." He positions himself as an isolated auteur and underscores the many hours, days, and weeks spent at the workstation transferring material. He recalls how he works, "transferring every shot from a film from one tape to another. I only take twelve frames from each shot. This is a lengthy process, so I can talk about other things. Metaphor means to transfer." Pointing to a control desk, a player, and a recorder, he informs the viewer, "This is a workstation, an editing station for the reworking of images and sounds." He also insists on presenting two images simultaneously, "one image in relation to another: image and counter-image." While he says this, he shows the digital editing complex on the left screen and the analog table on the right. Farocki continues, "When working with film instead of video you have to make an actual cut in the image or sound strip." This method, he explains, differs from video editing, where one copies "from one tape to the next, making an imaginary cut and not a real one." For Farocki, the analog process is both intellectual and tactile. He emphasizes film editing's haptic nature, which goes beyond seeing and hearing. He discloses that he touches the material when editing film: "I keep the tip of my finger on the running image or sound reel to feel the cut or the glue before I see or hear it. This is a gesture of 'fine perception' or 'sensitivity.'" This phenomenon contrasts with his video production, where his fingers do not touch the tape. "When working with video..., I only push buttons." Nevertheless, he concludes that both techniques require fingertip (digital) activity.

The double-screen montage technique, which Farocki refers to as "soft montage," allows associations to be suggested spatially and not mandated temporally. His use of this technique is directly related to conceptual and material transformations made possible by the shift from analog to digital editing and exhibition format changes due to the migration of moving images into the gallery. New spatial configurations allow the images to dialogue with each other. In *Interface*, Farocki explains, "One can grasp this duality that one image comments on the other. To date only words, or sometimes music, comment on images. Here images comment on image." However, it is not just still images like photographs that communicate with each other. Moving images do too. In his characterization of the essay, Adorno stresses that the genre is never static; each of its components contains movement within itself and with others in the constellation: "the elements crystallize as a configuration through their motion," becoming a moving thought image.[55]

Interface is structured chronologically, following Farocki's oeuvre. He replays the opening sequences of his better-known films, reworking and transforming them from single to double-channel projections. Repetition of the original commentary heightens the alienation effect that results from viewing Farocki analyzing and manipulating his earlier productions. The works shift acoustically from the past to the present. Farocki slightly delays his delivery, creating the same echo effect as he did two decades earlier in *Erzählen* (About Narration) (1975). In this manner, he underscores the temporal lag between *Interface*, on the one hand, and *Inextinguishable Fire* (1969), *Zwischen zwei Kriegen* (Between Two Wars) (1978), and *Images of the World and the Inscription of War*, on the other.

Farocki poses questions about his production in *Interface*. He also contributes pithy explanations of his previous productions. For example, in regard to *Inextinguishable Fire*, he asks if one could equate his editing work with scientific study. He concludes that the earlier films are models rather than portrayals. He notes that workstations do not look like this: "This isn't a depiction of an editing station, it's a model." Models, like index cards, are condensed, simplified representations of more complex systems. Film, for Farocki, is a model, a precursor to the virtual worlds of video games created by computer-generated images.

In *Interface*, Farocki edits film stock and explains how "montage may be used to invert images and recombine them." He analyzes *Workers Leaving the Factory* (1995), placing the found footage's documentary shots on the left-hand monitor and the ones from fictional feature films on the right. He wonders what his initial aim was when he began to study images of workers leaving factories. He recalls that he first understood "how to view images unintentionally, in one swoop until the blueprint of the film unfolded on its own." Later, while editing *An Image* (1983), he "learned how to reclaim from the images the text that would accompany them." "I spoke to the images and heard things from them," he says. In *Interface*'s analysis of *Between Two Wars*, Farocki, referring to himself as "the author," observes how, at the film's beginning, "the script jumps from the desk into the scenes of the film." This jump, he maintains, is "a jump back in time. The author brings to life a text handed down from history."

Interface ends with Farocki researching Alan Turing's inventions and contemplating a new project about encoding messages. Over the image of a coding machine, he explains that he relied on a simple program that combined and recombined shots when making *Images of the World and the Inscription of War*: "The program I used provided the film's order. At that time, I was thinking about both music's compositional rules and the wheel in a slot machine." Finally, he ends *Interface* with an elusive set of questions to challenge his films' viewers: "Does this editing station encode or decode? Does it unravel a secret? Or does it maintain its confidentiality?" For Farocki, editing is filmmaking's most crucial aspect. Unlike television's *cutterins*, he considers good editors authors who work directly with images. The competent editor communicates, thinks, argues, transforms, and translates ideas through weaving texts.

CHAPTER 2

Labor

The cinema, in documentary and other forms, has rarely filmed work.
—Jean-Louis Comolli, "Mechanical Bodies, Ever More Heavenly"

The first camera in the history of cinema was pointed at a factory, but a century later it can be said that film is hardly drawn to the factory and is even repelled by it. Films about work or workers have not become one of the main genres, and the space in front of the factory has remained on the sidelines.
—Harun Farocki, "Workers Leaving the Factory"

Following the example of the steel industry, where every waste product flows back into the production process and hardly any energy is lost, I try to create a compound of my works.
—Harun Farocki, "Necessary Variation and Variety"

Since relocating to West Berlin when he was sixteen years old, Farocki made work and labor issues a central concern. At first, it was a matter of how to support himself and retain relative independence from his parents (although, as mandated by the law, he still received a monthly stipend). During his early years in West Berlin, he held several odd jobs, including unloading freight at Tempelhof Airport and working in clubs. Farocki constantly worked, sometimes at multiple engagements, and throughout his adult life was always on the lookout for the next gig. He recalls, "There have been times when I've done several productions in several towns, ... times when I read my way through libraries for 5 months for a measly fee of 1,000 marks.... I realized that I was often putting myself in situations where I had to accept everything, where I really couldn't afford to have any scruples anymore."[1] Even as he grew older and established a steady income, the compulsion to work hard and for long hours was hard to shake. It is, therefore, not surprising that a politics based on the economy of labor grounded his filmmaking practice till the end.

One of Farocki's last projects, *Eine Einstellung zur Arbeit* (Labour in a Single Shot, 2011-14), co-realized with Antje Ehmann, revisits his decades-long commitment to labor politics.[2] To make this production, Ehmann and Farocki conducted fifteen video-production workshops in cities worldwide, from Moscow to Bangalore, Cairo, Buenos Aires, Boston, Mexico City, and many others. (Following Farocki's death, Ehmann has organized additional workshops in Chicago, Marseille, Vilnius, and elsewhere.) In each site, Farocki and Ehmann teamed up with local educational institutions. They invited students and instructors to participate in ten-day working seminars where they taught basic direct-filmmaking principles. The seminars' only provisos were that the topic had to focus on labor and the participants presented their footage without cuts. The format harkened back to the early *actualités* of the late-nineteenth century. Upon the completion of each workshop, Farocki and Ehmann posted the videos online.[3] This platform remains accessible to this day. The videos range in length from between one to two minutes. In addition, Farocki and Ehman sometimes install selections from the workshops in galleries, museums, and other art exhibition spaces as double-sided hanging projection screens. Currently, *Labour in a Single Shot* features over three hundred contemporary portraits of labor (both material and immaterial) and laborers. The latter often represent themselves.

Farocki has long been concerned with the invisibility of work, the lack of shots or staged scenes of labor in cinema, and the workers' effacement. His fascination with the cinematic representation of labor directly relates to his observation that work is everywhere and yet nowhere at once; it is the elephant in the room that few want to address. Labor permeates all industries, especially those from which it gives the veneer of having the greatest distance: entertainment, education, sports, culture, art, and war. Farocki traces this representational problematic back to the Lumière brothers' *Workers Leaving the Factory* (1895), cited by many as cinema's first production. For Farocki, the closing of the factory gates at the end of the Lumière brothers' short signals the onset of an ideological barrier against filming what takes place within factories. Cinema does not represent workers performing their labor; it represents their life only once the workday is over. On those occasions when cinema represents workers, it is as an anonymous mass. Farocki's eleven-channel installation *Workers Leaving the Factory in Eleven Decades* (2006) probes this phenomenon in film history.

Farocki's interest in representations of labor extends back to his early study of Bertolt Brecht and, in particular, to two of the latter's pronouncements. The first is Brecht's well-known statement that a photograph of a Krupps factory tells us nothing about the social relations within the factory.[4] The second is Brecht's poem "Questions of a Worker Who Reads," which evokes the unnamed laborers that undergird the success of all great humans and even build their memorials. The poem asks, "In what houses of gold glittering Lima did the builders live? Where, the evening that the Wall of China was finished did the masons go?" The last lines read: "Every page a victory. Who cooked for the victors? Every ten years a great man. Who paid the bill? So many reports. So many questions."[5] Factory workers appear in Farocki's first feature, *Inextinguishable Fire* (1969). However, the film leaves the question of what the workers produce unclear. They either manufacture vacuum cleaners that users can reconfigure as machine guns or machine guns that users can retool into vacuum cleaners. Like with the picture puzzle, the function of the commodity is a matter of perspective. The film presents workers metonymically as part of the larger military-industrial complex. At the core of Farocki's worldview is an ideological commitment to Marxism's insistence on the economy as the base that underpins all social relations. Finally, Farocki was attentive to his labor and, following the steel industry example (*Verbundsystem*), carefully ensured that none of it went to waste.

Farocki's awareness of the integral role of economics in everyday life is present in his earliest writings. He came of age during the height of the rebuilding of West Germany and its *Wirtschaftswunder* (economic miracle) culture. He was keenly critical of the deleterious effects of this consumer culture and the logic of advertising. One of his early reviews, "Glanz und Elend auf vier Rädern: Der Schrott in unser Landschaft" (Shine and Misery on Four Wheels: Scrap Metal in our Landscape, 1964), sardonically attacks the new *wegwerf* (disposable) society. In it, he describes the fate of an abandoned 1954 Buick: "Previously old cars were cannibalized, their metal was melted down, and people did not throw their cars into the field every Spring. There are about two hundred vehicles which expire every day. Cars made between 1950–1955 are left to die because those were weak years. Once the sixties generation has died there will be no one left to recycle raw material."[6] Farocki mobilizes the disposable fate of cars as a metaphor to critique the new West German consumer society. Instead of fixing or repairing cars barely a decade old or melting them down for their metal, they sit rusting in "car cemeteries," cast off without value. Hence, "a car cemetery [functions as] nothing but the ultimate proof of a prosperous society."[7]

TO TEACH

In the late 1960s, Farocki's writing integrated Marxist critiques of ideology and theories of capital. His 1967 trip to South America sparked an interest in "Third World" liberation politics and practices of decolonization. During these years, he reviewed translations of Regis Debray, Fidel Castro, and Ernesto Che Guevara for *Die Zeit* (the equivalent of *The New York Times*). By the end of the 1960s, Farocki stood at a crossroads marked by dual ambivalences regarding the efficacy of direct political action and the impact of political cinema. The ongoing question became how to translate Marxist theory into an effective cinematic practice capable of rendering the complexities of the socio-political-economic fabric. As his published reviews from these years indicate, Farocki was reading widely on contemporary theories of education, economics, and societal change. Increasingly, film's potential to educate and liberate became central.

In the 1969 essay "die agitation verwissenschaftlichen und die wissenschaft politisieren" (making agitation scientific and politicizing science), Farocki tackles the difficulty of introducing politics into both the classroom and film.[8] He confronts the limits of the cinematic and educational institutions. Learning is primarily material-based, with an instructor imparting specialized information to students. Farocki's goal is to break through this closed system to develop a pedagogical strategy that can connect to political agitation and change. Changes in pedagogy call for radically novel approaches. Farocki writes "making agitation scientific and politicizing science" in small-case letters (the German language capitalizes the first letter of all nouns), underscoring that a new politics demands a new form of writing or filmmaking, as the case may be. Farocki's concern is also with the role of film in education. He questions the material currently taught, to whom it is taught, the lesson plan's goals, and the medium the pedagogical mission employs: Books? Tapes? Films? He proposes that films have inherent instructional limits because "one cannot initiate a dialogue free of domination with the medium, at most through it. The flow of film is always hierarchical. It goes from one source to many recipients."⁹ In an unpublished co-authored typescript, Farocki and Bitomsky detail how they plan to break through the hierarchical system. They write, "We planned the films for teaching situations for school and training. We applied the so-called single content method. A few minutes of film are shown to the students and then prompt a discussion. There is a division of labor between film and teacher; the film needn't relate everything and thus become loquacious like a feature."¹⁰

In "making agitation acientific and politicizing science," Farocki surveys recent theories of pedagogy. He focuses on those that establish a link between systems of education and the capitalist economy, the former the product of the latter. Farocki turns to cognitive psychologist Sidney L. Pressey to bolster his claims regarding the interconnectivity of the two systems. He explains that "pressey wanted to organize learning the way taylor wanted to organize work. he wanted to track how it was organized in early capitalism; from the infantilization and bestialization of wage earners, to the strict division of labor, and short-term pay." He continues, "pressey's concept of a roll of paper composed of sheets of learning material, followed the idea of the early transport machines belts, on which is based the wage-dependent and now also the knowledge-dependent paid mechanical labor. the learning techniques of skinner and other behaviorists corresponded to capitalist relations from the early thirties on."¹¹ Farocki concludes that the current educational system is a product of capitalism, with theories of learning and pedagogy intimately linked to systems of work and productivity. There must be a corresponding change in education for a change in how people think. Farocki participated in a broader global dialogue that sought to radically reform educational institutions at all levels.¹² It is crucial, when teaching, neither to speak for workers nor to impose ideas and theories about their class oppression on them. Farocki's position resonates with that of Jacques Rancière's, whose *The Ignorant Schoolmaster* stressed the importance of non-hierarchical production of knowledge across classes. As Farocki forcefully underscores, "leftist agitation cannot develop a step system of consciousness, it can't speak to the workers the way imperialists speak to negroes [sic]."¹³ He continues, "Leftist agitation cannot take over the methods of didacticism, it must transform them."¹⁴ Adopting the Soviet theory of transforming society through media, especially film, stresses the importance of communication in learning.

The next step for Farocki was to translate these economic and pedagogical theories into film and television. The immediate result of these dual endeavors was two made-for-television films co-directed with Bitomsky: *The Division of All Days* (1970) and *Something Self-Explanatory (15x)* (1971).[15] In these productions, Bitomsky and Farocki attempt to render abstract economic principles in the audiovisual language of film. With their focus on Marxist economic theory, the films recall Sergei Eisenstein's never realized project to film Marx's *Capital* (1883), and Brecht's struggle to aesthetically represent the dynamic processes of finance capital. Indeed, Farocki recalls retrospectively that "Bitomsky and I planned to film *Das Kapital* by Karl Marx... We read Marx and Marx commentaries and texts on semiotics, cybernetics, didactics and learning machines. Our programme: 'to make film scientifically and make science politically.'"[16] The filmmakers set *The Division of All Days* in a seminar classroom. Farocki, garbed in a floral-patterned shirt, opens the discussion with a question about the meaning of exploitation. He writes the words "NECESSARY WORK/SURPLUS WORK" in block letters on the blackboard. Farocki encourages the seminar's participants to explain what exploitation means to them. He then has them watch a video clip addressing the topic. The clip, titled "Non-Capitalistic Exploitation," is a fictional sequence filmed by him and Bitomsky. It is composed of three scenes. The first is of a man buying an enslaved person, and the second of a carpenter building a chair. The latter complains that the material costs of building the chair exceed his labor costs, which makes the enterprise no longer viable. He concludes that factory production can execute the task more efficiently. The third skit, "housework," tracks social reproduction. Two workers, one female and the other male, go to work. However, once the day is over and they return home, the female puts on an apron and prepares dinner while the male sits at the table. The commentary states, "Both worked for the food. The half of the kitchen work the man benefited from without his paying for it." The brief sequence ends, and the scene shifts back to the classroom with Farocki introducing concepts of productive forces, wages, and social reproduction. He also introduces concepts of necessary and surplus labor. The seminar's participants contribute to the discussion.

The second section of *The Division of All Days*, "Capitalist Exploitation: The Factors of Production and Their Value," follows a similar schema. First, Farocki opens the seminar discussion, and various participants weigh in. Then, he screens segments of a didactic film that focuses on a product's changing units of value (u.o.v.) as determined by the ratio of raw materials, the facilities used for production, and the labor power expended to make the final product. Farocki and Bitomsky repeat the same factory sequence three times, suggesting the repetitive base

2.1 Hartmut Bitomsky and Harun Farocki, *The Division of All Days* (1970)

of Taylorism, with the result that there is a 1,000 u.o.v. in production each time. Yet, when one adds all three columns, the total is not 3,000 u.o.v. but 4,000 u.o.v., realizing a 1,000 u.o.v. (or 25 percent) surplus value. The commentary reads: "Capital makes a profit. To make a profit it has to exploit wage labor. How does this happen?"

The scene then features an image of a worker and a clock that indicates noon (lunchtime). The voice-over reflects, "If the worker stops working now, capital has made no gains, and if it couldn't make any gains, it wouldn't employ him." The clock then speeds forward to a sequence of a factory with a woman posing at a machine. The text reads, "Unpaid Labor." There is a wipe to the left as a man stands in front of his machine. The text reads, "The Unpaid Workday," and the clock is 7:35 a.m. The commentary explains that "unpaid work begins a few minutes after work starts." The camera tracks women working on the factory floor, making telephones. A sequence of workers leaving the factory follows this tracking shot. Over this scene, the commentary announces that "labor power is a commodity, its use value for capital is to create more value than it itself is worth."

The inter-filmic insertion ends, and the setting returns to the seminar room with Farocki at the blackboard.

The third and concluding part of the film is titled "Capitalism Is Progressive." A series of pronouncements introduce a fictional sequence, which is followed by a discussion. The declarative statements are as follows: "1. Capitalism develops world trade," "2. Capitalism internationalizes the proletariat," and "3. Capitalism develops productive forces and the intellectual forces that set them in motion." A break then occurs as documentary footage is introduced, which features images of striking workers. We learn that the workers will be "retrained"—a process that will be the focus of Farocki's film *Die Umschulung* (Retraining, 1994)—and the film shifts to a classroom where they receive education about economic theory. The workers learn how to organize their knowledge and make visible the contradictions inherent in their subject position. A van circulates through the city broadcasting agitational slogans, such as "We make the wealth, but it is his wealth," "We work on the machines, but they are his machines," and "We develop new ideas, but they become his ideas." At the end of this section, a character asks, "How can we abolish the exploiter and work for ourselves?" The film then cuts back to Farocki's seminar, concluding with his explaining Marxism's basic tenets.

The Division of All Days follows Brecht's concept of a "*Lehrstück.*" Just as Brecht's concept sought to break down the fourth wall between actors and audience through participatory learning scenarios, Farocki and Bitomsky's technique aims to facilitate an interactive seminar comprised both of those featured in the film set as well as those anonymous audiences viewing the film. The filmmakers insert formally staged sequences composed of actors playing types that reproduce attitudes and gestures rather than assuming characters' roles. Overall, the didactic film creates a model seminar or classroom in which Farocki and Bitomsky employ film tactically as a learning tool to teach students the basic tenets of capitalism. They shoot the film of the seminar as a documentary. The camera follows the speakers. By contrast, the film-within-a-film sequences are stilted-set pieces emphasizing their artificial and staged nature. Moreover, the filmmakers underscore the sequences' scriptedness by repeating them multiple times with only slight variations. Ideally both the staged seminar participants and the real viewers of the film will learn together.

Farocki first refers to the concept of "operational" in "making agitation scientific and politicizing science." At this point, the term still differs from "operational images," which he will later use to account for images not taken by humans, such as those from surveillance cameras. Farocki's encounter with "operational" language has two sources: Sergei Tretyakov and Roland Barthes. He writes, in "making agitation scientific and politicizing science": "tretyakov has coined the terms *beschreibend* 'writing as description' and *informierend* 'writing to inform' to distinguish literary genres. the agitational film or any part of an agitation is operational. the informing (operational) film can speak of anything, of its own speechlessness as well as of a political topic. the operational film can only speak of what is part of the operation.... teaching is operational."[17] Farocki evokes the Russian constructivist writer who was associated with a group of revolutionaries that followed the linguistic theories of Ferdinand de Saussure. Saussure divided language into "*langue*" and "*parole*" and explored the language of newspapers as mechanical, autonomized, and informational (operational) instead of the poetic language of poets and novelists. Tretyakov argued that the newspaper format overdetermines journalistic writing.[18] Journalists base language on pre-determined forms that resort to stereotypes and linguistic clichés to convey meaning. Tretyakov referred to this type of language as operational. "Revolutionary phrases—clichés like 'the onslaught of capital'—were linguistic readymades, prefabricated syntactic formulae that were fashioned for deployment in specific communicative contexts."[19] As I noted earlier, operational language appears in Barthes's *Mythologies*. However, at this point, Farocki does not address Barthes's language theory, also derived from Saussure's categories of langue and parole. For now, Farocki translates Tretyakov's concept to film and turns to nonfictional, instructive, or documentary films rather than poetic or fictional films to transmit abstract political thought. The set language of newspapers becomes equivalent to that of documentaries. Operational language must be strategically deployed as part of the class struggle, and it constitutes revolutionary language. This will be the focus of Farocki's *Die Sprache der Revolution* (The Language of Revolution, 1972).

The Division of All Days' reception was weak. The film came across to its critics as too dry and pedantic. It failed to expand on Marx's writings. This criticism led Farocki and Bitomsky to contemplate the film's shortcomings. They questioned how to make a compelling political film about abstract thought. As Farocki writes at the time, "The central difficulty in making political films is the transformation of abstract ideas into concrete examples and the transformation of concrete examples into abstract ideas. The relationship or placement of these two elements within a film must be such that it produces agitation. Agitation is a method of learning."[20]

The year following the production of *The Division of All Days*, Bitomsky and Farocki made *Something Self-Explanatory (15x)*. This time they dismissed the classroom structure in favor of a series of fifteen satirical skits once again reminiscent of Brecht's *Lehrstücke*. Each chapter loosely focuses on an aspect of capital. The disconnected scenes recall Eisenstein's plans for filming *Capital*. Recognizing that a conventional plot and narrative logic cannot render the complexity of Marx's work, Eisenstein proposed a composition made from thousands of fragments and details. This technique, he believed, would generate a new type of cinema. It would assemble "one point of view from many events."[21] As Bitomsky and Farocki explain in "Die Frage nach dem Kräfteverhältnis der Kämpfenden: Eine Art Lehrplan" (The Question of the Power Relations Between the Combatants: A Type of Curriculum, 1971), a pamphlet essay they wrote to accompany the film, *Something Self-Explanatory (15x)* is "a porous text" that approaches the matter from multiple perspectives. "We taught economic details, but we also brought in experiences that the reality of the law of value has shaped in cinema and life."[22]

Each chapter of *Something Self-Explanatory (15x)* comprises a tightly scripted scenario with characters who perform roles corresponding to the designated topic. Bitomsky and Farocki do not fully develop the characters; they serve only as types. Chapter 1, "Are the Wages Fair," opens with a man and a woman driving through a staged set filled with advertisements and images of consumer goods necessary for achieving middle-class status in the new West German republic. This opening shot repeats the first lines of Marx's *Capital*, "The wealth of societies in which the capitalist mode of production prevails, appears as an immense collection of commodities."[23] The point of view is from the backseat of the car. It positions the spectator as a passenger, perhaps a child, witness to the white hetero-normative couple that expresses its desire for the shiny commodities they drive by: furniture sets, a dishwasher, a fancy watch, a four-room apartment. The couple woefully questions, "How do we get the money to acquire these goods?" A benevolent voice of god responds, "You can sell your labor power—then you can buy things." The couple then asks where they can sell their labor power, and the voice instructs them to make a left-hand turn. An image of the couple with a new color television follows the wail of an air-raid siren. The couple will return in chapter 4 to recount all the goods they have purchased and try

2.2 Hartmut Bitomsky and Harun Farocki, *The Division of All Days* (1970)

to balance them against the money they have earned. They ruefully express their desire to "keep driving on forever."

Chapter 2, "When Is the Exchange of Things Fair?" represents the historical evolution of economic transactions. It depicts two Romans who compare the value of a capon to that of a pound of honey. A few centuries later, the comparison is between grain and a sickle and closer to the present between an object and two days' worth of work. In chapter 7, "What is the Commodity of Labor Power Anyway?," a man in a suit solicits the labor power of a young athlete. The athlete undresses and swims across the English Channel. His strokes in the waves are perfect. But the suited man tells him to return to shore, for he is wasting his labor power. This man speaks in deadpan to the camera: "[The athlete's] dumping eleven thousand calories in the waves of the Atlantic," yet nobody benefits from his labor power. The swimmer returns to land exhausted. He has expended his labor. He exclaims, "I was in that broth for sixteen hours, and now I feel like a dead fish." A litany of exhortations against labor power wasted on entertainment instead of on productive activities such as splitting wood or shoveling coal follows. The young man remarks, "My labor turns into everything that keeps us alive." The sequence's final inter-title reads: "Labor Power is a commodity whose use value creates more value than it itself is worth." The film proceeds with wry sketches, each explaining a facet of economic theory.

A particularly striking sequence in chapter 3, "What is the Value of Labor Power?" begins with a worker sitting at his machine. The voice-over states that the worker needs calories to carry out his job. Here, Bitomsky and Farocki split the screen. We see a succession of food images on the left and the laborer at work on the right. The commentary notes that the worker will need a break. Shots show him relaxing. He then needs a vacation. We see clips of water skiing and an airplane taking off (see figure 1.7). The split-screen continues with sequences of the labor performed on one side and what it produces materially for the worker on the other. This remarkable sequence advances a new type of montage that anticipates Farocki's later dual-channel installation work.

When he made *Something Self-Explanatory (15x)*, Farocki was working for television. He subsequently recollected how difficult it was "to do anything political in television, firstly because I didn't want to understand politics as simply content or discourse. I was looking for an advanced political practice as promoted by the Groupe Dziga Vertov or Tel Quel. For example, I was against intercuts or shot-countershots."[24] In search of an alternative way to present political material, Farocki conceived of a split-screen that avoids time-based montage sequences and is based instead on holding two different images simultaneously. Thus, two or three years before Jean-Luc Godard and Anne Marie Miéville presented multiple screens in *Here and Elsewhere* (1974), and long before he and Kaja Silverman theorized the notion of "soft montage," Farocki was already operating with a new form of cinematic juxtaposition.

In tandem with making *Something Self-Explanatory (15x)*, Farocki wrote a related essay, "Kapital im Klassenzimmer" (Capital in the Classroom).[25] This text begins as a history of learning technologies, cybernetics, and machines. It then develops a theory of the relationship between capital, knowledge, and educational institutions. Farocki closely reads Marx's *Grundrisse* (1858) and *Capital* to support his concepts. He emphasizes the connection between middle-class education (*Bildung*) and the reproduction of ideology through the production of culture that oppresses the working class. Capital, with its dictate of wealth accumulation, holds the bourgeois class under its sway as it extracts resources from the proletariat. *Something Self Explanatory (15x)* reinforces this concept. Bitomsky and

Farocki break with convention to produce a radically anti-bourgeois and anti-capitalist film.

Something Self Explanatory (15x)'s final sequence, "While the Law of Value Prevails the People Can't Determine Their Lives or Their Own Free Will. They Can Undertake Whatever They Want, but What They Can Undertake Is What They Have to Undertake, What Happens Is What Has to Happen," differs in style from the others. In this scenario, Farocki and Bitomsky imitate the genre of a 1970s popular television crime series. A man returns home after spending three years in jail. In need of money, he decides to rob a small café/bar. His elder mentor warns him that there will be distractions (the "what happens... has to happen" of the title). The scene plays out as the older man predicted. Fortuitous events impede the heist: customers enter the establishment to place orders. Farocki introduces the element of happenstance and the difficulty of preparing for it.[26] He uses these planned chance occurrences to develop a formal style tightly controlled in post-studio production editing. His fictional and nonfictional films adhere to rules and regulations, while also admitting possibilities of programmed chance. Farocki's 1992 text on the essay film, "Unregelmäßig, nicht regellos" (Uncontrolled, but Not Without Rules), touches on this conundrum. The German title, which may be translated as "unruly, but not without rules," alludes to Adorno, who underscores the importance of the element of chance in the essay. Farocki leaves little room for error, plotting and rehearsing each scene carefully. The only exceptions to this method are his observational documentaries, for which he trains his camera on allegedly unscripted scenes, letting individuals speak freely and unpredictably. However, even in these, he takes control during the editing stage.

The year after *Something Self-Explanatory (15x)*, Farocki examined the role of calculated or pre-programmed chance in the culture industry (a topic that resurfaces in *Parallel I–IV* [2014]). In *Remember Tomorrow Is the First Day of the Rest of Your Life* (1972), he compares playing records to listening to songs on the radio. The difference, he states, drawing the following analogy, is like "Essen Machen vs. Essen Gehen" (Cooking Dinner versus Going Out to Eat): "One is a pleasure we plan for others; the other is a pleasure given to us." The short is composed of sequences of a 1960s powder-blue Citroën sedan driving through Berlin. On the radio, American Forces Network (AFN) plays "hit" songs such as Neil Young's "Heart of Gold," Don McLean's "American Pie," and the New Seekers' "I'd Like to Teach the World to Sing." The commentator observes, "Hearing music we like after an eternity has passed gives us a special kind of joy. The AFN, using advertising strategies, perpetually repeats, creating fondness by repetition, turning the present into eternity, so to speak. By means of its repetitions, the station supplies the coordinates of memory.... The AFN transforms the present to nostalgia." Farocki underscores the radio broadcast's ideological power in delivering pleasure "from an unknown source, as if one dreamt something pleasant, but didn't know what." *Calculated chance* is the operative term. The disk jockey must play songs from the station's top-one-hundred charts, and each piece must play five times a day or three times an hour. Decades later, computer algorithms will generate this planned arbitrariness. In *Remember Tomorrow*, the broadcast station is a foreign military occupying power, and the music transmitted is part of a soft-power mission. The seemingly innocuous repetition of pop songs invades the listeners' unconscious. The high-fidelity sound (one of the AFN's trademarks) lures those eager to hear music to tolerate the programmed "messages" targeting the dangers of smoking, especially marijuana. As Farocki notes, AFN does not have direct advertising. Indeed, it doesn't need it since its superior sound quality sufficiently promotes its consumer-based profile and an American way of life. With *Remember Tomorrow*, Farocki produces an incisive critique of the culture industry that bridges his earlier written reviews. All highlight the systematic and totalizing effect of the commodification of culture. Mass entertainment distracts. The real and false memories it evokes transport the listener across time and space. But much of its success depends on chance. At the conclusion of *Remember Tomorrow*, Farocki reflects, "One aspect of happiness is chance; the AFN produces happiness under calculated conditions." Filmmaking functions in a similar way.

Farocki's full-length television broadcast *Einmal wirst auch Du mich lieben: Über die Bedeutung von Heftromanen* (Someday You Will Love Me Too: About the Meaning of Dime Store Novels, 1973) focuses on pop culture's escapism. The pulp fiction publishing industry and the formulaic romance novels it churns out have replaced the radio and popular music. Farocki depicts two co-existing narratives: he relays stories and events from the lives of those who consume the novels and how the stories represent unachievable dreams and goals. Like Hollywood's "dream factory," the stories generate unrealizable fantasies necessary to keep consumer society functioning. As Farocki notes, "The texts express what the readers believe they don't experience in daily life: fame, money, and a lot of leisure time. Work doesn't exist in these novels."[27] The split self between the worker and their fantasy world recalls the split screen in *Something Self-Explanatory (15x)*, where the laborer imagines luxury vacations and beautiful companions while working.

68 Labor

The Division of All Days and *Something Self-Explanatory (15x)* constitute broad-based studies of Marx's economic theory. With their highly stylized acting and their didactic lecture-style presentation they are *learning films*. In their construction they oscillate between short fictional skits that are illustrative, and factual or proclamatory parts, that together correspond to Tretyakov's division of language into the two genres of poetic and operative. Further, in *The Division of All Days*, there is the discussion generated amongst the seminar participants in response to Farocki's instruction that constitutes an everyday language. Overall, both films constitute the ABCs of capitalism, a primer, as it were, that shows how ideology is constructed and permeates all aspects of everyday life.

TO NARRATE

None of these earlier works of Farocki may be said to have a sustained narrative. They are treatises on capitalism that show how ideology functions and how the modern subject is constructed through consumerism. They are neither specifically anchored spatially by regional or national location markers, nor temporally by exact dates. The scenarios are abstract, without characters, only types or agents. They show capitalism and its effects but do not tell its history or story. And, as Farocki learned at the DFFB, popular film is about telling stories.[28] But how does one tell a story about a class or ideology and not resort to documentary? Such was the conundrum facing Farocki in the early 1970s.

Farocki directly tackled these issues in *About Narration* (1975). Farocki co-directed and starred with Ingemo Engström in this quasi-narrative film that considers the relationship between images, text, and narration. It questions how one can balance reality and fiction, imaginary narratives and historical records. The directors frame facts as still images. They place photographs, diagrams, books, and other documents into a narrative continuum that moves across time and space.

About Narration centers on three main characters: a writer (played by Engström) researching the life of Larissa Reissner, a director (played by Farocki) who wants to make a film about the steel and coal industry, and a professor of narrative theory (Hanns Zischler). In a shot that evokes Godard's contemporary productions, *About Narration* opens with Farocki sitting at his desk before a typewriter. He gets up, lights a cigarette, and removes a copy of *Stahl aus Luxemburg* (Steel from

Luxembourg, 1942) from the bookshelf. There is a cut. The next scene has Farocki behind the wheel of his car as he drives onto the sidewalk to post a letter into a mailbox. The sequence sets the tone of the film. It is a cinematic flourish, an excess of visual detail, that does not directly relate to the production's narrative.

In the following scene, Farocki and Zischler sit on the banks of the Spree. Farocki flips through the pages of *Steel from Luxembourg*. He explains the workings of an integrated *Verbundsystem* and his interest in writing a treatise on the topic. Zischler advises, "You shouldn't write [the treatise] as an academic paper. You should narrate it like a story. Then people who wouldn't read an academic book can read it." Farocki responds, "I don't really know what a story is." There is a cinematic shift in tone. Nondiegetic romantic music plays as the camera follows Farocki's gaze onto the water. A ferry carrying Engström floats downstream. She stands on the deck with her hair blowing in the wind. The scene mimics the codes fictional films employ to signal the beginning of a love story. *About Narration* concerns the complexities of storytelling and, in a self-reflexive gesture, of transforming a story into a screenplay.

2.3 Harun Farocki, *About Narration* (1975)

The film's following sequence depicts a television moderator interviewing Engström on Larissa Reissner. Engström explains to the moderator that Reissner was a Russian writer and revolutionary who spent time in Berlin as a child and later as an adult in the early 1920s. Engström admits to her interlocutor that she struggles to find the proper form to tell Reissner's story. The interview is filmed from multiple perspectives. Zischler operates the mixing booth. He shows Farocki the many cameras that simultaneously record the discussion from different angles. He also monitors the images. He glosses over a glitch with an alternate recording if there is a pause or technical error. His job is to cohere the narrative from the many disjointed shots. The screens on the walls of the editing booth hark back to Farocki's writings that describe television editing and production processes and prefigure the guard control tower in *I Thought I Was Seeing Convicts* (2000). The numerous cameras will also reappear in *Deep Play* (2007), which explores the advanced techniques used to film significant sports events such as the 2006 World Cup finals.

Engström, Farocki, and Zischler debate narrative theory and strategies. Zischler draws a circle on a chalkboard, divides it in half, and explains that the basic principle of a narrative consists of the movement of actants from one half of the circle to the other. There is no narrative without movement and a change in position. Farocki questions Engström about her Reissner project, "Do you plan to invent what has been forgotten?" She responds, "That is a different type of storytelling. So far in my work documents have been available—diary entries, conversations, interviews, transcripts of audio recordings, curricular vitae. Now I have to make a life clear and transparent with the help of fiction." Engström resorts to speculative fiction to write history. She uses conjecture to fill in gaps and holes when there is no readily available data. But, she continues, "it is not enough to achieve only an imaginary creation. The usual meaning of literature is limited to that form of storytelling. To write, you need to develop a style, to look for a way to grasp life. And that means not just creating from the imagination but also recognizing what we are in reality." For Engström, fiction must be based on fact to resonate.

Farocki and Engström tell different types of stories in *About Narration*. These include the Cinderella fairy tale, the Hollywood story of King Kong, an Angolan folktale, an oral history of World War II, and the lyrics of B. B. King's "How Blue Can You Get?" (1964). Farocki includes a shot of Walter Benjamin's *Über Literatur* (On Literature), and Engström quotes from the latter's "The Storyteller" (1936).

In the passage quoted, Benjamin laments the demise of storytelling in industrialized society. He attributes this demise to various factors, including information's proliferation through multiple media forms. The flood of information stifles imagination and suffocates creativity. A powerful scene in *About Narration* features Engström sitting by the river listening to a reel-to-reel tape recording. She speaks into the microphone and listens to her voice's playback through the headset. A slight delay creates an echo effect. This echo leads her to reflect, "I speak in the present [but] what I hear is the past." Both her recorded words as well as all the quotations add temporal layers to the film, creating a palimpsest. People tell stories to maintain the relevance of records, narratives, and memories. The stories present the past; they render the past present.

In one anecdote, an older woman recounts the fate of six hundred communists arrested by the SA in the oral history of World War II. The woman remembers that the SA immediately sent four hundred of the detained to prison camps. The SA beat the remaining two hundred with clubs when they did not follow its soldiers' orders to sing "The International." The prisoners joined hands and arms during the beating, forming a single body. As the group fell to the floor, a single voice sang the anthem's first two stanzas. The SA soon silenced the singer. The older woman recounts the story from memory. She does not provide a specific location, dates, or names. Her story is not a verifiable narrative, rather it serves as a parable of resistance. In contrast to the anonymous woman's story, Farocki and Engström include an interview with a historian, Retzlau, who authored a book on the Spartacus revolution. The historian matter-of-factly recounts the two times he encountered Reissner. He describes her charismatic personality and commitment to the revolution. Unlike the tale the woman tells, Retzlau's narrative is based on fact, but it is craftless, styleless, and lacks creative tension.

About Narration is structured like a Bildungsroman in which Farocki learns how to tell a story. He explains, "When I examined the pattern of stories, I searched for a new magical formula. But there is no magic. Depictions develop rules over time." Resisting classical storytelling, he tells Engström, "The form is known. It involves harmony and closure. We need to develop it further. Let's get back to work." Farocki returns to the desk featured in the opening sequence. He takes a red marker and draws on a piece of paper the diegetic circle Zischler taught him. He divides the circle in half and traces how actants move from one side to the other as he narrates a story of the steel industry's internal production process.

When he finishes, he makes a proclamation that alludes to Benjamin's and Tretyakov's theories of objects: "From the life of things. My story's hero is the gas in the blast furnace. When the story starts, the gas flame burns relentlessly."[29]

VERBUNDSYSTEM

That story forms the base of Farocki's most ambitious film to date: *Between Two Wars* (1978). The film runs eighty-five minutes long and Farocki lists himself as director, writer, producer, and narrator. The production dates are 1971–1977, indicating not just the duration of, but also the labor involved in, the film's production, which was made while Farocki was otherwise employed directing programs for television and other projects. *About Narration*'s focus on blast furnaces and the coal and steel industry anticipates *Between Two Wars*. Farocki uniquely promoted the latter. The year before its completion, he produced a radio broadcast, "Das große Verbindungsrohr" (The Large Connection Tube, 1976), that included several of the same characters in the film. He also devoted an issue of *Filmkritik* to the film and published no less than eight essays on it, placed advertisements in film journals, and wrote graffiti promoting it on a West Berlin wall the year the film was released.[30] (He later advertised *Etwas wird Sichtbar* [Before Your Eyes— Vietnam (1984)] on the same wall.) Farocki's writings on *Between Two Wars* articulate the film's historical complexity alongside the aforementioned expenditure of time and labor. They also contextualize the scenes and function as extended captions to the cinematic images. The result is a diptych-like production of texts and moving images that co-exist separately but are brought together in a *Verbundsystem*.

Farocki declares in an information leaflet accompanying *Between Two* Wars that he "made this film against television and cinema."[31] He was thoroughly disgusted with conventional television and questioned "how you should live according to this television image[;] I can only defend myself against it through not looking at it."[32] Further, he asserts that the film formally, stylistically, generically, and thematically challenges television's and cinema's dominant conventions. His written and filmed critiques of television demonstrate that he was thoroughly versed in the medium's operation. He was not only aware of television's rules but also of how to break them systematically and productively.

Like *Inextinguishable Fire* and *On Narration*, *Between Two Wars* is neither a feature film nor a documentary. It is a highly performative essay film that combines fact and fiction to shed light on the German working class's embrace of fascism. Farocki seeks to redeem the workers and explain their adoption of extreme right-wing politics by explaining the economic conditions and developments that transformed the industrial landscape in the late 1920s and early 1930s. As he explains somewhat plaintively, "German culture has lost much since the Jews, anti-Nazis, scientists, and artists left the country in 1933. However, there is hardly any awareness of the destruction of another culture. Before 1933, there were hundreds of thousands of people who studied literary and scientific tracts, newspapers, price lists, and sang songs on the railroad everyday." Fascism, he continues, destroyed these people and "cut us off from the past.... Whoever does not want to talk about capitalism should be silent about fascism. I want to speak directly about both topics with this film."³³

This passage is troubling. To refer to the brutal persecution and annihilation of Jews and anti-Nazis as a mere departure from the country ignores the facts. Claude Lanzmann's *Shoah* (1985) captures a similarly willful ignorance when contemporary Polish citizens state that the Jewish residents formerly in their communities "left" their homes in the 1930s and 1940. Farocki's positioning of the German worker as a victim of fascism on par with Jews is also highly problematic. When Farocki made this statement, it was unheard of to suggest that Germans were victims either of fascism or Allied bombing raids, such as those that destroyed Dresden. However, one must view Farocki's comment in the context of West Germany's cultural discourse in the 1970s. As Thomas Elsaesser has argued, until the late 1980s and 1990s, German filmmakers rarely addressed the Holocaust and, when they did, only indirectly. The NBC mini-series *Holocaust*, first broadcast in 1979, made the Holocaust accessible to Western television audiences. In its wake, Edgar Reitz produced a West German rejoinder *Heimat* (1984), that begins in 1840 and follows the lives of a German family in a small town. The Holocaust is only one event in a long historical continuum. Some explain that the Germans' inability to discuss the Holocaust in depth is due to an inability to mourn. Others, like Adorno, developed a theory of a *Vergangenheitsbewältigung* (a failure to come to terms with the past).³⁴ Indeed, both in writing and filming, Farocki is silent about the Holocaust in the first two decades of his career. It is not until 2010 that he reflects on this omission. Addressing *Between Two Wars*, he explains, "My film doesn't deal with the Jews and what was done to them. The only person I show as a victim of Nazi terror is a worker who has gained insight into historical processes. The left was often unable to speak about the Jews when they tried to prove something—the same with me."[35] Farocki first reflects on the concentration camps a decade later in *Images-War* (1987), a precursor to *Images of the World and the Inscription of War* (1989). Even here, though, he summons the camps obliquely. Both films center more on vision and imaging technologies than on what those technologies depict. *Aufschub* (Respite, 2007) is the first film in which Farocki directly identifies the Holocaust's Jewish and Romani victims.

Between Two Wars is based on sociologist Alfred Sohn-Rethel's *Ökonomie und Klassenstruktur des deutschen Faschismus* (Economy and Class Structure of German Fascism, 1973). As noted by Tom Holert, Farocki extensively researched and read most of Sohn-Rethel's writings after the latter returned to Germany in the 1970s following decades in exile. Sohn-Rethel's *Geistige und körperlich Arbeit* (Intellectual and Manual Labor, 1970), *Materialistische Erkenntniskritik und Vergesellschaftung der Arbeit* (Materialist Critique of Knowledge and Socialization of Labor, 1971), and *Warenform und Denkform* (Commodity-Form and Thought-Form, 1971) all had a profound influence on Farocki.[36] *Between Two Wars* tracks significant steel and coal production changes during the first third of the twentieth century. The film opens with a still shot of a man (Jürgen Ebert) holding a gun to the head of another (Michael Klier) who kneels with his back facing the camera. The scene is staged in a factory and reappears in the film's final sequence. We hear the clatter of hooves on cobblestones as a police officer on horseback rides into the courtyard below. A voice-over, spoken by Farocki, announces: "A film about class wars that isn't about the pain of the wounded and the agonies of the dying." Nondiegetic music by Gustav Mahler then fills the soundtrack. The music serves as the transition to the next scene. This scene is composed of a closeup of a woman's long elegant fingers typing in rhythm to the music. The commentary continues, "A film about the organization of work, but not about the pain and agonies of the workday." There is a repetitive, looping structure to the sentences, which mirrors Mahler's composition. Several images also repeat throughout the film. The credits follow a black screen, which appears at regular intervals to indicate scene shifts, mark periods, break the narrative's flow, and underscore the work's episodic nature.

In the sequence that follows the typist's fingers, we recognize Farocki sitting at his work desk, cluttered with books, photographs, papers, and documents. He directly addresses the camera, "Because I couldn't get any money for this film, I had to do other work. I earned money in the cultural sector as usual." The camera focuses on photos of various pin-up girls. Farocki explains that his job is to compose captions for these images, such as "Eva loves death," "Mona likes freedom," or "Ina loves life." In an apologetic tone, he admits that "as usual," he "covers up sensuality with words." Suddenly, he sweeps everything off his desk onto the floor and picks up a notebook. *Between Two Wars*' narrative begins.

These first few minutes foreshadow the active role Farocki *as auteur* plays in the film. His voice and commentary guide the viewer and provide narrative coherence. His physical presence as a filmmaker at different intervals in the production anchors the disembodied voice-over and self-reflexively stresses the difficulty of making a film and the extensive labor filmmaking involves. Farocki, here cast as the character "Farocki the filmmaker," introduces the problem of representing the self. As he looks at his reflection in a mirror, he observes, "A story can't be about two people; a story can't be about two worlds; a story can't be about

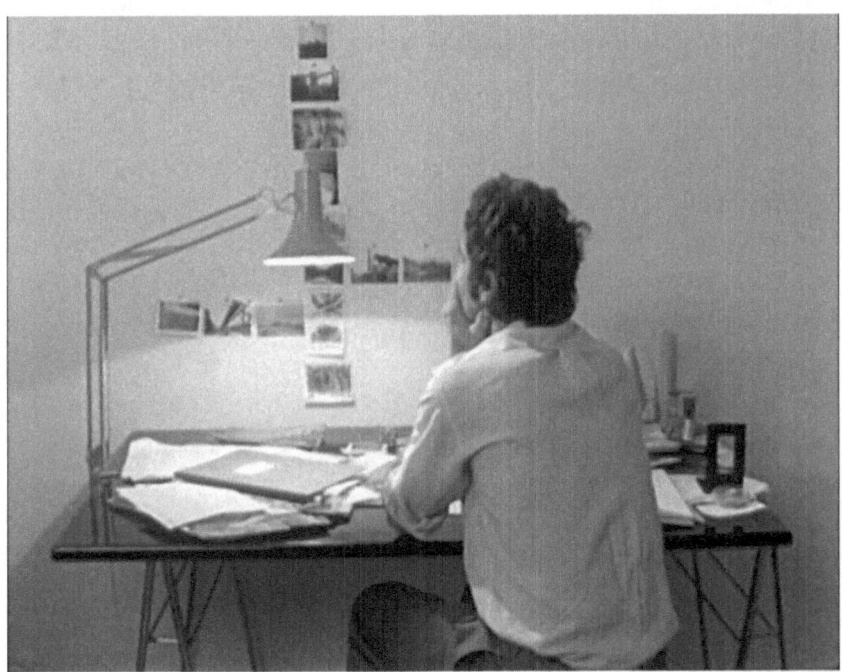

2.4 Harun Farocki, *Between Two Wars* (1978)

two classes since two is the totality." The mirror reflection splits the image of the self, like that of the subject.

Farocki interweaves multiple narrative threads in *Between Two Wars*. He orders the film chronologically, beginning in 1917 on the Western Front and ending with Hitler's rise to power in 1933. One story is of a nurse (played by Engström) who collects the dying words of soldiers on the battlefield. She asks each, "For what do you fight, for what do you die?" Her motive is to preserve: when the soldiers are gone, they will vanish, but their words will remain. "What I saw and heard I tried to understand materialistically. That means I tried from the dying of the dead to teach life for the living." At the end of the film, the nurse recalls that "in the Second World War that began at the latest in 1933," her diary "remained empty" since "learning was discouraged, and the dead have nothing to pass along to the living." The grand-narrative history books obscure the voices and "minor" stories of workers. As Farocki explains in a press release, by shifting the focus to work and economics, "you can get another picture of history just like you would get a different picture of a city if you went through it on a train and not a car."[37]

Farocki declares, over an image of himself smoking, that he aims to bring forth "a story of the time between the two wars that will not leave out the history of the twenties." That history is not of the Weimar Republic's revolutions, intellectuals, and vibrant cultural scene but of the enormous changes in economic production and their impact on the worker during these years. According to Farocki, except for Sohn-Rethel, this story has been ignored by historians. Perhaps the only film that seeks to make sense of the devastating conditions facing the worker—mass unemployment, hyperinflation, lack of food—and the dangerous political options on the horizon is Bertolt Brecht and Slatan Dudow's *Kuhle Wampe, oder wem gehört die Welt* (Kuhle Wampe, or Who Owns the World, 1932). Farocki references *Kuhle Wampe* thematically, formally, and stylistically in *Between Two Wars*. As evidence of his continuing admiration of the film, in 1986, Farocki introduced *Kuhle Wampe* for WDR (*Film Tip: Kuhle Wampe* [1986]). In his six-minute preamble to the film, Farocki focuses on several key sequences, including workers on their bicycles, the suicide of a young unemployed man, and the mass sports competition staged by workers. Over a sequence of a man reading a newspaper description of the courtesan Mata Hari while his wife seeks to balance the household's budget, Farocki states, "The film desires a different political world. The film reveals ideas and compares them to each other. What is the relationship between the cost of living and beauty?" For Farocki, Brecht and Dudow's film, made in the years immediately preceding the Nazis' rise to power, "captures hope"—a hope that will be short-lived. *Between Two Wars* depicts the other, verso side of the picture, the dark side that led to the embrace of fascism.

Kuhle Wampe is structured episodically and filmed on location with a majority of non-professional actors who deliver their lines and play their roles according to Brecht's alienation techniques. Farocki explicitly references his predecessor's work. Twice, he restages the gesture of the young unemployed worker, Bönicke, who removes his wristwatch and carefully lays it on the windowsill before committing suicide. The repetition foreshadows the death of progressive movements during the rise of National Socialism. The last image in *Between Two Wars* features the chalked outline of Bönicke's body on the pavement. Rain falls on the chalk marks. They gradually dissolve, suggesting that National Socialism and its aftermath washed away all traces of a worker's history. Farocki ends his film with the finality of death. This characteristic contrasts with Brecht's staging of the suicide at his film's beginning to offer hope for a better future. *Kuhle Wampe* also

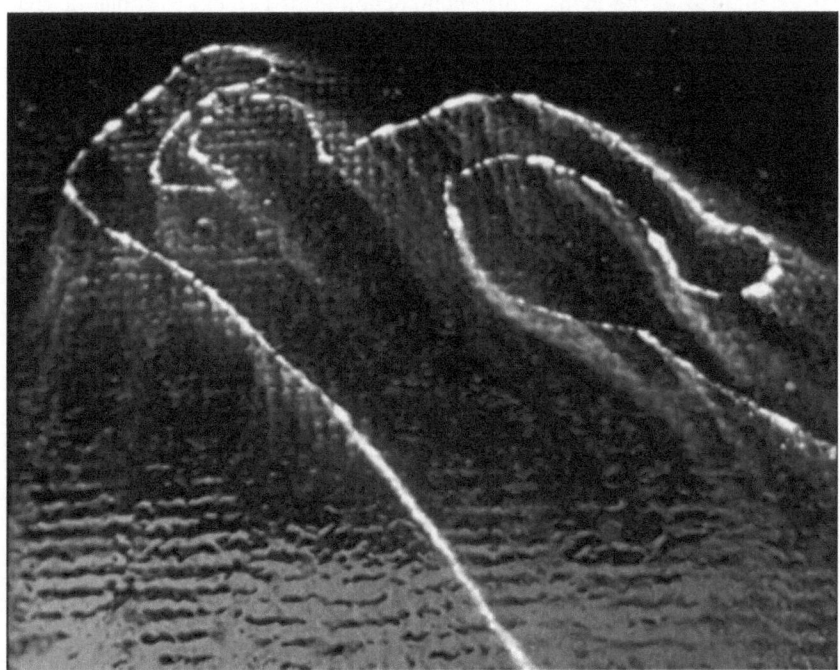

2.5 Harun Farocki, *Between Two Wars* (1978)

ends on an optimistic note. The film's final sequence features thousands of young workers singing Hanns Eisler and Brecht's "Solidarity Song," with its powerful refrain, "Forward and never forget, wherein our strength lies, in hunger and in eating, forward and never forget: solidarity!" Farocki's film fulfills the "never forget" pledge and recalls the enthusiasm, hope, and optimism of fifty years earlier. Farocki exclaims, "The hope awakened after the First World War was then deeply buried. We need to find it again, where it was lost, even if we now occupy a different place."[38]

In addition to its subject matter, what made *Kuhle Wampe* particularly striking was its formal style that translated the principles of silent Soviet montage theory into a sonic contrapuntal composition.[39] Whereas Brecht focuses on workers and their families, Farocki's primary subject is economics and the type of industrial production developed in the 1920s. As he explains in *Between Two Wars*, "I am telling a story, and its hero is neither a person nor a group of people. Instead, it is what one calls an organization of energy, *Energieverbund*." In the film's commentary, he adds, "I wanted to tell this story with the machines that produced it." However, those machines were barely accessible. Only a vast industrial wasteland remained in the 1970s. This phenomenon leads Farocki to conclude that "things disappear from sight before they are only half understood." He takes on the task of reconstructing what transpired in these now dilapidated factories, telling their stories, and restoring a forgotten history. Accordingly, cinema functions as a redemptive tool. Similar to the challenge of filming *Capital*, making a film about changes in the coal and steel industry that steered clear of the documentary genre posed significant problems. Farocki created imaginary characters (e.g., the nurse), plot lines, and micronarratives capable of attracting the viewers' attention and propelling the historical narrative forward to transgress the limits of nonfiction.

A coal factory engineer (Stefan Mattusch) and a steel factory blast-furnace worker, "Hochöfner" (Jeff Layton), play central roles in *Between Two Wars*. The year is 1919, and the two characters share a living space. They work opposite schedules. When the engineer comes home at 5:00 a.m., the Hochöfner gets up and leaves for his shift. The two need only one bed, since they will never occupy it simultaneously. The Hochöfner dreams about a bird that eats its eggs to gain the energy necessary to brood. He relates the dream to the engineer, who tells it to others in the factory. The engineer comes up with an idea: since the amount of high-quality gas necessary to heat the coal factory is less than that available, they could use the excess efficiently if they produced coal and steel together instead of separately. The Hochöfner pronounces, "Science must be merged with the dreams of the workers." The scene then shifts to a meeting between the engineer and a colleague at dinner. The engineer asks his fellow worker to explain to him (and to the viewer) exactly how the current factory system heats coal. When his colleague informs him that the current system wastes 3,000 kcals, the engineer relays the Hochöfner's dream. Thus, the engineer extracts a productive idea from the worker's unconscious.

Four years pass, and in 1923 we see the engineer proudly displaying a model factory designed to redirect surplus gas to heat the city, a steel factory, and mining tunnels. The engineer even harnesses the excess steam. He ensures that the model factory wastes nothing. Similar to the efficient manner in which the engineer and the worker shared a living space, the engineer's model factory uses resources in a "logical" way. A wealthy landowner and an industrialist set out to realize the engineer's designs. Together, by 1925 they have developed an integrated production system (*Verbundsystem*) of ore and coal. At this juncture, the engineer and the Hochöfner discuss the possibility of combining coal production with a steel factory. They note that while France has plenty of ore and Germany plenty of coal, their nations' competition might lead to war unless the workers internationalize in solidarity. Farocki introduces a new character, "Genosse Nau" (Peter Nau), a communist who complains about people's unwillingness to discuss the difference between a worker's life and that of an exploiter. An image of a hand-drawn sketch of a brooding bird with two eggs appears. One of the two eggs bears the words "our future," and the other "our world." A scene of the Hochöfner and Nau drinking follows. The two discuss politics and warn that "in times of upheaval, a worker might well follow a demagogue instead of a true revolutionary." A glass overturns, and the camera tracks the liquid flowing off the table, onto the floor, under the door, into a street gulley, and down a drain. The passage evokes the lost hopes for an international workers' movement.

The integrated coal/steel factory system begins operation. However, the economic crash of 1929/30, that hits Germany particularly hard, hinders its success. A flaw becomes apparent: the *Verbundsystem* only works if the factories operate at 100 percent capacity. The voice-over explains that 1929/30 proved more difficult than in previous years. If the furnaces cut back their production, there will not be enough gas for the ovens, and a decrease in productivity means less gas for electricity. Farocki provides the analogy of a luxury car. He notes that the vehicle can only engage the fourth gear if a long stretch of straight highway permits it to run at full throttle. Without such a stretch of road, the car will sputter and stall. Farocki accompanies this metaphor with an extended shot from the passenger side of a powerful car. The car's hood ornament figures prominently in the foreground as the vehicle glides over the roadway. The image evokes historical footage taken from Hitler's motorcade as he traversed Germany in the late 1930s to generate popular support. The film further references Hitler's rise to power when a woman announces, "He is speaking in Düsseldorf today." The woman refers to Hitler's famous speech to the Industry Club on January 27, 1932, in which he promised total production capacity. The following commentary follows the woman's announcement: "One could say that the industry raised the production platform and was at a loss of how to make better sales, one could say also that they put a *Verbundsystem* into the world, so that the new capacity could be enforced. This is the development of production force that forces production relations to change—war."

Between Two Wars is a highly self-reflexive essay film. In one fragment, a woman says to her interlocutor, "I heard you were planning a film . . ." There is no follow-up; her words are left hanging like a wisp of smoke. By foregrounding the filmmaking process, Farocki breaks down the fourth wall and highlights the role images play in producing historical memory. Nau states in his dialogue with the Hochöfner, "I have begun to take photos of the fragments of everyday life. Thoughts and machines are preserved in history books—small work is lost." Small work, those activities and gestures that, like the toils of workers, are deemed too insignificant to be preserved and recorded in history.

About mid-point in *Between Two Wars*, a sequence opens with a close-up of a brick wall. The camera then tracks back slowly to reveal the figure of Nau with a camera. An eye-line match establishes that the image of the bricks is from his perspective. The voice-over explains Nau's fascination with walls: "[Walls, for Nau,] are impenetrable, insurmountable, enclosing the logic of capitalist production. They are something the owner cannot surmount. [The owner's] walls prevent him from seeing the society as a totality." A long, slow tracking shot moves along the length of the wall. Nau, now standing in for the filmmaker, states: "I started taking photos—one photo is too few, you need a minimum of two photos of everything, things are so much in motion that minimally you need two images to see the direction in which they move." For Farocki, then, film as a series of moving images can overcome the still photograph's limits that Brecht signals in his observations on the Krupps Factory.

A few years later, in *View of the City* (1981), Farocki discovered how to "make images argue." Film is a time and movement-based medium. Editing and montage techniques put together individual shots and images and place them into a continuum that allows for a more complete vision of "society as totality." The filmmaker's job is to make the connections between the shots and images, weaving an argument. In a memorable sequence in *Between Two Wars*, we see Farocki framed by black leader, cutting up images at his worktable. He delivers one of his signature quotations: "When one doesn't have money for cars, [film] shooting, or nice clothes..., when one doesn't have money to make images in which film time and film life flow uninterruptedly, then one has to put one's efforts into intelligently putting together separate elements, one has to produce a montage of ideas (*der Montage der Ideen*)." Farocki required over six years to make *Between Two Wars*. He did not have the means to shoot the entire film in a concentrated period. He made different parts when possible. The film was assembled out of many fragments. The editing process took a considerable amount of time and skilled labor. The final product reveals the significance of montage.[40]

Immediately following *Between Two Wars*, Farocki made *Industry and Photography* (1979), a nonfiction film drawing on material not used for the former project. *Industry and Photography* returns to the certitude of facts, photographic evidence, and documentary records. Farocki employs the photographic medium to access the coal and ore industries' histories. *Industry and Photography* is almost entirely comprised of still photographs, and references are made to the series of industrial prints taken by the Düsseldorf conceptual photographers Bernd and Hilla Becher.[41] Farocki links the terms industry and photography by noting that they are both production technologies. The former generates energy, and the latter produces images. At the film's beginning, Farocki focuses on a 1930s series of documentary photographs by Czech photographer Jaromír Funke featuring factories. With their skewed angles and intense lighting, Funke's artistically staged photos prompt Farocki to remark that "these images speak for themselves and nothing else." Farocki's focus then shifts from these professionally executed images to disorderly, anonymous ones "that are poorer and therefore have more to say."[42] The next battery of photographs pictures the depths of a coal mine circa 1900. Farocki explains that the reflection of metal in the earth produces the luminescent light that emanates from the photos. He also relays how each gesture or pose photographically captured had to be held for minutes for the machine's imaging process to take effect. The photograph's maker and the workers pictured remain anonymous. Farocki muses that when these pictures were taken, the industries of photography and mining were yet in a relatively "primitive" stage. He then presents photographs from twenty years later. These pictures reveal men working alongside powerful machines. The mines featured are now large industrial complexes.

However, alongside these images of large industrial production there is another history. Farocki presents a book of photographs taken by an amateur photographer in 1935 that features "small mines." He explains that these mines are usually privately owned, located on private property, and family operated. Their production output is relatively small: the mines only supply energy for the surrounding community. Farocki draws an analogy between small mines and businesses like blacksmiths and shoemakers. He explains that small mines flourished during the postwar years when resources were scarce. They continued to operate until the mid-1970s. However, the mine structures of those years were not built to last much longer than a half-century and soon became obsolete. This phenomenon reminds Farocki of another postwar industry, scrap metal, that would also soon vanish.

Farocki refers to the amateur photographs of 1935 as "memory on the periphery." He describes them in a tone mired in romantic nostalgia. In one example, "a man emerges from a mine shaft located in the middle of a field. He shields his eyes from the sun like a sailor." Farocki observes that baking bread and extracting coal may have been everyday occupations on the farm in which the small mine is located. The commentary notes, "Hopefully these age-old mines will be preserved as testament to the diligence of our ancestors." Farocki detects a holistic synthesis between life and work in these photographs. The synthesis recalls the natural rhythms of communities that he considered a few years earlier in his analysis of *The Song of Ceylon* (1934). For Farocki, the photographs represented in the 1935 book preserve a minor history. The film medium stores the memory of that which is about to disappear. It embalms time and mummifies that which the lens records.[43]

Unlike small mines discretely dug directly into the earth, industrial mines have large aboveground shafts. The shaft towers metonymically signal the vast underground network of industrial activity below. Farocki makes quick links between that metonymic example and that of a single image frame to a celluloid strip, a cathedral's spire to a city, a face on an identity card to a human subject. The film then sequences a series of photographs of soon-to-be-obsolescent mine shafts by the Bechers. But Farocki's display of multiple styles and variations of industrial architecture also evokes Alain Resnais's photographic survey of the architecture of concentration camp guard towers in *Night and Fog* (1955).

In *Industry and Photography*, Farocki recycles footage of the factory wall from *Between Two Wars*. He reiterates his concern that "work has disappeared behind walls ... and become invisible." Labor may be described in words but is seldom pictured. Farocki recalls that whereas craftsmen used to work in storefronts with their labor in plain view, the emergence of mega-industrial workplaces placed that labor behind walls.[44] Over the years, architects of industrial structures have even covered up the blast furnace that motors the coal and steel industry. Farocki provides a fascinating history of the blast furnace's evolution from its early iterations as a brick oven to its present-day encasement in concrete to enable its cooling, ventilation, and exhaust systems to function more efficiently. Farocki's images offer "an exploded view of [the blast furnace's] pieces," and underscore the relationship between the fragment and the whole.

Relying almost entirely on filmed still images, *Industry and Photography* offers an intermedial comprehensive history of the evolution of the coal and steel industries. The photographs Farocki employs trace the gradual erasure of images of workers. He uses early-twentieth-century pictures of miners working to show how difficult it is to reconstruct the work process through images. He notes that today it is easier to make photographs of the products of industry, such as railways and bridges, than of the production process itself. This leads him to conclude that "photography collaborates with big industry" in obscuring the latter's inner workings. He attributes this collaboration to scale, noting that cameras have been designed "with the view of the human eye as their basis." With industry spreading out over vast expanses of space and labor dividing into many forms, an individual photograph can no longer image the production process. A new medium is necessary to visualize work. Farocki remarks that "perhaps images of industry can only be captured on an industrial scale, in pictures that cannot fit in any apartment, on any walls, in anyone's pocket." *Industry and Photography* ends with an extended traveling shot taken from a car as it drives through a vast industrial complex. This scene is accompanied by the music track from Tony Conrad's recording in *Single: Ein Schallplatte wird produziet* (A Single: A Record is Being

Produced, 1979). (The same music is played in *Der Geschmack des Leben* (The Taste of Life, 1979), and Farocki links the three disparate films through this sonic signature.) In contrast to still photography, film's time-based quality extends its range and compresses distances, uniting time and space.

CULTURAL WORK

Between Two Wars depicts a complicated new system of work and industrial production. Although it presents the figure of the worker, it fails to capture scenes of his actual labor. To that extent, *Between Two Wars* is more about the conceptual work of invention, the *Verbundsystem*, rather than manual labor. To redress that lacuna, Farocki's *Single: A Record is Being Produced, An Image* (1983), and *Jean-Marie Straub und Danièle Huillet bei der Arbeit an einem Film nach Franz Kafkas Romanfragment "Amerika"* (Jean-Marie Straub and Danièle Huillet at Work on a Film Based on Franz Kafka's *"Amerika"*, 1983) all highlight work. However, much of the labor pictured in these films takes place in the culture industry and not in factories. The productions' further investigations were begun a decade earlier by Farocki in *Make-Up* (1973), a short detailing the work of make-up artist Serge Lutens as he meticulously transforms the bare face of a model into a powdered mask upon which any expression the producer desires may be painted. *Make-Up* tracks only the labor behind Lutens's artistry, not that of the model, who patiently remains immobile as Lutens transforms her visage into a blank canvas. In creating a face to be photographed, the make-up artist renders her faceless. He erases her individual features and turns her into a depersonalized worker. Her anonymity is further highlighted by the fact that her identity is not even credited. The film stresses the work of Lutens, who wields his craft to produce an image that will sell commodities.

In *Single*, Farocki concentrates on the music production industry. Specifically, he details the lengthy process of recording the song "A Time to Love," by the band Witchcraft, on a twenty-four-track mixing deck. Farocki films the individual recordings of the various instruments, including drums, guitar, and bass. He then assembles these clips and shows how they will eventually be brought together to form the integrated whole. Farocki conveys the sense of work entailed in a recording process that extends over days to produce a product that will be listened to for an average of three minutes. Labor time is radically compressed into the speed of consumption. Parallels to Jean-Luc Godard's *One + One* (1968), which follows the Rolling Stones' recording of their hit "Sympathy for the Devil," are apparent. And like Godard in *One + One*, Farocki does not play the finished version of the song in its entirety. The viewer only hears instrumental fragments and isolated verses. Farocki heeds Adorno's caution about a totalizing aesthetic pleasure, and wholeness is systematically thwarted and frustrated.

In *An Image*, Farocki shifts from the acoustic entertainment business back to primarily visual pleasure. He films a photoshoot of a Playboy centerfold model in Munich. The agency obliges the model to hold excruciatingly long poses. She obeys the photographer's commands, shifting and positioning her body to produce the optimal erotic still image. Farocki compares the soft-porn production process to medical surgery: "The photos of women stand for something else. Similar to every representation there is a large disparity between the sign and that which it represents . . . An art director and a makeup artist for the body and face are close at hand. The entire process resembles a medical operation."[45] Farocki exposes the reification of the woman's body required to produce pleasure for the (heterosexual male) consumer. The glossy photographs' perfection is superficial. The model's objectification is as flawless and slick as the photo of an automobile in a BMW advert. "It's very much about respectability, the sex should become a solid brand, it must stand out against the no-man's-land of pornography. As with the black BMWs that usually appear in the magazines, the girls must have a perfect finish."[46] Both *Single* and *An Image* were commissioned by public television. In both cases, Farocki claims he was given insider access to the production process because the producers, in one case of music and in the other of pornography, believed he was making an advertisement for them. Farocki enters the systems, like a mole, and produces a critique of labor from the inside, a form of institutional critique.

The most direct and self-reflexive of the three films is *Jean-Marie Straub and Danièle Huillet at Work*; the production directly confronts the labor of filmmaking. Farocki films the rehearsal process of one brief sequence from Straub and Huillet's 127-minute *Class Relations* (1983), which features Farocki acting in the role of Delamarche. The directors instruct the actors to repeat the same lines multiple times to get the cadence, rhythm, and intonation just right. The subtle shifts in tone, timing, and breathing are barely discernible, and perfection for the directors is only achieved after multiple tries. The arduous process tasks the patience of the actors, directors, and audience. However, for Farocki, his film *Jean-Marie*

Straub and Danièle Huillet at Work does more than merely record labor. It also teaches how to work with actors, how to film actors, and how important rehearsal and repetition is in achieving the perfect synthesis between the movement of the human body, language, the camera, and the editing process. As with the mixing of the twenty-four tracks in *Single*, Farocki emphasizes the extensive labor required to perfect actors' timing in *Jean-Marie Straub and Danièle Huillet at Work*. Farocki also plays with the double sense of the French *répétition*, which means both repetition and rehearsal. He demonstrates that the space of rehearsal is one of freedom before a rigorous process diminishes the intervention of chance.[47]

LOOKING

In *As You See* (1986), Farocki applies the conceptual strategy of the *Verbundsystem* to his filmmaking practice. This film represents one of the first works he made entirely out of recycling pre-existent footage and materials. (The first was *The Trouble with Images* [1973].) As he explains, "I compose a new text out of these scraps and thus stage a paper-chase. My film is made up of many details and creates a lot of image-image, word-image, and word-word relationships. So there's a lot to chew on. I searched for and found a form in which one can make a little money go a long way."[48] Farocki assembled the 72-minute essay film from an archive of clips, photographs, drawings, plans, designs, art, and other historical sources and weaved together multiple narrative strands. The trope of weaving is central both to grasping some of the fundamental subjects in *As You See* and providing a formal lens through which to decode it. Farocki summons Adorno's conceptualization of the essay as a type of weaving together of ideas. The philosopher wrote, "Thought does not progress in a single direction; instead, the moments are interwoven as in a carpet. The fruitfulness of the thoughts depends on the density of the texture. The thinker does not actually think but rather makes himself into an arena for intellectual experience, without unraveling it."[49] In *As You See*, weaving is enacted by a complicated system of editing, a "montage of ideas." Farocki stresses, "The work at the editing table converts colloquial speech into written language. The pictures are put in a file marked cutting or montage."[50] Indeed, *As You See* is a masterpiece of montage. Speaking of his production process, Farocki explains, "On location you can place the camera here or there; the decision just takes a minute and it's made with a ponderous expression. Later in the editing studio an entire week is spent appraising where to put this one-minute shot."[51] Amongst the multiple lines of thought Farocki traces in the film, three dominate and recur. The first examines the concomitant development of war and technology; the second tracks the shift in labor from handcraft, to mechanized production lines, to complete automation; and the third explores systems of recycling, reuse, and repurposing that challenge consumer society's wastefulness.

As You See begins with what appears to be a drawing of a plow that resembles a canon, though perhaps the drawing represents a canon that looks like a plow. The visual ambivalence of the picture-puzzle recalls the vacuum cleaner/machine gun conundrum in *Inextinguishable Fire*. The voice-over, spoken by a woman, relates that "war begins from daily bread." A series of images unfold that track the importance of crossroads since the beginning of civilization. In theoretical terms, Farocki's focus on crossroads recalls Adorno's disparagement of Benjamin's methodology at "the crossroads of magic and positivism." "That spot is bewitched," Adorno complains. "Only theory could break the spell."[52]

The crossroads imagery, culminating in a pornographic image of a naked woman with a star superimposed on her anus, segues to archival photographs

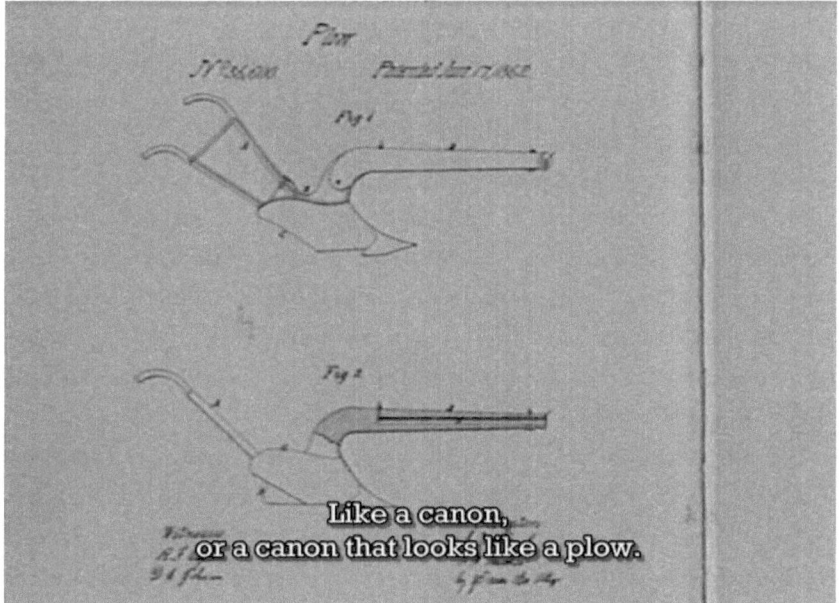

2.6 Harun Farocki, *As You See* (1986)

from the U.S. Civil War. The film features Alexander Gardner's and Matthew Brady's graphic pictures of corpses on the battlefield. The commentator notes that the first machine gun, invented by Gatling, was designed for this war. Images and commentary explaining the development of the autobahn and the gradual implementation of the cloverleaf design at crossroads follow the U.S. Civil War sequence. Farocki details how the autobahn evolved as automobile technology advanced and the machines were able to perform at higher speeds and take curves at accelerated rates. Significantly, when Farocki made this film, the West German autobahn was lauded worldwide for its ability to accommodate unlimited speed, a phenomenon celebrated in the music group Kraftwerk's 1974 hit "Autobahn," with its refrain: "*Wir fahren, fahren, fahren auf der Autobahn*" ("We drive, drive, drive, on the highway"). But Farocki grounds the autobahn in its initial function, which was to facilitate troop movement and unite the Third Reich—a subject more fully explored in Bitomsky's *Reichsautobahn* (1986). The autobahn images in *As You See* shift to depictions of German colonies in Africa and the colonialists' use of the machine gun to control the colonized population. Farocki reflects on German troops' annihilation of an entire population of Muslims in Sudan in 1898. The film then focuses on the role of machine guns in World War I, noting that one of these guns could wipe out entire battalions. Farocki turns to a 1919 photograph of workers resisting military control, an image that was rare to find from this time. Analyzing this picture, he refers to it as a "counter image" of a "counter action." A series of black-and-white archival images follows, one upon the other, as the film continues to unfold.

Three filmed color sequences stand out in *As You See* from the still images. One shows a young man weaving at a hand loom, another the testing of a prosthetic hand, and the third an interview between Farocki and a British engineer who we learn has invented a bus that can operate on both roads and rails. These three seemingly disjointed sequences follow Peleshyan's logic of distance montage as they recur repeatedly in *As You See*. Farocki waits to the film's end to reveal the logic of their interrelatedness.

Weaving, one of the oldest forms of human craftwork, is a central trope for Farocki in this film. *As You See* produces a fragmentary history of the loom. Farocki includes footage of an early cloak preserved in a museum and a 300-BC Egyptian relief of a pedal-operated spindle. He notes the way the Egyptian relief casts the foot, like the hand, as an instrument. The loom, Farocki emphasizes, was the first craft to be mechanized. It stands at the threshold between handwork and mechanical work. We learn that in 1733, English engineer John Kay invented the flying shuttle, a key contribution to the industrial revolution. The Jacquard machine, patented by Joseph Marie Jacquard in 1804, incorporated chains of punched cards laced together into continuous sequences to produce elaborate designs. Farocki draws an analogy between the Jacquard machine's complicated technology and that of television, which also translates dots into images. Despite his earlier trepidations about using writerly quotations in films, he includes several citations in *As You See*, including one by Goethe's Mephisto on the mechanization of thought by a system of logic: "Truly the fabric of mental fleece resembles a weaver's masterpiece, where a thousand threads one treadle throws, where fly the shuttles hither and thither. Unseen the threads are knit together, and an infinite combination grows." A film sequence of an adolescent boy at a handloom repeats at regular intervals amidst the archival still images. Toward the film's end, the voice-over explains that the boy is mentally disabled, and the handloom assists his focus, concentration, and manual dexterity. The commentary also reveals that the boy is "not a real worker." The loom's original function is no longer to make cloth, but to serve as an educational instrument. This representation of a change in function foreshadows Farocki's study of the shift in video game technology from war preparation to treating soldiers with Post Traumatic Stress Disorder in *Ernste Spiele* (Serious Games, 2010).

Concomitant with and related to his investigation on the loom, Farocki also takes up the development of the spindle and the spinning wheel. He explains that spinning is as important to making thread as notation is to the operation of a combustion engine. He then diverges to discuss attempts to develop more efficient engines, concluding that the piston engine's one-hundred-year dominance solidified its staying power: "Like the Capitalist system that has been optimized and supported for so long, even a better system could not replace it [the piston engine]." At this point, Farocki subtly shifts his historical account to an ideological critique that reflects on contemporary conditions. Better systems, be they technological, mechanical, economic, or ideological, remain marginal as people rely on the "trusted and true." Farocki returns to an earlier sequence of a British engineer who provides details about the efficiency of a bus-rail-combination vehicle. The hybrid brings two systems of transportation together and relates to other resourceful inventions that Farocki refers to as *"praktische technische Kritik"* (practical technical critique). He films in a small factory that manufactures replacement parts for washing machines enabling them to be repaired rather than thrown out. He interviews an engineer who has constructed an automobile from especially durable parts, facilitating its decades-long lifespan instead of the three to four years dictated by the market's planned obsolescence. He informs us that in Britain there are cooperatives that design wind turbines and other generators that "counter" the hegemony of a capitalist system based on consumer goods that rapidly become obsolete. Farocki cites the mathematician and engineer Michael Cooley who advocated for the development of what he referred to as "products for life instead of weapons for death." Farocki, following Cooley, suggests an alternative in which "the system would reproduce work without reifying it. The producer would govern the production. The talent and invention of the craftsman and the intellectual worker would be involved simultaneously, continuing development of the process itself. This would link human intelligence and advanced technology."

Adorno and Horkheimer's theory of the "Dialectic of Enlightenment" guides Farocki in *As You See*. The positives that technology provides come with their negative corollaries. Farocki tracks the evolution of craft work to mechanized labor, and on to industrial production, through research on the loom. He includes a print of two workers, one who operates a loom and the other who watches the former. With industrialization, a new type of worker, the overseer, emerges. The latter, literally the one who watches, functions as a segue to modern surveillance systems. The commentary adds the following similes over a series of still images of a bridge, a train station, and a factory with whimsical towers: "A bridge like a fortress, a train station like a temple, a factory like a castle." The voice-over continues, "Capital enlists labor and hides behind thick walls. To represent its might as law, the walls become decorative. Hannah Arendt wrote that work is hidden away because the social order is ashamed of itself." Work is concealed as a new substitute image is made, one that is false and occludes what happens behind the walls. *As You See* shows company promotional advertisements of happy smiling workers from 1937.

The punch-hole system prefigures the emergence of computer technologies. This leads the commentator to state that "today, instead of more colonies and *lebensraum*, we need a microchip industry." Computers threaten certain types of workers and labor. The voice-over notes that the textile industry was the first to be computerized. Over a sequence of a computer-drawn graphic plans of machines, the film narrator observes that "ever since work became math, the eye, ear, and nose of the worker were no longer necessary, the machine looks more like household goods." The film pictures a slick machine that resembles a toaster oven on the screen. A covering protects the devices from inept hands. Careful packaging is key. Like with the Suhrkamp edition of Mayakovski, *Schein* or appearance is more important than substance. A stylish exterior obscures the labor that produced the everyday product. Farocki recalls Adorno's question at the end of the "Picture Puzzle": "Where is the proletariat?"[53] In *As You See*, the filmmaker details a history of computers, locating their emergence in Germany in 1941. The voice-over self-consciously observes, over the image of a pin-up girl and an airplane, "I jump to the USA and back to Europe." It continues, "Computer, rockets, nuclear technology developed in Germany when there were more slave laborers than ever before. These technologies came from the USA back to Germany after the war. To and fro: as if wiping away traces of a path like money that is laundered overseas."

As You See then jumps back to the theme of replacing human labor with machines, suggesting that computer technology will be the next logical step. Farocki refers to (and includes an image of) the German translation of David F. Noble's "Social Choice in Machine Design, 1979" to bolster his argument that recording devices teach machines to replicate handwork so they can replace workers. Farocki thus shows how machines are gradually making human labor redundant through a process of replication: "The machine replicates by carefully probing an object, which a worker's hand created." Following this logic, he suggests machines will eventually take over the production of images, prefiguring the domination of operational images and AI. Once again, a dialectic emerges. A series of filmed sequences of the development of a prosthetic hand punctuates *As You See*. The sequences show progressive improvements as the device "learns" movements, beginning with a crude machine engaged in a repetitive grasping motion. At this stage, the hand is only pieces of metal and unrecognizable. A more sophisticated model sheathed in plastic resembling skin and fingers follows. The following scene shows a fully developed hand with a programmer "teaching" it to perform gestures and functions. Minutes after Farocki underscores the positive value of the mimicry technology the commentator asks, "Is it possible that the technology of the interaction of hand and mind could be used in dangerous ventures like mining and blast furnaces?"

As You See ends with a return to an earlier clip from a dubbing studio in which a man and a woman provide the acoustic track for a pornographic scene's visuals. The two follow the commands of a sound editor and carefully pace their moans of pleasure to match the visuals. These are paid actors. Their labor contributes to the reality effect the entertainment industry seeks. They work in the service industry. Their work is literally invisible and can only be heard while consuming a composite product. *As You See* primarily concerns visuality and the construction of still and moving images. Farocki focuses on what is rendered visible and what is occluded, masked, hidden, and veiled from sight by walls, substitute images, and other ideological constructs. Labor, while mostly obscured, may be detected through close readings and analyses constructed in an audiovisual montage that encourages viewers to see and understand critically.

Two years later, in *Georg K. Glaser: Writer and Smith* (1988), Farocki asks, "How do you explain that society hides work behind its walls?" This process documentary's eponymous subject responds: "You can't show what you are ashamed of." For this film, Farocki traveled to Paris to interview the expatriate German writer Georg Glaser. Glaser authored several memoir-based novels including *Schluckebier* (1932), about his dissident youth and early membership in Germany's Communist party (KPD), *Geheimnis und Gewalt* (1950), that relates his wartime experience imprisoned by the Germans, and *Jenzeits der Grenzen: Betrachtungen eine Querkopfs* (1985), which recounts his life as both an independent metalsmith and a writer.[54] In his remarkable portrait of Glaser, Farocki allows his subject to speak freely while he smiths a copper bowl. Glaser's relationship with his work is organic. He pounds the metal rhythmically, each beat seemingly timed to his heartbeat. As he manipulates the material in an effort to, as he puts it, "outwit" it, he explains that copper can be recalcitrant and unyielding. Unlike a machine's brute force, his calculated hammering is resourceful, not violent. He warns that "mistreated material takes revenge." In contrast to a shiny mass-produced object, the surface of Glaser's final product evidences his labor. "My hammer strokes are visible. Their traces remain, which is how I think it should be." Glaser's labor is never alienated; his product bears an intimate relationship to its maker from start to finish. Glaser nostalgically recalls seeing artisans performing their trades during his youth. He reflects that whereas in the recent past one would decide which line of work to pursue depending on interest, skill, and other factors like physique, this is no longer the case.

Glaser explains the process of smithing an object: how the metal is heated, cooled, expanded, and contracted. He elaborates on an array of tools that, when used, become extensions of his hands and arms. Farocki intersperses Glaser's practical account with passages that the smith reads from his writings. In one instance, Glaser notes that he "once described what happens during just one of the ten thousand hammer strokes necessary to raise a jug. It took days to come up with the sentences that elucidate the coordination of brain, hands, eyes; illustrated the suitability of the necessary tools; and made it clear what it means to apply oneself so as to outwit the reluctant raw material." We hear his wordsmith practice while we see his handcraft as he makes the pitcher. This overlap runs through the entire film.

George K. Glaser resonates with other process films by Farocki, such as *Zum Vergleich* (In Comparison, 2008) that documents how bricks are fabricated.[55] Glaser self-identifies as a craftsman and not as an artist. He notes that craftsmen make things that have use value, whereas artists work material to express the "battles of their souls." Farocki asks Glaser leading questions. To "Why should goods be durable?," Glaser offers a lengthy response that explains his holistic relationship with his work. He uses the analogy of a table made from the wood of a tree. He states that the duration of the table's use value should equal the length of time it took the tree to grow before it was felled. He grounds this ethical principle in what he refers to as carpenters' "contract with the earth" and metalsmiths' responsibility to the finiteness of their material.

Continuing the conversation about why work is hidden behind factory walls, Glaser opines that the modern-day factory destroys the workers' dignity. He recalls that, even when starving, workers used to muster the consciousness of their own value. As he puts it, "Confident craftsmen who have wanted to be recognized for their skill and in their wage value by those who benefit from them have always formed the vanguard of insurgencies." Farocki's documentary on Glaser echoes this respect. When he speaks with Glaser, Farocki's tone is gentle and reveals a genuine interest. At one point, the smith details the array of objects he makes. Some are commissioned pieces, such as a facsimile of a ship made for a fishmonger's storefront or a rendition of a cow's head for a Kosher butcher. Others are everyday objects like bowls and ashtrays. Glaser singles out an archaic 1-liter pitcher made of one piece of metal that has a large spout but no handle. He notes that the vessel is perfectly weighted and shaped so that the user can easily grasp it around the neck when pouring liquids. However, these vessels, he continues, are no longer used. They have been replaced by jugs or carafes. For Glaser, to continue to manufacture these archaic pitchers is to preserve historical memory. He makes them to ensure that object-forms that have existed for millennia do not entirely disappear. Likewise, Farocki's film of Glaser's workshop and skillset preserves a way of life that many will consider anachronistic. At the same time he was filming *Georg K Glaser*, Farocki was making *Images of the World and the Inscription of War* (1989). One sequence in particular resonates with subject of the loss of artisan labor. This occurs when Farocki includes images of a dusty old metal press factory that had not been operational since before the Second World War. Over footage demonstrating the use of old pieces of equipment, the narrator notes: "War production equals mass production, which is certain death for small enterprises."

Farocki opens *Georg K. Glaser* with a shot of Glaser's back. The latter sits at his desk while reading from one of his memoirs. We hear about the life of an outcast youth who struggled to find a place in society. Glaser recalls that to overcome extreme isolation he had "to narrate himself." "In keeping with that intent, my endeavor from the first syllable was marked by the concern of credibly reporting my truths. So my sentences only succeeded when they were based on events perceived with my own senses." This passage echoes Farocki's own attempts at the autobiographical genre, first with "Als ich 22 war" (When I was 22, 1979) followed by "Written Trailers" (2009), and finally the incomplete *Ten, Twenty, Thirty, Forty* (2017). Yet, whereas Glaser was a wordsmith and metalsmith, Farocki was a wordsmith and image smith.

OBSERVATIONAL WORK

In sharp contrast to the dignity and respect that permeates his portrait of Glaser, Farocki's dozen or more observational documentaries made between 1987 and 2013 are cynical and ironic. They focus on advertising and the selling of consumer goods. Their breadth spans from children's shoes in *Image und Umsatz oder: Wie kann man einen Schuh darstellen?* (Image and Sales: Or How to Depict a Shoe, 1989) to architectural designs in *Sauerbruch Hutton Architects* (2013). Some, like *Die Bewerbung* (The Interview, 1997), promote the self to potential employers. *Die Schulung* (Indoctrination, 1987) centers on a five-day seminar designed to teach executives better self-marketing skills, and *Der Auftritt* (The Appearance, 1996) focuses on the promotional strategies of an executive of a Berlin advertising agency. Some films are compiled of numerous disparate but related sequences that Farocki edits together to comment on a larger phenomenon. Taken together, they study contemporary life's transformation by commodity culture. Moreover, they record the emergence of the entrepreneurial self in the 1980s neo-liberal democracies in remarkable ways. Farocki labeled each a "documentary film" in the beginning credits. The films adhere to Direct Cinema's documentary style. This style follows the premise that the director is a "fly on the wall" who listens and records what takes place with no discernible intervention or interaction with the subjects. These documentaries do not have an overarching voice-over that guides a narrative. According to Michael Renov, observational cinema is "an approach to documentary filmmaking... characterized by the prevalence of indirect address, the use of long takes and synchronous sound, tending toward spatiotemporal continuity rather than montage, evoking a feeling of the 'present tense.'"[56] Like Klaus Wildenhahn's *The Tirecutter and His Wife* (1969), Farocki lets his subjects speak for themselves. In each instance, he directs the camera on a situation and films as events unfold.

Some of Farocki's observational documentary films are compiled of numerous disparate but related sequences that Farocki edits together to comment on a larger phenomenon. Examples include *How to Live in the FRG* (1990), which surveys a panoply of role-playing structures that teaches individuals to become better-functioning citizens. It features mock scenarios which range from child-birthing classes and self-presentation strategies to military exercises and educational tools. What unites the activities is that they are rehearsals and substitutes for the real. In all these examples, a separate language and set of rules emerges that marks each bureaucratic system—they are microcosms unto themselves. As Farocki notes in 1980, "Bureaucracy is a language; and able to reflect upon itself like a language, it brings about its own philosophy of language. The task dreamt of by this philosophy is the question whether the relationship between the language and reality is arbitrary or mimetic—a reality which can only be formulated and indeed only exists in these bureaucratic terms. Offices thus become a metaphor for production of meaning."[57]

Image and Sales tracks the design process for the launch of a fall advertising campaign for a children's shoe company. The passage of time is marked by intertitles that announce the month and day of the week a segment is filmed. The shoe manufacturer's executives meet with representatives from a Berlin advertising agency. As they discuss the fall "look," they contemplate the best ways to highlight muted seasonal colors, while making the shoes stand out, and the models' age, gender, and overall appearance. Budget constraints also emerge. The executives speak freely about their concerns. At one point, as the group leafs through a portfolio of models, they reject a girl with dark hair and eyes who made the initial cut on the grounds that consumers might see her as "Turkish." Her look is too "oriental." In her stead, the group scrambles to find a "blonde one" who will better represent the product in Germany. Yet, they keep the dark-haired model in reserve to use in international marketing. They reflect in a similar way about her male counterpart. The company will use a blond-haired model for domestic audiences, and a darker man for its international campaign.

The focus of *Indoctrination* is a week-long seminar in Bad Harzberg. The seminar assembles businessmen who want to learn how to sell themselves better. The workshop director repeats the phrase *"Alle Neger laufen barfuß"* (all n*****s run barefoot) unselfconsciously to illustrate the mantra "It doesn't matter what you think, but how it's perceived." The camera films the men's impassive expressions. None react to the phrase. However, their homogeneity as a group of white middleclass males is plainly apparent. That both this discussion and the one in *Images and Sales* take place with no self-reflexiveness or irony is remarkable. This is perhaps why Farocki loved this genre—it allows a rare unscripted glimpse of how subjects are constructed and ideology operates.

Critique slips in through the cracks of these observational documentaries. At one point in *Image and Sales*, a shoe factory official remarks that he will be taking a day off because of a factory holiday. One of the advertising executives (who the film has already shown working on a Sunday) responds, "Nice, you have the life." Farocki then inserts a sequence of women at a shoe factory assembly line. A red ticker tape affixed to the back wall counts their progress: they have to make 222 shoes, as well as an additional backlog of 30 shoes from a previous shortfall. Farocki encourages the viewer to read between the lines in this montage.

In *The Interview*, Farocki uses highly distorted music to highlight the contradiction between what is scripted and what is experienced by the interviewees. The music comes from Neil Young's soundtrack for Jim Jarmusch's *Dead Man* (1995), a film about the "living dead." Guitar feedback plays as interviewees demonstrate their skills at effacing and erasing all aspects of their individuality. Their "lifelessness" makes them ideal for the post-industrial workforce. *Indoctrination*'s theme is similar. The film opens in *medias res* with a man, whom we later learn to be the lead instructor, asking students "what vampires drink." The students respond in unison: "Blood, blood, blood, blood." The man repeats the same question five times. On the sixth round, he asks, "When do you cross the street?" The students respond, "On the red!" The exercise shows how repetitive behavior leads to automatic responses. Farocki chooses this opening sequence to shape how the audience receives the following material. He mobilizes the well-known analogy between capitalism and vampirism to prepare viewers for the transformation of these businessmen into effective bloodsuckers.

Farocki uses the identical ruse seven years later in *Retraining*. The same instructor featured in *Indoctrination* leads a workshop at a ski resort in Engadin, Switzerland. The workshop's participants come from former East Germany. They seek employment at West German companies. The course aims to teach the participants how to sell things (and themselves), practices unfamiliar to the East Germans. The participants must learn how to squeeze blood out of potential clients. The mostly male participants reveal their distrust in the slick Western businessmen who they see as more willing and able than them to exploit the average person. The instructor repeatedly describes the group's sympathy and respect for potential clients as a "weakness." He insists that they be clear about the differences between those who sell and those who buy. At one point, the instructor exclaims in exasperation, "You haven't realized yet that the customer is king." The film features humorous scenes in which the participants try to outwit the West German instructor. A case in point is when, in an exercise that aims to market flat roofs to potential homeowners, the participants playing the role of potential homeowners insist that the roof be able to support a large garden!

Retraining makes evident how deep the chasm is between the two systems, the West and the former East, and how many former tenets of communism remain residual. The film opens with a self-reflexive moment when one participant responds to the question of what he would have done in a different life: "Maybe if the DFFB hadn't stopped taking students in 1968, I'd be behind the camera." The participant's hailing of Farocki and his team, which included DFFB graduates Ingo Kratisch and Thomas Arslan, ironically recalls how Farocki's cohort's attempt to close the Academy may have inadvertently shut down the dreams of many potential filmmakers.

Farocki organizes each of these documentaries around a rigorous structure. *Indoctrination* follows the days of the workshop. If his earlier film on labor studied "the division of all days," the principle is now "the day as division." Farocki enumerates the parts of the day relegated to labor. These include not just labor hours but also preparing for and decompressing after work. Labor takes up the greatest portion of the workers' waking hours. When filming *Retraining*, Farocki organized the seminar according to the "natural" rhythms of a day. He marked time through shots of the sun setting over a picturesque landscape or the moon shining above a snow-covered mountain crag at night. The shots recall advertisements, or scenes from high-production feature films. They are highly unusual in Farocki's work, which typically features offices, classrooms, shop floors, urban milieus, and operative images. *Retraining* suggests that capital has now colonized even the splendors of nature. As Farocki underscores in *Workers Leaving the Factory* (1995), post-industrialism structures even leisure activities as work. His compilation film *A Day in the Life of a Consumer* (1993), made at the same time as *Retraining*, takes place over a 24-hour cycle during which commercials target specific activities connected to times of the day. The advertisements feature waking up, showering, going to work, exercising, shopping, relaxing, eating, and sleeping. Farocki montages these activities together to demonstrate the commodification and commercialization of all aspects of everyday life.

At the end of *Retraining*, the seminar leader closes the workshop on a fresh note. Instead of congratulating the participants and offering them certificates, as he did seven years ago, he reads an Aesop fable. The parable recounts Aesop sitting by the side of a road between Athens and Argos. Two travelers approach him from Argos and ask about Athens's citizens. Instead of a direct answer, Aesop responds with a question about the character of the people of Argos. Upon receiving the travelers' reply, he flips it and says, "You will find that people in Athens are the same." The seminar leader chooses this anecdote to reinforce national solidarity and underscore that the differences between the former East and West are not as fundamental as they might seem.

Following reunification, Berlin became ordained as the *Bundeshauptstadt* (capital of Germany) in 1990. However, the government remained in Bonn till 1999, after which Berlin became the *Regierungssitz* (seat of the government). Throughout the 1990s, Berlin was a site for unprecedented speculation and investment. Despite being heavily subsidized by West German taxpayers, West Berlin had been a relatively neglected outpost prior to unification, left behind economically, financially, and industrially. Farocki witnessed the city's transformation from isolated bohemian island to vibrant center attracting artists, bureaucrats, financial investors, speculators, and contractors searching for opportunity. The new transformation erased many fascist and communist remnants.

Berlin's revitalization fascinated Farocki, especially the influx of investment and venture capital (VC). He filmed scenes of the city's new class of "workers": investors, consultants, negotiators, contract lawyers, and financial advisors. In *Nothing Ventured* (2004), Farocki hones in on negotiations involving a company, NTCE, that manufactures contactless torque sensors. NTCE sought 750,000 euros in funds from a VC firm. In exchange, the VC investment company insisted on 34 percent control of NTCE. This insistence insulted Lutz, NTCE's prinicpal owner, who felt that the potential buyers were undervaluing his company. He held fast to a 20 percent share. Farocki filmed two days of negotiations, revealing the negotiators' posturing and role-playing strategies, likely learned in executive seminars similar to the ones featured in *Retraining* and *Indoctrination*.

Nothing Ventured shows how the white-collar professionals operate with purposeful obfuscation tactics to put opponents off-balance. Myriad other rhetorical ruses and lies compound these tactics. Farocki draws on the type of tension developed in a feature film to get the audience to wonder who will triumph. In the end, NTCE proposes a seemingly risky maneuver. The company will settle for a five-hundred-thousand-euro loan with 20 percent of control. However, if it needs additional funds in the first four years, it must turn to the VC company, which will in turn increase its share portfolio to 34 percent. The negotiators bet on futures. NTCE has extraordinary potential, but it is a high-risk venture.[58] Farocki thus shows that post-industrial manufacturing has developed from producing tangible products to speculation. Capital now grows through transfers and investments. Explaining his decision to follow the edicts of observational documentary in making *Nothing Ventured*, Farocki states, "Free from commentary or any other literal explanation, a film of this kind seeks to avoid disintegrating into good or bad generalities."[59] He observes the often invisible phenomenon of financial transactions and makes them visible and understandable. For Farocki, *Nothing Ventured* represents a new stage in capitalism, one that has not yet been represented in film. As noted by Petzold, in reference to *Nothing Ventured*'s influence on his feature film *Yella* (2007), Farocki's "premise was the insight that we do not even have any new images of capitalism yet. Sure, we have these airport boarding zones, where we see modern people with laptops, reading high-gloss magazines, wearing Rolexes and Burberry clothes. All this is only a surface, but we do not have images for how this new form of capitalism *operates*." He continues, that Farocki "approached his task ethnographically, rather than assuming a priori a denunciatory perspective, [which meant] the film managed for the first time to render visible the flexible, modern people who are involved in these operations."[60]

Farocki's *Sauerbruch Hutton Architects*, produced for Zweites Deutsches Fernsehen (ZDF), leaves behind the business of simulation and role-play to focus on workers at a Berlin architectural firm. From July–October 2012, he followed members of the firm's team. We see clips of them in their offices as well as at locations where their designs are actualized. The various spaces captured on film correspond to the stages in the development of their plans. The team draws up initial designs and a VR rendering for a building in France and displays them in their Berlin office in a seminar-style room. Farocki includes scenes of the firm's co-owner, Hutton, negotiating with representatives from the University of Potsdam over a project they've commissioned, who are evidently disappointed. Following numerous revisions and presentations, the two sides finally reach an accord. A young female employee presents her chair designs to her male boss, Sauerbruch, whose criticism is scathing: "This looks like a student project!" Farocki's film subtly reveals how traditional gender, class, and racial norms are perpetually rearticulated in white-collar intellectual and creative workspaces. The firm's female employees require the male boss's validation. Even Hutton seeks Sauerbruch's approval, and her name is subordinated to his as the name of the firm ignores alphabetical order. Moreover, the firm's personnel is uniformly white, not a reflection of Berlin's diverse population.

The genre of Direct Cinema closely approximates observational images. It reveals much that the filmmaker did not intend to show, the optical unconscious, as it were. *Sauerbruch Hutton Architects*, for instance, captures Berlin's newly designed perfection. Like the workplace, which is ostensibly the film's primary concern, the city as a whole seems to be in order. This overall neatness is a far cry from the difficult labor conditions and the grimy, dilapidated, forlorn, and neglected urban spaces of the 1960s. The transformation of work and architecture is in lockstep.

In these observational films, workers labor in office spaces far removed from factories. White-collar workers predominate. They train others in the codes and conventions that govern their profession. Farocki's films track the transformation of work as the imperative to act like an entrepreneur becomes ubiquitous. The worker is driven to improve constantly, change, and adapt to a workplace only capable of accommodating those who comply with its rules and regulations.

WORKERS

Farocki pondered the worker's representation in cinematic history throughout his career. He made the short compilation film *Workers Leaving the Factory* for the centennial anniversary of the birth of cinema in 1995. Scenes taken from film history comprise the film. The production method recalls Godard's compilation of film clips in *History of Cinema* (1988). Farocki uses footage from feature films, including *Intolerance* (1916), *Metropolis* (1927), *Red Desert* (1964), *Deserter* (1933), *Grube Morgenrot* (1948), *Accatone* (1961), and nonfictional footage from industrial documentaries and newsreels. The first iteration of *Workers Leaving the Factory* was made for and broadcast on television. However, Farocki re-edited and remixed the footage in 2006, inserting additional clips to make a twelve-channel installation, *Workers Leaving the Factory in Eleven Decades*. He placed the dozen monitors chronologically by the decade represented. The artwork encourages the viewer to follow the evolution of cinematic language's representation of workers and factories. Although the sequences on each monitor vary, several details repeat. For instance, filmmakers almost always show workers entering or leaving the factory and rarely at work inside. This detail leads the film's commentator, Silverman, to note, "Factories have not attracted films. Rather they have repelled them."[61] As Farocki's earlier work emphasizes, factories in films are usually represented by walls and gates, like fortresses. Farocki underscores these workplaces' impenetrability by including contemporary footage of electric steel gates, with signs bearing "Protection of Property," and automated roadblocks designed to prevent vehicles from breaking through the perimeter. Anticipating his *I Thought I Was Seeing Convicts*, Farocki suggests that factories have come to resemble prisons more than anything else. He remarks that in film history, there have been more shots of prison gates than of factories. With the industrialization of factory work comes technologized surveillance. The figure of the overseer watching laborers perform their duties in *As You See* has been replaced by a surveillance camera that records factory floor activities. As Farocki observes, "In 1895, the Lumières' camera was pointed at the factory gates; it is a precursor of today's many surveillance cameras which automatically and blindly produce an infinite number of pictures in order to safeguard ownership of property."[62]

Workers Leaving the Factory opens with the Lumière brothers' eponymous 45-second film. Farocki closely analyzes the single-shot sequence, drawing attention to the workers' carefully choreographed movements and interactions. "Disequilibrium and balance, this is the law of cinema narration," the narrator informs the viewer. Farocki stresses the workers' flow out of the factory and matches the scene to sequences in film history, such as 1926 footage of workers leaving a Ford factory in Detroit and 1934 footage of Berlin workers dismissed from a Siemens factory early so that they can participate in a Nazi rally. Sometimes workers meet acquaintances, such as in the clip from *Clash by Night* (1952) showing Marilyn Monroe quarreling with her boyfriend after a hard day's work. But most films show workers steadily entering or leaving factories. Farocki muses, "The visible movement of people is standing in for the absent and invisible movement of goods, money, and ideas circulating in industry."[63] Though the specifics of the shots differ, what unites them is the way they mirror or visually rhyme movement, angles, lighting, and staging. The commentary observes, "If we line up one hundred years of scenes of people leaving factories, we can imagine that the same shot had been taken over and over." This homogeneity, repeatability, and predictability of specific image sets intrigues Farocki. Like a stock phrase, this phenomenon's extreme form verges on a visual cliché. However, though the images resemble each other, their employment in film is determined by variegated factors that shift meaning. Such iterability leads Farocki to pronounce, "An image is like an expression that can be suited to many statements," followed by, "An image is like an expression that is so often used it can function blindly and doesn't have to be seen." Farocki theorizes a lexicon for moving images. This taxonomic system will undergird works such as *The Expression of Hands* (1997) and *Parallel I–IV* (2012-14). As he notes regarding his research process for *Workers Leaving the Factory*, "A new archive system is thus on its way, a future library for moving images, in which one can search for and retrieve elements of pictures. Up to now, the dynamic and compositional definitions of a sequence of images—those things which are the decisive factor in the editing process of converting a sequence of images into a film—have neither been classified nor included."[64]

Farocki shows that as the twentieth century progresses, films increasingly picture workers running: e.g., a 1926 sequence shot in Detroit, 1975 footage of a VW plant in Emden. In contrast to the Lumières's sequence, which removes any sign of power from the laborers, workers in subsequent films begin to run. They seem headed for confrontation. Farocki remarks that the earlier tendency to depict workers as passive was likely largely due to memories of the Paris Commune (1871). But as the history of film progressed, so too did images of workers moving rapidly. Farocki includes footage of a 1933 strike at the Hamburg docks showing a dynamic clash between strikers and strikebreakers who are "obliged to take on any kind of job without honor." Farocki follows this scene with one from Charlie Chaplin's *Modern Times* (1936), in which the protagonist, played by Chaplin, demands to be treated respectfully by a police officer. Another sequence features documentary footage from a 1956 strike by British carmakers. Farocki describes the extensive battle between workers and the industrial reserve army rendered in D. W. Griffith's *Intolerance* (1916) as perhaps the most remarkable strike sequence in film history. He tells the viewer that "the dispute resembles a civil war with the largest shootout in front of a factory gate in one hundred years of history."

Representations of labor changed in the West as the prevalence of information processing and the service industry sector increased. The worker is now less distinct. The commentary remarks, "Nowadays one cannot tell whether someone in the street is coming from work, sports, or the welfare office." At the same time, labor itself is everywhere and nowhere. Its manifestations have fused with everyday life activities, making it difficult to discern. This difficulty is even greater in moving images. To detect labor's presence within images, astute viewers must carefully analyze what they see, separating everyday life flows from sites of production.

Farocki's two-channel 16-mm film installation *Vergleich über ein Drittes* (Comparison via a Third, 2007) and its cinematic version, *In Comparison*, tracks the evolution of production processes.[65] The film follows Farocki as he visits nineteen different sites in five countries (Austria, Burkina Faso, France, Germany, and India) where workers produce bricks. The work is presented both as a single-channel film and a double-channel installation. Shot on location, diegetic sounds emanating from the mise-en-scène predominate on the film's soundtrack. The nature of the sounds differs remarkably according to location. In clips featuring scenes in the Global South countries, we hear snippets of dialogue, children's voices, animal noises, music, and the hustle and bustle of everyday life. Sounds generated by humans or nature are less common in scenes of the post-industrial Global North. Instead, the hum and clang of machines dominate the acoustic scape. Instead of dialogue, interviews, or voice-over, Farocki includes twenty intertitles in *In Comparison*. The intertitles are informational: e.g., "Construction of a school building"; "Nothing is imported for this building and only human energy is expended"; or "This robot is translating an image into stone, one break equals one pixel." The intertitles appear at regular intervals. Animated diagrams designed

104 Labor

by artist Andreas Siekmann further mark the section breaks. These graphic designs are simple drawings of bricks made with white lines against a black background. Siekmann begins the series with a single brick. The bricks multiply as the production processes become more complicated and extensive. A progression develops. First, we see one unit, then two, then entire walls and buildings made

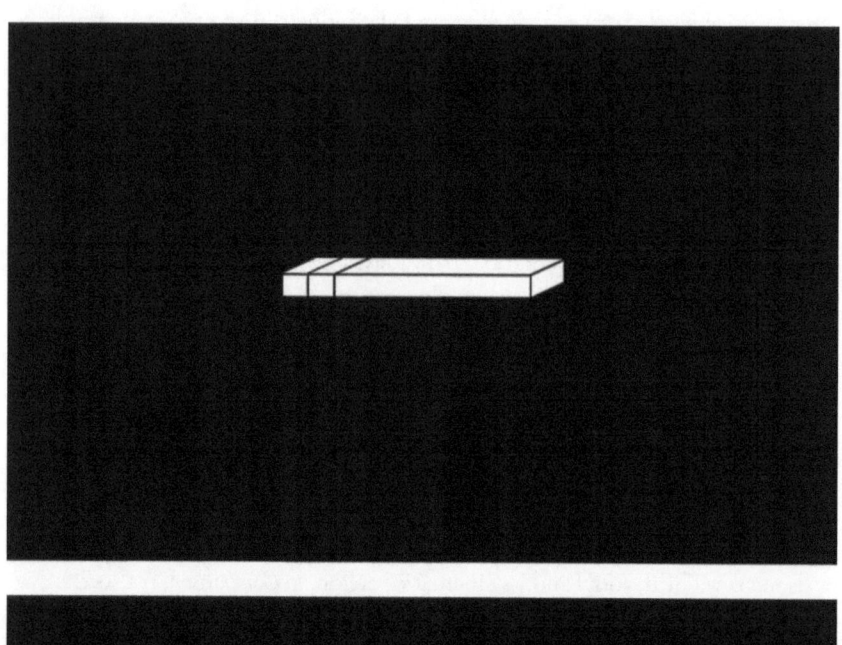

2.7 Harun Farocki, *In Comparison* (2009)

2.7 (continued)

from bricks. The graphics recall Farocki's motif of assembling a structure piece by piece in *As You See*. The bricks function metonymically.

The technology for making bricks emerged almost simultaneously in different areas around the world, and brick production continues robustly to this day. Farocki begins *In Comparison* with a simple brickmaking process in Gando, Burkina Faso. Workers mix mud and clay in an earthen pit, pour it into a wooden mold, and bake it in the sun. The scene highlights men's and women's roles in the production process. Women haul water for the clay and carry the dried bricks on their heads to the construction site. There, the bricks are handed, one by one, from one man to the next as bricklayers erect a wall. The wall reaches a height of about two meters after two days. When the structure's base is complete, women cover the exterior with a stucco-like substance, creating an adobe-type design.

The film then turns to Hinjandi, India, where workers add an additional step to the brickmaking process. We see bricks fired for two days. In Mumbai Powai, workers introduce another device: a mechanical belt. The latter assists laborers in the transportation of bricks. Women no longer need to carry the bricks on their heads. Clips from Puducherry, India, reveal workers introducing yet another variation. Here, we see laborers building a house of unfired bricks. The workers cover the structure with stucco, fill it with coal, and carve air vents into it. When they seal the opening and fire up the interior, the house turns into a kiln. After a few days, the workers crack the hard stucco shell encasing the brick building and chisel it open, revealing a sturdy red brick edifice. They remove the coal and other material inserted into the structure earlier, prompting the intertitle: "The socially minded idea: a building is fired, and the heat is used to fire bricks as well." The process is a *Verbundsystem* without waste. A second intertitle stresses, "The bricks fired along with the building can help to finance its construction."

In these sequences, shot in eight different places in the Global South, entire communities are involved in the building process. Children play on-site as adults engage in labor while talking, singing, and exchanging stories. There is a rhythm to their work and social exchanges that recalls those identified earlier by Farocki. The documentary camera tracks the entire process, from mixing mud to forming bricks and using them to build the structure in question. Farocki then shifts the setting to Western European brick factories. The first shot is of a 1930s production plant. The intertitle reads, "Same routine now as then." A shot of a factory in Leers, France, built in 1945, still in use in the early twenty-first century follows. The brickmaking has been mechanized, and North African workers operate the machines here. The laborers examine each brick before its storage. The film then moves from France to a fully mechanized factory in Dachau Pellheim, Germany. The only worker visible in this factory is a foreman who oversees operational controls. Each part of the production process is automated, including the final plastic shrink wrap encasing large units of bricks. The film also features a plant in Cologne where machines make prefabricated brick walls, package them, and prepare them for shipping to a plant in Zürich where computerized robotic production translates bricks into pixels. These large production sites are stark. Hardly any workers are visible. The immense machinery dwarfs even the few computer programmers.

In Gando, where each brick bears the labor of the multiple hands that made it, Farocki details the intimate relationship between the worker and the finished product. This gesture recalls Glaser's ruminations on the vital connections between a tree and a wooden table or raw metal and a copper bowl. Following the completion of the building in Gando, the inter-title stresses, "Nothing is imported for this building and only human energy is expended." What happens to "human energy" during the process involving alienated labor? Farocki closely examines brick production, like he does the weaving loom, to cast light on a much larger topic about the evolution of the relationship between humans, work, and production processes. But whereas he presents a diachronic account of the history of the loom, he studies contemporary brick production synchronically, as manifested in different geographies across the globe today. He uses double-screen projections that encourage viewers to observe and process two sets of images simultaneously to reinforce this spatial configuration further.

When assembled with others, single bricks culminate in architectural structures such as houses, schools, and clinics. Alone, they have no function. The modular units' meaning changes according to how they come together with others. This phenomenon parallels the way individuals, when brought together, form communities. In both cases, collectivity produces new structures. This pattern is also operative in filmmaking, which sutures discrete shots into whole forms. In filmmaking, each image is like a brick, and the film is like a building. Dziga Vertov observes, "*Kinopravda* [film truth] is made with footage just as a house is made with bricks. With bricks one can make an oven, a Kremlin wall, and many other things. One can build various film-objects from footage. Just as good bricks are needed for a house, good film footage is needed to organize a film-object."[66] Farocki builds his films image by image, shot by shot, brick by brick. Some of the images are crafted by hand, while machines make others. Farocki reflects on the evolution of his image-making career in *In Comparison*, and a parallel may be drawn from the different bricklaying processes (hand-made to fully automated) to Farocki's production arc: the exacting process of analog filmmaking with which he began, his work with larger film crews in the late twentieth century, and the greater flexibility the twenty-first-century digital programs he mobilized allowed. Whatever the system, Farocki's filmmaking practice puts together images that think and produce thought.

While Farocki's focus on labor mostly tracks nineteenth- and twentieth-century Western history, in 2010, he accepted an invitation by Alice Creischer, Max Jorge Hinderer, and Siekmann to participate in "The Potosi Principle: How Shall We Sing the Lord's Song in A Strange Land." The large group show, which opened at the Reina Sofia Museum in Madrid and then traveled to Berlin and La Paz, focused on the founding of colonialism in the sixteenth century and the plight of the indigenous populations the Europeans marshaled to extract local resources. The curators asked the participating artists to one or more of the twenty-two colonial paintings included in the exhibition. For his part, Farocki produced the double-channel video installation *The Silver and the Cross* (2010), which painstakingly analyzes Gaspar Miguel de Berrio's *Descripción del Cerro Rico e Imperial Villa de Potosí* (1758). De Berrio's panoramic painting depicts the wealth, citizens, and laborers of the colonial city of Potosi, Bolivia. Farocki's video production addresses the Andean city's vexed history and contemporary legacy. If *Nothing Ventured* represents capital's virtual life in the twenty-first century, then *The Silver and the Cross* goes back to capitalism's material beginnings in imperial conquest, slavery, and primary accumulation. *The Silver and the Cross* is both a stand-alone discrete work and part of a larger group project. Its relation to other exhibited works in the installation largely shapes its reception. Like a single frame in a film or a brick in a wall, meaning and function are determined by context and positioning within a larger narrative structural scheme and inter-textual dialogues.

Farocki divided *The Silver and the Cross* into two sets of images. One features sequences from present-day Potosi and the other details of de Berrio's painting. During the sixteenth century, Potosi was one of the wealthiest cities in the world, with a population exceeding that of London. It was the capital of silver production and a conduit for the global transportation of enslaved or indentured laborers. During the initial years of the mining operation, the Spanish exploited the indigenous population. When the Spanish decimated the population, they replenished the labor pool with people from West Africa and later with Chinese people who also perished in large numbers due to the hazardous work conditions. No one has yet recorded the exact number of deaths, but there is plenty of evidence of genocide. Farocki studies every square inch of the painting with his camera. His detailed iconographical analysis exposes what the picture leaves invisible. The canvas depicts Potosi during its heyday. We see a lively and vibrant city full of commerce, religious icons, and ceremonial processions. The commentary of Farocki's video, delivered by Cynthia Beatt, informs the viewer about the complex system of waterworks developed to produce sufficient energy to pulverize the rocks from the mines. The painting pictures many dams and piles of crushed ore mixed with mercury neatly arranged next to the processing mills. Yet, Farocki's probing camera cannot find a sign of the Spanish exploitation of the labor force anywhere in De Berrio's composition. De Berrio does not even show the mines' entrances. Farocki's film thus underscores those crucial historical details' absence, which the voice-over claims speaks of the "large-scale genocide" wrought upon the mines' laborers. Whereas de Berrio's painting reflects an effort to capture a history that was already over two hundred years old, Farocki's video installation brings the "losers of history" back to consciousness, *pace* Walter Benjamin. The double-screen projection, with images from both the past (the painting) and the present (video imaging), sets up a dialogue. Beatt's voice forges a sound bridge to her delivery of the commentary in *Images of the World and the Inscription of War*, an earlier film about the recto/verso of in/visibility. Beatt's reading is factual and neutral as she presents Potosi's hidden history. Her voiceover observes that, as we contemplate the invisibility of the laborers in the painting, "it is important to bear in mind that the philosophers of the European Enlightenment also made no mention of slavery or of the slave trade." With *The Silver and the Cross*, Farocki partially restores the history of enslaved peoples who lost their lives mining silver so that the Spanish Empire could flourish and exert its might around the globe. His mobilization of two parallel sets of images juxtaposes the contemporary with history. The political critique emerges in the interplay of imagery on the two screens and the regular insertion of blacked-out screens to give the viewer time to pause, think, and contemplate the commentary. The production reveals the relationship between modernity and colonialism and the role this binary played in capitalism's development. Over five hundred years old, the fateful dynamic continues as current conditions force millions of migrants and refugees to risk dangerous journeys and working conditions to survive.

What is work today? How does one render its various modes, motives, and profits in an image without giving it an order of fatality that renders it natural? From different forms of manual labor to service providers, furniture designers, machine technicians, and computer programmers, Farocki historicizes labor. As a result of his ongoing interest in work he tackled a new production, exhibition, and distribution format for what turned out to be his last project: *Labour in a Single Shot*. This work, still live at the time of writing, brings together several of Farocki's concerns: his commitment to teaching, his exploration of ways of filming, and his egalitarianism. He and Ehmann are less auteurs than curators, pedagogues, and programmers. They teach practical methods and conceptual tools necessary to put the ball into play. At a time when Farocki was an international star with gallery representation, the exhibition format's online open-access quality gestured towards his and Ehmann's steadfast devotion to the politics of practice. With *Labour in a Single Shot*, Farocki sidestepped the global art market and produced a work that, like his earlier television broadcasts, had the potential to reach a large non-elite public. With it, he continued his ongoing project of rendering workers and their labor visible, making economic relations and structures comprehensible, and restoring respect and dignity to work.

CHAPTER 3

Critic as Filmmaker

In all modesty, I've tried to find means in which not only additional words shape the idea of cinematography's discourse, but somehow the shape, the montage, the form of film contributes to it. It can sound a little bit poetic to say "having images that think" and "having films that think," but it's in this sense one of my ambitions: to find some autonomy in the cinematographic form, in which you don't just repeat things which already exist on paper and try to translate them to film form, but you try to give some autonomy to the cinematic medium. That is one of my aims.

—Harun Farocki, "Keep the Horizon Open"

Farocki extended economic theory to images beyond human, animal, and factory labor. For him, images also must "work" collaboratively to produce critique. He was particularly interested in how newspapers, photojournalists, and film books strategically deploy images in tandem with written texts. As a filmmaker and cinema critic, he was concerned about the paucity of film publications. However incisive and influential his film commentary for the journal *Filmkritik* from 1974-1984 was, Farocki felt the need to supplement it with analyses performed through the film medium. He did not want to rely exclusively on static words and images. Thus, in addition to directing films that critiqued television, he shot several that focused on film. These productions, intended for a mass audience, apply his critical dictum to make "work better." They are part of his overall dissatisfaction with popular film publications.

112 *Critic as Filmmaker*

3.1 Harun Farocki at the Arsenale Movie Theater. Permission courtesy of the Harun Farocki Archive

FILM CRITICISM

In *Filmbücher* (Filmbooks, 1986), Farocki poses as a reporter sitting at a desk reviewing recent publications on various cinematic subjects. These include books on Rainer Werner Fassbinder's *Querelle* (1982) and Wim Wenders's *Kings of the Road* (1976), as well as Pauline Kael's study of Orson Welles, a biography of Erich von Stroheim, and many others. All have a large number of photographs that accompany a written text. In each case, Farocki faults the authors' use of these illustrative images. Sometimes, the quality of the reproduced pictures falls short; in others, the cropping for publication, which focuses on individuals and faces at the expense of backgrounds, is the problem. In still others, it is the author's use of images taken by set photographers during production rather than actual film stills that Farocki finds misleading. In some egregious examples, he shows that the photographs were mislabeled and are unrelated to the written text.

3.2 Harun Farocki, *Filmbooks* (1986)

Farocki's critique then moves to the textual content, especially in autobiographical works that recall production processes and provide "indiscrete details" about set romances but remain silent on more significant matters, such as finances. In one case, he points out that the book's author is the film's publicist and producer, making the publication part of a promotional strategy. Why, he muses, should a reader pay ten Deutsche Marks for an advertisement? In his selection of source materials, Farocki does not consider examples of serious film theory and criticism targeted at academics and specialists. This omission is because his focus is on popular books meant for the general public, whom he believes are purposefully being fed misleading and inane material similar to that delivered by television documentaries. Part of Farocki's mission is to provide a corrective or counter-product to this mass-delivered "educational" fare.

Farocki's critique of these popular film books contrasts with the attention he pays to films in the eight programs he produced for television between 1974 and 1987. These programs consider films he respects and admires. The first, *Über 'Gelegensarbeit einer Sklavin'* (About: "Part-time Work of a Slave," 1974), focuses on

Alexander Kluge's eponymous 1973 film. Unfortunately, television did not broadcast the production. Broadcasts concentrating on Slatan Dudow's *Kuhle Wampe* (1932) and Danièle Huillet and Jean-Marie Straub's *Death of Empedocles* (1987), an interview with the author Peter Weiss (*On Display: Peter Weiss* [1979]), and an introduction to Weiss's experimental films, *Kurzfilme von Peter Weiss* (Short Films by Peter Weiss, 1982), followed. French filmmaker Robert Bresson is the focus of the collaborative film *"L'Argent" von Bresson* ("L'Argent" by Bresson, 1983), which involves several editors of *Filmkritik* (who were then preparing a dossier devoted to Bresson).[1] Hartmut Bitmosky was among these editors.

Farocki's approach was slightly different for each program. He selected distinct aspects that make these films or directors significant. For example, his analysis in the collaborative film on Bresson centers on narrative codes and scenic constructions. The color film opens with Bitomsky systematically going through a series of black-and-white frame photographs from Bresson's film while providing a narrative account of the making of *L'Argent*. The flipbook effect breaks the film into narrative blocks and still images. Bresson's proposition for a "cinematographer's film where the images, like the words in a dictionary, have no power and value except through their position and relation," is put to the test in this sequence, whereby each images is presented as part of series of stills and their meaning is gleaned through a continuous *défilement*.[2]

About "Song of Ceylon" by Basil Wright (1975) was the first of Farocki's film critiques to be broadcast on television. Farocki introduces several concepts of film history and technique developed by Wright and John Grierson's GPO Film Unit in this short. Filmed on location in Sri Lanka, Wright's *Song of Ceylon* (1934) is an early travelogue essay film that depicts life in the former colony through a series of disjointed tableaus reminiscent of *Kuhle Wampe*.[3] The GPO team, including Walter Leigh (a student of Alberto Cavalcanti) and Paul Hindemuth, composed and designed the soundtrack in London. Wright's film was funded in part by the Ceylon Tea Propaganda Board. It conveys the tea industry's colonialism as an integral part of Sinhalese culture. Farocki's short opens with a crudely drawn image of a television set. The drawing recalls the similarly handwritten words "Telekritik zu" in *The Trouble with Images: A Critique of Television* (1973). Farocki's voice announces, "We are going to examine films, in order to learn something about today's television—something about watching television and creating television." The voice-over's pedagogical tone supports Farocki's belief in television's potential as an instrument for instruction. It declares, "We will make you aware of a few cinematic methods, and we will look at the results of a few cinematic methods." Accordingly, Farocki produces, expanding on Bertolt Brecht's concept of *Lehrstücke*, what could be referred to as "learning television." A form of the medium programmed for education and instruction instead of entertainment.

As if riffing on the German *Fernsehen* (to see faraway), Farocki opens *About "Song of Ceylon"* with a discussion of travel films that feature exotic images and pictures. His program consists of sequences from Wright's film interspersed with illustrative watercolor paintings that resemble those typically found in a journey's logbook or a filmmaker's storyboard. He explains that in his film, "there are also the small drawings made by a graphic designer that function as subtitles. The commentary rests within them; it does not accompany the drawings."[4] Casting viewers as tourists, Farocki reminds them that every picture they brought back was valuable when they took the trip. He argues that films made during travels are even more valuable than still photographs or drawings because they transmit movement. Farocki's production stresses shots in *Song of Ceylon* that feature people in motion. He suggests that these people's internal rhythms connect to nature and intercuts footage of swaying trees and palm fronds with clips of people going about their everyday activities. He comments on how people connect to one another in this community, with their shared movements bringing them together.

Farocki shifts from his moving picture lecture on *Song of Ceylon* to Sergei Eisenstein's *!Que viva Mexico!* (1931). He replays a scene from the Russian director's unfinished film in which a young woman's partially obscured face gradually becomes recognizable through the dense foliage. Farocki explains that Eisenstein used a mirror to reflect light off the girl's face. What initially appears as a natural interplay of sun and shadows is an artificially produced cinematic effect. Farocki relates that Basil Wright had studied film aesthetics and montage with Eisenstein and probably followed Eisenstein's advice to young directors: "Go the way the material calls you. . . . The scenario changes on location, and the location shots change in the montage."

Wright divided *Song of Ceylon* into four unrelated chapters. Each chapter, Farocki remarks, in a nod to Jean-Luc Godard's *Two or Three Things I Know About Her* (1967), promises to show and tell "two or three things" instead of attempting to depict a totality. He underscores that a few particulars displayed in detail might generate "an idea of a whole." Following Wright's lead, he shows only a few details of *Song of Ceylon*. He explains how Wright and his team bring together several types of image, each of which they make differently. They fabricated some of the images of foliage in the film studio. He notes how this production method makes the "forests of the past look synthetic." This observation proleptically connects to his four-channel installation *Parallel* (2012–2014), which traces a genealogy of artificially generated images of trees. Wright's team also shot on location. This footage is documentary and less prone to manipulation. It includes symbolic images of giant Buddhas and religious temples as well as shots of the landscape. In addition to the documentary footage, *Song of Ceylon* is replete with micronarrative sequences shot with multiple cameras and scenes staged and performed explicitly for the filmmakers. All of these different images were woven together by Wright and his team and organized into constellations of meaning.

Two interrelated characteristics of the film stand out for Farocki: movement and sound. Movement is related to sound, for unlike images that filmmakers can present still as well as moving, sound travels in waves and requires motion. Farocki imparts in *About "Song of Ceylon"* that one of the most remarkable aspects of Wright's film was its elaborate post-production sound design. Besides pointing out the various ways that Wright adds music and other sounds to the images to create a flow and higher degree of realism, Farocki isolates a couple of sequences that epitomize the production's overall musical structure, generating what he refers to as its "song." He notes that how Wright scored and arranged images recalls how composers place notes in musical compositions. This observation leads him to describe the resulting production as "a music of images." Halfway through *About "Song of Ceylon,"* Farocki inserts the intertitle "Song," as he announces: "A film like a song, a film like music." His commentary continues: "The subject crystals that are generated for an instant and then disintegrate again. To make music from the images, there are the dissolves. Dissolves match the pictures to each other, make them smooth, allow for disparate things to come together." Farocki illustrates this observation by replaying a series of dissolves in Wright's work. He stresses the importance of rhythm and motion as structuring devices, as represented by the opening sequence of Walter Ruttmann's *Berlin—Die Sinfonie der Großstadt* (Berlin–Symphony of a Great City, 1927). Farocki introduces Ruttmann as a member of a 1920s movement that treated images and pictures according to their own properties and edited them together not according to a preconceived narrative plot to which they had to conform, but rather to one that emerged from the images themselves. Ruttmann used a rapid montage to impart the effect of travel, the speed of modernity, and the vibrancy of urban life. Farocki refers to this tactic as a "montage idea" but quickly undercuts his praise of Ruttmann's film with the assessment that the result is a "trivial philosophical idea that is a pretext for a montage of ideas." Farocki's preoccupation with the historical development of complex editing is clearly apparent in his focus on *Kuhle Wampe*, *Song of Ceylon*, and *Berlin—Symphony of a Great City*, all of which advanced new forms of montage.

A post-production team comprised of Walter Leigh and Alberto Cavalcanti in London created *Song of Ceylon*'s formal musical structure. Non-diegetic music, Foley sounds of nature, and other background noises compose the sound design. These noises include a playful passage matching tones from an oboe-like instrument to an elephant, making it seem like the majestic creature is speaking. Sound's careful employment imbues the animal with the power of speech. In *About "Song of Ceylon,"* Farocki pauses over one sequence, "commerce," and replays it several times. The clip depicts a young man scaling a coconut tree and reaping ripe coconuts. Once the nuts fall to the ground, the man gathers them, splits them in half, and extracts their fruit. Other villagers harvest, process, and store grain. Farocki observes that the multiple forms of labor represented capture Ceylon's vibrancy. Nevertheless, he cautions that there are limits to this cinematic method. "One can't tell from the look of the work whether its goal and speed were specified by the commercial director. One can't simply distinguish the difference between the commercial and the working village community by looking at them." Farocki then replays the sequence but remains almost silent, allowing the original soundtrack to punctuate the clip. Against the rural pre-industrial imagery, disjunctive non-diegetic sounds emit modernity's din. Voices conduct business transactions and trade information bits. They provide statistics about stocks, transportation, and commerce. The colonizer's presence is transmitted from afar through telephones, radio broadcasts, and announced recordings. There is discordance between what we see on the screen and hear on the soundtrack. Visual dissolves and sonic overlaps create an audiovisual palimpsest. A sound bridge spanning time and space connects images of age-old work practices with the commerce of colonization.

Farocki returns to the musicality of Wright's composition throughout *About "Song of Ceylon."* He observes that Wright focuses on small movements detected only through "patient observation." A recurring sequence of a fisherman methodically pulling his net out of the water and rhythmically folding it to prepare for the next cast prompts Farocki to ask about the creation of melody, to which he responds that Wright tried to find it in the material. Wright, he observes, "uses music to make the material dance." He replays the sequence of the fisherman, but this time he adds the directly preceding and proceeding images, situating the sequence in a larger filmic continuum. We see a young man sitting by the water, the fisherman, and a man pounding laundry. The men's movements rhyme, uniting the different activities in harmony. In his television critiques, Farocki strives to achieve what Wright has already accomplished: "not ideas built into the material but ideas found in it." In the last section of About "Song of Ceylon," "Learning for TV (4 - 00)," he explains that Wright's film prioritizes images and their placement within the film's totality. He stresses the importance of demanding image clarity. One should be able to discern immediately what the image depicts, including when the filmmaker made it and why they are now using it. For Farocki, all images are significant; they are never fillers or placeholders. In the end, he writes, "No final word. A final picture."

And for this final picture, Farocki includes a watercolor of a pair of feet, standing in a lagoon, that dissolves into a sequence from Song of Ceylon with two feet of a young man in water. Wright's camera slowly pans up to reveal the young man's body and upward-tilted face. It follows the man's gaze as he looks toward the mountains. Farocki repeats Wright's commentary at this point: "This was a high mountain to worship." Ambiguity about why people needed to worship the mountain generates drama, especially given Farocki's claim that one must demand that the function of each image be clear. One cannot easily discern that clarity since colonialism is not critically summoned anywhere in Wright's 1934 film or Farocki's analysis forty years later. As with Ruttmann's production, Farocki is primarily interested in Wright's formal sound, movement, and montage innovations. He does not take up why the director created it and for whom.

Made a decade later, Farocki's *The Double Face of Peter Lorre* (1984) approaches cinema history from the perspective of Viennese actor Peter Lorre (aka László Löwenstein). Farocki addresses several films in which Lorre featured and investigates the actor's peripatetic condition of exile in the mid-twentieth century. Lorre starred in over seventy roles. Farocki singles out several of these to construct a larger argument about the intersections of history, politics, and cultural practice. *The Double Face of Peter Lorre* contrasts the "old world" of Weimar cinema with Hollywood's commercial dream factory.

Farocki shows that Lorre began his career as a successful stage actor in Berlin in the 1920s. The actor's first significant film role, as the child serial murderer in Fritz Lang's *M* (1931), defined him for the German public. Farocki highlights *M*'s many extraordinary features. The production was Lang's first sound film. The director tactfully employed sound as an active agent in exposing the killer's identity. Farocki shows that Lorre first appears as a shadow and then as a voice in the film. A blind beggar recognizes the villain later through his telltale whistle.

Lang's depiction of new types of mapping and surveillance systems in *M* is also significant for Farocki. He shows that the state, as represented by police and detectives, and civil society, represented by organized crime and beggars, each divides urban space in their own unique ways. The observation leads him to argue that *M* anticipates the proliferation of surveillance systems that some describe as the emergence of "control societies." The year before *The Double Face of Peter Lorre*'s release, Michael Klier made *Der Riese* (The Giant, 1983), a film composed entirely of surveillance images. In his review of Klier's film, Farocki notes that "electronic cameras are everywhere now." Many of these cameras picture from above to better monitor goings-on. The surveillance occurs "day and night, year in and year out."[5] The endless stream of footage is constituted of operational images produced by machines.[6] As Gilles Deleuze underscores, in "Postcript on the Societies of Control" (1992), the "disciplinary societies" that exercise power within discrete institutions outlined by Michel Foucault are dying, and their spirit of control is now permeating through all of society.[7] Surveillance systems are just one manifestation of this control; social networks are another. Farocki locates his interest in the power invested in those who watch in *As You See* (1986)'s factory supervisor and *I Thought I Was Seeing Convicts* (2000)'s prison guards.

For Farocki, the political unconscious of Lang's masterpiece is the rise of fascism. He also takes up National Socialism's impact on Lorre. After *M*'s success, and Hitler's ascendancy, Lorre, who was Jewish, first moved to England, where he acted in Alfred Hitchcock's *The Man Who Knew Too Much* (1934) and *Secret Agent* (1936). Then, as safety in England became increasingly uncertain, he fled to the United States where he joined a vibrant exile community in Hollywood. Two of his first roles in the United States were in Karl Freund's grisly horror film *Mad Love* (1935), scenes from which Farocki featured in *The Expression of Hands* (1997), and Josef von Sternberg's *Crime and Punishment* (1935). Director Norman Foster and others then cast Lorre as the Japanese detective Mr. Kentaro Moto in seven films from the titular series between 1937 and 1939. Farocki pauses on the harsh irony of this turn of events: a native German-speaking Jewish actor playing an East Asian character who is a skilled judo expert. In Hollywood, producers increasingly typecast Lorre as an outsider, an alien, and a suspicious foreigner.

Farocki draws a parallel between casting based on stereotypes and prejudices and the reliance by television editors on a limited database of clichéd images.

Following his exploration of Lorre's role as Mr. Moto, Farocki turns to the actor's part in John Huston's *The Maltese Falcon* (1941), where he portrays the shady character Joel "Joe" Cairo, who helps steal the falcon. Lorre then acted in Michael Curtiz's *Casablanca* (1942), cast as the sleazy Italian black-marketeer Signor Ugarte. Farocki highlights Lorre's prolificness during these years by including many posters from films in which the actor starred. He remarks on the similarity of many of Lorre's roles, revealing the extent to which directors cast him as an eternal outsider, a sinister foreigner with whom few would sympathize.

Farocki returns to the beginnings of Lorre's career as a stage actor in the 1920s to explain why directors so quickly typecast the actor. Brecht placed him in the lead role of Galy Gay in the premier of *Mann ist Mann* (Man Is Man, 1926). Farocki stresses that Brecht first introduced his "epic theater" style and the notion of "gestus" in this play.[8] Farocki explains that epic theater repeatedly and deliberately reminds spectators that the events depicted are not events to which they can relate. He defines this style in the terms of what Brecht named the *Verfremdungseffekt* (alienation effect). A typical characteristic of the alienation effect in film is the filmmaker (or narrator) explains what happens on screen. Other characteristics include exposing set functions like microphones, takes, and extras, screen projectors or placards, intentionally stilted or ironic acting, and actors speaking the screenplay directions or summarizing the events that have just played out. *Gestus* or "gestic thinking" is an acting method that encodes social and class positioning that emerges in gestures. It may include contradictions that are transmitted through highly formalized stilted performances. Such a distanced stylized acting that discourages audience identification is critical for Farocki's conceptualizations of how subjects act, move, and express themselves. Farocki observes, like his detection of patterns of set images and sequences, the repetition of gestures and movements on screens across time.[9] He discusses Brecht's Los Angeles exile and the playwright's intent to work with Lorre again. Unfortunately, the U.S. House Un-American Activities Committee (HUAC)'s decision to subpoena Brecht in 1947 rendered this plan impossible. The Committee suspected him of being a member of, or sympathizing with, the Communist party. Immediately after his hearing, Brecht returned to Europe and never again visited the United States. Farocki includes this anecdote to highlight the degree to which U.S. politicians persecuted leftist thinkers during the Cold War.

Farocki's excursus on Brecht also touches on the exile's return home (a rare theme at the time), an experience that Lorre, too, underwent. Back in West Germany, Lorre wrote, directed, and acted in *Der Verlorene* (The Lost One, 1951). This remarkable film addresses how fascism was absorbed into the banal practice of everyday life, corrupting even science and medicine. Lorre stars as a scientist who conducts secret research for the Nazi government. After hours, outside of the lab, he is a serial killer who victimizes young women. Accordingly, the character triggers an intertextual dialogue with Lorre's role in *M*. *The Lost One* ends with the scientist after the war, overcome by guilt about his crimes. We see him standing on train tracks as a locomotive rushes towards him. Farocki summarizes the extent to which Germany's history changed cataclysmically during the years of Lorre's film career: "No film showed pre-war fascism like *M*, and no postwar film showed fascism like *The Lost One*." He uses Lorre as a vehicle to reflect on the effect of Germany's fascist past on the psyche of individuals and cinema's history.

INTERLOCUTORS

In addition to his film critiques, Farocki produced several interviews with prominent intellectuals for television. These include *On Display: Peter Weiss*, *Interview: Heiner Müller* (1983), and *Catch Phrases-Catch Images: A Conversation with Vilém Flusser* (1986). Each of these individuals held a particular interest for Farocki. Weiss and Flusser were part of an earlier generation forced into exile because of World War II. Müller, a celebrated playwright, was a contemporary of Farocki's residing in East Berlin. Farocki had staged, filmed, and recorded a radio broadcast of Müller's *Die Schlacht* (The Battle: Scenes from Germany, 1951-1974). He and Müller identified as cultural workers in the same divided city. They met several times and exchanged views about their shared heritage in the now fractured country. Both, too, acknowledged the tremendous impact of Brecht and Godard on their own work. As Müller observes, "After forty American films, *Pierrot le Fou* seemed extraordinary just because it seemed like thinking."[10]

Like Müller, Weiss was a dramatist internationally renowned for *Marat/Sade* (1963), and his documentary plays *Die Ermittlung* (The Investigation, 1965), and *Vietnam Diskurs* (Vietnam Discourse, 1968).[11] Farocki found Weiss's genre of documentary theatre that integrates archival material and documents into stage productions attractive. Weiss based his groundbreaking *The Investigation* on court testimonies from the Frankfurt Auschwitz trials 1963-1965. Of particular interest for Farocki was Weiss's engagement with the Vietnamese people's anti-colonial struggle against the United States in the 1960s and 1970s. Like Weiss, Farocki viewed the U.S. war in Indochina as formative to understanding capitalism's imperialist methods of power and control in the late-twentieth century. His interview with Weiss in Stockholm begins with the latter's trip to North Vietnam. Weiss reveals the extent to which the Vietnamese people's consciousness of a history of participation in cultural life struck him. He notes that poetry, theater, dance, opera, and other arts activated the population culturally and militarily. Weiss credits the Vietnamese people's knowledge of what they were defending for their success against the U.S. war machine. In Vietnam, he observes, culture is an organic unity, with each component essential to the functioning of the whole. It is not the sole property of a particular class. Accordingly, it constitutes the basis of the nation's unification. Weiss's epic three-volume novel, *Die Ästhetik des Widerstands* (The Aesthetics of Resistance, 1975-1981), is founded on this organic model of culture. Weiss had only completed the first two volumes of the novel when Farocki interviewed him. The trilogy interweaves documentary material and fictional stories to examine the rise of fascism and various forms of opposition to it. In particular, Weiss, like Farocki, hones in on the defeat of the workers' party. Historical characters like Herbert Wehner, Willi Muenzenberg, and Brecht play parts in the novel.

Farocki asks Weiss about his efforts to translate Brecht's concept of the *gestic* from theater to literature. Weiss explains that the *gestic* encodes condensed memory and history for him. The formal structure of *The Aesthetics of Resistance*, of which each volume is written in a single block where none adhere to a conventional division of chapters, follows Brecht's tactic of eschewing traditional Aristotelian order and translating the epic form of poetry into drama. Farocki further highlights Weiss's affinity to Brecht by recalling that the two sought exile in Sweden. One of exile's most challenging aspects is the loss of belongings. Weiss remembers that Brecht always traveled with his books and that his library was his most cherished possession. Weiss paraphrases Brecht: "Life is lost if one doesn't like books or loses an appreciation of them." What impresses Weiss and Farocki is that "Brecht lived in between books." Not coincidentally, Farocki's films prominently feature books and his living spaces brimmed with volumes.

Farocki and Weiss discuss the difference between writing fiction or poetry, which, like painting (Weiss's first profession), are solitary activities, and staging theater, which, like film, is a collaborative endeavor. Farocki films Weiss's office. A white desk with a typewriter sits in front of a window. Shelves of varying sizes filled with notebooks, index boxes, papers, and books line the walls. Each document on the shelves refers to a topic in Weiss's novel. Also in the office is a large, meticulously drawn-to-scale picture of the factory compound where the first-person protagonist of Weiss's novel works. Weiss explains that the replica helps him imagine his character's everyday work life and the character's movement through spaces such as a courtyard, a canteen, offices, and workshops. Weiss works from a documentary-like constructed reality. Farocki adds that because a workers' culture is no longer visible, producing accurate representations of a milieu is imperative. Geographies, he insists, contain "invisible" worlds and languages. The artist must visualize that which is hidden. Weiss reminds Farocki that a documentary filmmaker must replicate a setting since settings frame actions and make events palpable. In his role as painter, playwright, and filmmaker, Weiss adheres to "the constant search for images, for visual frames that are tangible in all details and give the actions a certain weight." He acknowledges the importance of describing how people interact with each other. However, he maintains that describing "what space they are located in and in what country, in what society, and under which historical circumstances" is equally important. Perhaps in an attempt to test Weiss's theories, the same summer that he interviewed the author, Farocki made *The Taste of Life* (1979). The 29-minute film is composed of seemingly random shots from everyday life. Sequences are edited together without a plot or narrative. The film features visual details of the city only.[12]

Weiss states that his work is fundamentally dialectical about the class struggle, which he sees as eternal. He reveals that he decided to write *The Aesthetics of Resistance* during a visit to the Pergamon Altar in Berlin: "The visit sparked the development of the entire novel. I realized then that artworks are perfect starting points because class relations culminate in them. This is why I used artworks throughout the novel; they serve as examples of a certain time period's consolidation." The Pergamon Altar was built in the second century BCE by King Eumenes. It was excavated by the German engineer Carl Humann in 1878 and relocated to Berlin where the monumental structure was first housed in the museum for antiquities, before the construction of its own eponymous museum in 1930. During World War II, the Altar was removed for safety and later stored in the Hermitage Museum in Leningrad before it was returned to East Berlin in 1959. It encodes a subsequent history of imperialist domination, aside from its initial historical significance, and power—it was removed from Turkey by the Germans, ostensibly to save and preserve it from ruin. The fate of the Pergamon Altar is by no means unique and echoes that of hundreds of thousands of artworks that were taken from their places of origin by foreign Western powers. The Pergamon Altar thus represents Western entitlement, and the unquenchable capitalist thirst for domination and ownership over objects, peoples, and natural resources. Farocki's interview with Weiss loops back to the Vietnam War. Weiss affirms that this war was a "defining event" for him, equal to "the Third World people's struggle for independence from imperialism, which constitutes the most powerful oppressor today." Micro-struggles by individuals should parallel macro-struggles "against powerful neo-colonial oppressors," he contends. "The struggle of individuals includes decisions about political affiliations and ways to align to common causes." For Weiss, these causes encompass the continuous pursuit of justice and truth through aesthetic practices that locate one's historical place.

Farocki interviewed Flusser several years after he spoke with Weiss. Like Lorre and Brecht, Flusser was an exile. He was born in Prague and escaped the Nazis, eventually settling in Brazil where he lived for several decades before leaving the military dictatorship there and returning to Europe. *A Conversation with Vilém Flusser* marks a noticeable shift in Farocki's interest. Brecht, social history, politics, the Vietnam War, and the plight of workers are now absent. Instead, Farocki turns his focus back to images, text, and their role in media. He and Flusser rigorously analyze the front page of *Bild Zeitung*'s November 26, 1985, edition. *Bild Zeitung*, published by media mogul Axel Springer, is the German equivalent of the *National Inquirer*. "Bild" means *image*. Their conversation, which revolves around questions of how images and text function to deform and sensationalize what passes for news, harkens back to Farocki's earlier short *Their Newspapers* (1968). In the interview with Flusser, Farocki introduces him as the author of two important texts: *Für eine Philsophie der Fotografie* (Towards a Philosophy of Photography, 1983) and *Ins Universum der technischen Bilder* (Into the Universe of Technical Images, 1985).[13] He summarizes this: "For Vilém Flusser, photography is as equally profound an invention as print. With photography, the development of technical images began; film, electronic images, computer graphics."

A Conversation with Vilém Flusser presents Farocki and Flusser sitting at a small table in a café. Farocki pulls out the tabloid, and the two lean in to examine the contents. Flusser states that, conventionally, when images and texts appear together, the image illustrates the text, or the text explains the image. However, he observes that a new relationship occurs in *Bild*: the text functions as an image, and the image a text, with the two keeping each other in check. The camera reveals that the newspaper's front page features a photograph of a corpse positioned so that an arm cuts into the space reserved for text and functions like a word. Flusser notes that the letters, instead of the more conventional black against a white background, are the opposite, giving them an imagistic quality. He remarks, "Writing is a code to criticize and consider. Writing develops a diachronic message, which should synchronize our gaze. When we synchronize a diachrony, we criticize the event. Therefore, writing is a code of critical thinking. However, here it has been reversed into the opposite. Writing is made into an image." These reflections resonate with Farocki, for whom an image becomes a code with which to think critically.

3.3 Harun Farocki, *Catch Phrases-Catch Images: A Conversation with Vilém Flusser* (1986)

Farocki and Flusser then turn their attention to a report at the bottom of the page. The story details the murder of a woman and a child. Flusser argues that semantic analysis of a newspaper article is only possible if one studies the totality of the page on which the article appears. The importance Flusser places on viewing a part in its relation to the whole echoes Farocki's earlier critique of television editing, which spatially and temporally extracts images from their original context and continuum. Flusser describes the two different processes involved depending on whether we see words or images: "We read a text in a linear fashion to feel a historical event. By contrast, our eyes scan images in any which way to impose our own meaning on them." Images symbolize concepts. However, according to Flusser, images also feature an added value called "noise," or "an excess of information or data." This noise is what most concerns him. He points out that a photograph's indexical nature prompts the mistaken belief that a "so-called reality is somehow represented." In short, for Flusser, by the late twentieth century, images have come to generate rather than merely represent events. As he puts it, "It's the image that now causes the event."[14]

The interview ends abruptly when Flusser self-reflexively calls attention to his and Farocki's performance in front of a television crew. "You are, of course, aware," Flusser remarks in the café, "that we are not just speaking in normal circumstances here, but in front of a television crew. In other words, the setting is far from neutral. Therefore, everything that we say is plunged into an image, which 'magicizes' it for the recipient." Television technology transmits and transforms the images it records. Flusser continues, "We need to acknowledge that to be recorded on television is to know we are being watched and encourage viewers to use their critical ability against us."[15] The same sign system that provides photographs with a mislaid appeal to veracity is at play with televized images. Both assert an unquestioned "truth" that requires dismantling. The interview format, especially when featuring "experts" such as Flusser, stages a false veneer of authority. Understanding its operation demands the same critical lens as the front page of *Bild*.

The interviews with Weiss and Flusser reveal two of Farocki's running concerns. First, as a figure, Weiss appeals to his Marxist attentiveness to class struggle, economic inequity, and exploitation. Weiss sparks his interest in understanding capitalism's history of crushing and devouring whatever gets in its way. As a German raised in the postwar period, Farocki seeks to understand the proletariat's embrace of National Socialism in the 1930s. Intellectually and culturally, Brecht represents for him a cultural worker who foregrounds class struggle and provides tools to combat liberal bourgeois aesthetics. Weiss, Müller, Huillet, and Straub continue Brecht's political project.

Second, Flusser appeals to Farocki's semiological interest that emerges from Barthes's writings. This concern examines signs and codes rigorously. For Farocki, Flusser is a crucial philosopher of the technological image. He probes this technological image's ontology and questions its impact on language and knowledge production. Farocki gears his practice primarily towards an unrelenting interrogation of image production, utilization, evolution, and distribution in contemporary society. Some argue that Farocki's Brechtian side is prominent in his earlier work, while a Flusserian approach dominates the later output. My argument is that these two facets are present throughout his production and that Farocki intertwines them in most of his work.

BETRAYED

Between his interviews with Weiss and Flusser something else changed in Farocki's filmic practice. Namely he returned to his initial ambition, on entering film school, to become a feature filmmaker. Farocki's first attempt at fiction was *Brunner ist dran* (Brunner Is Next, 1973), loosely adapted from Charles Baudelaire's prose poem *Le mauvais vitrier* (The Bad Glazier). The short, which aired on the regional Nord 3 television channel, was not a success and Farocki did not make another purely fictional film for over a decade until *Betrayed* in 1985. *Betrayed* constitutes an anomaly in Farocki's oeuvre for a number of reasons, not least of which is that the filmmaker completely disavowed the entire project. While he was still alive, few even knew about the existence of *Betrayed*, and even fewer had ever seen it. He refused to discuss the work, and in one of the rare instances in which he addresses it, it is with marked disdain, "I had to take more criticism and scorn for this film than for any other one.... Today I don't want to see or show *Betrogen*. Some of it is really silly."[16] And it was in part because of the failure of *Betrayed* that he turned to making documentary films. As he states unequivocally: "The attempt to make a feature film that adheres to rules was a complete failure. Hence documentary films."[17]

And yet, in a 1986 review of noteworthy films from 1985, film journalist Kraft Wetzel cited one significant "surprise": Harun Farocki's *Betrayed*. Wetzel, though very impressed by *Betrayed*, was aware that "it will be overlooked," and that "film historians will be puzzled by this (oversight) in thirty years."[18] Despite Farocki's stance of seeming indifference approximately twenty years after its release, at the time of its making, Farocki's position on *Betrayed* was just the opposite. He had invested all his resources—material and emotional—into its production. He was convinced that it would catapult him into the field of feature filmmaking. For, despite his prolific output as both an independent filmmaker and a writer, Farocki yearned for the international fame and success of those other German filmmakers such as Fassbinder, Herzog, and Wenders whom he had decried in his writings. It was not enough to be "the best-known unknown filmmaker in Germany."

In advance of the production of *Betrayed*, in November 1983, Farocki wrote a letter to his friends, colleagues, and staff at *Filmkritik* to say goodbye. He had never abandoned the journal for any of his other film projects and had consistently used it as a venue to promote his work. Farocki's stated reasons for resigning are understandable and to a certain extent predictable: problems with understaffing, financial instability, and the general institutional precarity of the "independent" film, television, and writing culture in West Berlin. The letter is written in the tone of a somewhat exhausted and beleaguered individual who quite simply cannot continue under these circumstances. Towards the end, he states, "With my departure, I would like to impart the futility of this endeavor...."[19] Such hopelessness from someone who had devoted the past twenty years of his life to building and being part of an extremely tight-knit community was surprising, for there were always hard times. However, it is perhaps more understandable considering the new film project he was about to undertake. A project that would lead to many such breaks with what had come before. After his farewell to *Filmkritik*, Farocki's writerly output slowed considerably—in 1983 he published no less than thirty-three pieces whereas in 1984 he wrote two, and in 1985 only one. His departure from *Filmkritik* was but one of several goodbyes during that period. Perhaps even more significant was his dismissal of his steadfast production team. However, he was embarking on his, to date, most ambitious project; making a commercial feature, *Betrayed*, with a professional cast and crew where there was no place for personal friends and colleagues.

Betrayed opened at the nineteenth International Hofer film festival in October 1985. The subsequent year, it had a limited festival run with screenings at the Edinburgh Film Festival (August 1986), Journées Cinematographiques D'Orleans (November 1986), and the International Festival for New Cinema in Montreal (November 1986). It was broadcast on television in 1989, and screened once in

Berlin in 1990, after which point, for all intents and purposes, it disappeared. When it first premiered, the reception of *Betrayed* was rather neutral. Up to this point, Farocki was known primarily as a writer, editor, and maker of experimental documentary films and television programs. Viewers were surprised when, instead of seeing yet another powerful essayistic meditation and ideological critique, a film-noir thriller—based on a love story gone bad—a false-identity narrative, and murder unfolded on the screen. As Wetzel remarks, "With a dreamlike certainty, Farocki uses material from everyday life that had formerly appeared as 'big themes' in his essay films about National Socialist economics. The truth of complicated facts is presented in an amazingly simple way with suggestive metaphors."[20]

Although noted at the time as not uninteresting, *Betrayed* was not selected for international release and quickly sunk into obscurity. This lack of immediate acclaim by the professional film public led Farocki to pen a short text in October of 1985, "Ich habe genug!" He opens with the harsh pronouncement, "I don't want to meet anymore film people (*Filmmenschen*)." He continues with an acerbic critique against such film people, including filmgoers, writers, critics, students, and the like. "The film people call themselves filmmakers . . . as if they were craftsmen, as if a film was an everyday useful object like a shoe. As if it was easy to make a film. As if film came from being something useful into being an art by itself."[21] The rejection of *Betrayed* and Farocki's bitter disappointment resound throughout the essay.

Five years later, when *Betrayed* was screened in Berlin at the FSK Kino, its reception was even worse. Instead of being overlooked, it provoked scathing critiques that ensured that its revival would be short-lived. As noted by critic Katrin Bettina Müller, "When diving for hidden treasures, many rusty cans have seen the light of day. With the screening of Farocki's, previously unscreened in Berlin, 1985 feature, *Betrayed*, the FSK theater was hoping to resurrect a previously commercially censored film that might have the potential for being mentally stimulating. However, the dusting off of these film cannisters was not worth it."[22] Another critic concludes that it is "totally blah (blaß) and very boring."[23]

The panning of *Betrayed* by the critics had an enormous impact on Farocki; not only was he unwilling to discuss or screen it, but he also attempted to erase it from his life. As a visit to his archive attests, Farocki was meticulously organized and saved every piece of information, correspondence, and documentation for each of his projects in a double system of files that were organized by the title of the project as well as by calendar year. In these files, there are informal notes and comments, screenplays, and reviews, as well as bills for food and transportation, funding applications, and personal letters in the form of postcards (he loved receiving postcards) and faxes, including copies of those he sent.[24] He was obsessed with the establishment of a record of his life and work and its careful organization. As a documentary filmmaker, Farocki knew well the proleptic significance of an archive. Therefore, it is striking that all files, logbooks, and binders connected to *Betrayed* for the period of its making—roughly 1984-1985—are missing. Yet, one significant letter by Ingo Kratisch remains. Kratisch was Farocki's cinematographer and, at the time, had already made several films with him including *Before Your Eyes—Vietnam* (1982), *An Image* (1983), and *Jean-Marie Straub and Danièle Huillet at Work on a Film Based on Franz Kafka's "Amerika"* (1983). And after *Betrayed*, he resumed working with Farocki until the latter's death. In the brief letter, Kratisch asks Farocki why he has dismissed his entire loyal production team of the past several years and instead contracted a new team of workers and producers for *Betrayed*. The tone of the letter is less marked by confrontation than by confusion and hurt. Kratisch voices that he feels let down and *betrayed* by Farocki. Unlike his other films, for which Farocki served as the primary producer with financial support cobbled together from various sources, including television, *Betrayed* had the external backing of Helmut Wietz, whose production company, Common Film, retained the rights to the film. Additional co-producers included Bayrische Rundfunk, Helmut Herbst, and Adolf Winkelmann. For the first time in his career and possibly the last, Farocki gave up his authorial rights to make this feature. He put everything into it and even broke with his Berlin-based network of friends, colleagues, and workers.

Despite a generous production budget and a cast of professional actors and crew, *Betrayed* was a commercial failure. Why? A contemporary viewing without the specific historical context does not provide any clues. At face value, it seems like a perfectly viable film. And indeed, it made it onto critic Piero Scaruffi's list of one of the top movies from 1985.[25] *Betrayed* is a finely crafted film noir thriller and is not overtly genre-bending. The narrative revolves around a case of stolen identity and duplicitous role-playing. It is evocative of Christian Petzold's *Phoenix* (2014), for which Farocki wrote the screenplay. The plot had its roots in a newspaper story that Farocki read in which a man killed his wife and, for a while, successfully substituted her sister in her place. In his review essay "Vertauschte

Frauen" (Exchanged Women), from *Filmkritik* in 1980, Farocki focuses on examples in film and literature in which one woman replaces another, and the substitution goes undetected. He begins with Agnés Varda's *Le Bonheur* (Happiness, 1965): "In the story of Happiness a woman is substituted for another, and the exchange goes without a hitch. A story is rarely told, about the substitution of a woman, in which the exchange doesn't work."[26] He discusses thematically similar films and novels ranging from François Truffaut's *Mississippi Mermaid* (1969) to William Irish's *I Married a Dead Man* (1948). Farocki concludes by citing a newspaper article about a British soldier in Singapore who killed his wife and replaced her with her sister. The sister successfully takes on the identity of her murdered sibling; however, she has four children whom she must now adopt as if she were the soldier's spouse surviving the death of *her* sister. It all goes according to plan. Here we find the germ of Farocki's *Betrayed*. As he recalls, "I carried this newspaper clipping around with me for a long time. The paper has become yellowed and wrinkled over time."[27] Farocki explains the recourse to a newspaper or factual story for inspiration in the following: "Poe wrote stories in such a way that life is only communicated by the metaphors that are contained within them. That is the beauty of newspaper stories too."[28] For Farocki, the stripped-down or "operational" language of factual reporting may be read simultaneously as a metaphor that symbolically points to something else. In this instance, through an exchange of identity, performance and appearance become the reality. He concludes, "An exchange is also a ghost—one existence takes over another. There is an arrangement behind this, that is the rule of the game. So that the process of illusion-disillusionment is not empty, the illusion must establish and assert its own reality. The exchange is a powerful metaphor. That one person can step into the outline of another and has to live something out of the life of the other: that is too good an idea to easily become a good story."[29] (It is interesting to note that Farocki never mentions Daniel Vigne's immensely successful *Le Retour de Martin Guerre* (The Return of Martin Guerre, 1982) that centers on the return of a soldier from war who takes on another's identity.)

Betrayed is contemporaneously set in late-1970s–early-1980s Hamburg, after its successful rebirth following the "economic miracle." Throughout *Betrayed*, there is meticulous attention to the details of everyday life and the changing landscape of West Germany. The protagonist, Jens (Roland Schäfer), works as a technician for air conditioning units, postwar American imports, reinforcing notions of U.S. imperialism that even extend to controlling and regulating the environment. In his profession as a "*Kilmatechniker*," he makes enough money to *buy*—thanks to a new mortgage system for financing—a contemporary condominium by the sea. Anna (Katja Rupe), his love interest and future wife, is employed in a high-end club, where she supplements her bar income as an "escort" to wealthy clients. When he is not working, Jens spends his time watching Anna at work and grows increasingly obsessed with her until he finally makes contact. The film focuses on his desire.[30] Anna's sister, Edith (Nina Hoger), lives alone with her two young children. She is on the run from the law (we are not quite sure why) and studies court cases in preparation to try and defend herself. Anna provides her with both financial assistance and help caring for the two children. Jens's marriage to Anna is doomed from the onset. She does not respond well to her new isolated existence in the modern apartment. In contrast to the vibrant life of bars and clubs, here she wanders through the various empty rooms without a purpose. The contrast between the two spaces is stressed by the lighting; the nightclub is shot in warm colors and earth tones whereas the apartment is represented in cool lighting to stress its soulless character. The new building is without a history or past and seemingly provides the ideal stage on which to begin a new life. The functional and antiseptic nature of the building mirrors the middleclass marriage in which Anna finds herself and it is only a matter of time before she returns to her former haunts. Anna's nightly absences and emotional distance fan a jealous fury in Jens. He seeks her out and tries to force her to return home with him. She wavers and seems to acquiesce to his demands and gets into his car to return to their home. However, as Jens begins to rail against her and become enraged, she gets out—even as the car is still slowly moving. What happens next is ambiguous. Farocki masterfully films the key scene from the perspective of someone in the car, closely aligned with Jens's point of view. We see Anna walking in the road in front of him; there is then a cut to a shot of her purse that she has left on the car's passenger seat. Jens reaches for the bag, and in that instant, it is not clear whether he swerves the car intentionally to hit her or temporarily loses control as he goes for the purse. Consciously or not, Jens has mortally injured Anna. However, instead of taking her to a hospital to get medical attention, he lets her die. He disposes of her corpse, though it is not revealed how or where. The next step in the plot is for Jens to convince Edith, who is about to lose her children, to move in with him and assume Anna's identity. In exchange for the charade, he will provide her and the children with a safe home environment and solidly middle-class existence. *Betrayed* then follows a series of sequences in which the successful masquerade is performed. Edith slips into Anna's role and files an application for herself and her husband, Jens, to adopt the children of her "disappeared sister." The custodial exchange works without a hitch, and even later, when the social worker visits the children in their new home, the family manages their performance perfectly. Everything goes according to plan except for one glitch, one character, who sees through the facade.

From the outset of the film, Jens is not the only person interested in Anna. There is a strange clownlike figure, Eddi, who exists at the margins of the bar, sometimes selling flowers and cigarettes. Eddi's significance is underscored as Farocki opens *Betrayed* with a shot of him organizing his wares on a display board that he wears. Eddi thinks of himself as Anna's special friend and carries her photograph with him. Around Anna's marriage and departure from the club, he enters a mental institution for treatment. Upon his release, over a year later, he returns to the bar and sees Edith acting Anna's role. As Edith and Jens leave the club, he immediately recognizes the deception and calls out, "No!" followed by, "You have forced her down, you have snuffed her out." Eddi's last words echo, uneasily, as he collapses in a paroxysm on the ground: "I have picture... have picture... picture." The next shot is of him receiving electroshock therapy, succeeded by a closeup of a crowbar prying up a cobblestone. The camera pulls

3.4 Harun Farocki, *Betrayed* (1985)

away and pans out, and the final scene of the film is revealed to be that of a police crew digging and searching the banks of the Elbe with the visual suggestion that they are looking for Anna's corpse.

As this description reveals, the plot and story are quite compelling, a fact that several of the critics immediately acknowledged. However, they are quick to condemn Farocki for ruining an otherwise great story. According to one, "In some films, doing without the usual narration is a creative convenience rather than an avantgarde choice. With Farocki it is worse: a first-class story falls by the wayside."[31] Though many exciting elements are brought into play—crime, passion, emotion, deception, melodrama, and suspense—they are not properly calibrated and do not fit together. And Farocki, who had so carefully studied the rules of filmmaking, was betrayed.

Betrayed is about mimicry, acting, and simulation. All the agents in the film are engaged in forms of performance and role-playing. Their interactions are part of an intricate game that revolves around capital and commodity exchange. If Edith wants financial security for herself and her children, she must adopt a new role and adhere to certain conventions and guidelines. The same bourgeois contract was offered to Anna, who refused to play by the rules. An early exchange between Jens and Anna reveals her self-awareness as a commodity. Jens, like a spectator or voyeur, comes to watch Anna every night. Finally, she sits down to talk to him, but first demands that he buy her a drink since "that is what is done if one wants a woman's attention." Jens criticizes this ritual, and they have the following exchange regarding payment for a woman's time and attention: Jens sanctimoniously declares, "I find whores more honest. Here the girls act as if men had a chance; they act as if they are really in love with men," to which Anna retorts, "Men know that women will pretend to be in love with them when they spend money on them. That is what they pay for. One also goes to the movies though one knows that the actors don't really die." In other words, we willingly pay for our illusions to be upheld. For Anna, Jens, and Edith, their livelihood depends on the successful performance of their roles, just like in a film. Games and role-playing are integral features in Farocki's oeuvre, extending from prominent works such as *Serious Games* (2009-2010), *Deep Play* (2007), and *How to Live in the FRG* (1990) to the children's games of *Bedtime Stories* (1977-1978). In his autobiography, Farocki remembers significant moments in cinema and their impact on his way of being. For example, in his early twenties, he recalls seeing Paul Newman in the role of Eddie in *The Hustler* (1961) and observes: "His false play consisted in showing them that he belonged to them. Also I participated in a false play and paid close attention to see that the others also played by the rules."[32]

In *Betrayed*, as with Newman's character, role-playing and acting have become a profession. For Anna, Jens, and Edith, their livelihoods and that of all hustlers depend on the clientele's successful deception. To that extent, they are no longer, according to game theoretician Roger Caillois, players but rather workers. Mimicry is instrumentalized.[33] And yet, Farocki underscores, in a Lacanian gesture, desire is produced in the consumer of the game even as they are aware of being taken. It becomes like going to a film—the grandest of illusions. Through his memories of Newman and his navigation of everyday life in *Betrayed*, Farocki underscores parallels between filmmaking and game-playing. Cinema is about the successful mastery of creating different imaginary worlds in which the spectator momentarily loses themselves despite the knowledge that the world on screen is not real: *Je sais bien, mais quand même*.... (I know very well, but nevertheless....) In an explicit nod to Lacan, Farocki demonstrates that Jens, by violating the implicit rules and conventions of fantasy through his attempt to possess his fetishistic object of desire, is doomed to failure. In *Betrayed*, human relations are harshly reduced to economic transactions where both parties know the value of the negotiated "goods." One has to pay to play the game.

The story of Jens and Anna is thus transformed into a metaphor for cinema and a metonym for life more generally. Such self-reflexivity is not new in film and abounds, for example, in classic films by Jean Renoir and Orson Welles. Still, the question remains, what accounted for *Betrayed*'s failure at the box office? The narrative was compelling, but how it was told—its form—was decried as being too "avantgarde." As one critic laments: "The artificiality is intentional," while another charges that "Farocki's characters are so artificial to the extent that their dialogue is ready to be printed thereby diminishing any interest in either them or the newspaper article from which their story was taken."[34] Specifically, critics were responding to a stylized form of acting and the distanciation effect that Farocki had developed from Brecht. The actors act in a way that reflects on itself and draws attention to the fact that they are playing roles that have been crafted for them by society. Such a method is intended to break the fourth wall with the audience and to produce a new state of social awareness. However, in the case of *Betrayed*, the reception to the actors' performances was roundly condemning, speaking of "abysses that open up with every word. The unspeakable hides behind the banality. The actors themselves don't believe the lines they deliver."[35] The actors are faulted for breaking the conventional code of make-believe and drawing attention to the fact that they are acting and not *believing*. Two years prior to the making of *Betrayed*, Farocki had worked as an actor with Brechtian filmmakers Huillet and Straub in their film *Class Relations* (1983). In this adaptation of Franz Kafka's *Amerika* (1911-1914), Farocki plays the role of Delamarche. Farocki details their rigorous rehearsal process and work with actors in his *Jean-Marie Straub and Danièle Huillet at Work on a Film Based on Franz Kafka's "Amerika."* Here, every phrase, word, and syllable is meticulously calibrated and rhythmically measured so that the actors' lines achieve at once a natural but stilted delivery. Because Huillet and Straub repeated exactly Kafka's original literary language from the novel, the formality of the exchanges is already built into the dialogue. Similarly, in the case of *Betrayed*, with its contemporary setting and original corresponding screenplay, the awkwardness of the dialogue manifests both in Farocki's scripted language as well as in the delivery of the lines.

The Brechtian alienation effect is further reinforced by Farocki's recourse to an acting technique based on *gestus* that further reveals the embeddedness of bourgeois ideology. For example, the fatal act of leaving her purse in the car when she leaves Jens underscores Anna's willingness to abandon a particular way of life and to resume her status outside of society. Additional Brechtian influences in *Betrayed* manifest in the execution of the narrative, which instead of flowing smoothly unfolds in a series of, at times, disjointed episodes. It is left for the viewer to connect the dots and fill in the gaps; thus, it is never shown how or where Jens disposes of Anna's corpse or why Eddi is institutionalized. As one anonymous reviewer remarks in a blurb used to promote the film, "The most important aspects of his film take place between the images, that is to say in the black holes between edits."[36] Other critics were not as generous in their assessment: "Instead of just telling a story, Farocki (and he shares this with many German filmmakers) insists on an analysis. For most other German films this comes at the expense of the narrative, however, Farocki's script stands on its own, only his narrative style ruins what could have been brilliant."[37] Early on Farocki perfected a Brechtian filmmaking style in essay films such as *Inextinguishable Fire* (1969), *Something Self-Explanatory (15x)* (1971), *Between Two Wars* (1978), and *Before Your Eyes—Vietnam*; however, the translation of these effects into a feature film was not met with success. Instead, the response to this unconventional presentation of the story combined with an artificial style of acting lead to the following withering assessment: "They act as if they were in a 20-Minute TV series between commercials."[38]

In addition to Brecht, another important influence at the time on Farocki was Bresson. Immediately prior to making *Betrayed*, Farocki been deeply immersed in researching the films of Bresson both for a television broadcast, *"L'Argent" by Bresson*, and for a special issue of *Filmkritik* devoted to the French director. In his contribution to that volume, "Bresson ein Stilist" (Bresson a Stylist, 1984), Farocki singles out several characteristics that distinguish the director. First, he notes that "Bresson never uses long shots, and never provides an overview of the entirety before focusing in on a small detail."[39] And in *Betrayed*, Farocki too eschews establishing shots or compositions that would provide a totalizing view. The film begins with a disorienting over-the-shoulder shot of Eddi arranging cigarettes and flowers, followed by a cut to part of Jens's light-blue car with partially obscured words printed on it, followed by a cut to the bar, in which Anna is first presented from the back, her face reflected, but barely discernible, in a mirror. After this rapid series of shots, the camera tracks back, and a greater depth of the sequence is provided. The reveal is slow, like the erotic stripteases performed in various clubs in Hamburg's Reeperband where *Betrayed* is set. Bresson's second stylistic tendency that impresses Farocki is the French director's way of "tight cutting," quick shots containing a sparse cinematography, that further pronounces the fact that the totality is assembled out of shards and fragments. Farocki's editing style is commented on by reviewers both positively and negatively. As Katrin Müller recognizes, "In the interface between shots, the blind spots of perception, the truth lurks." In his essay, Farocki also notes that for Bresson, one of the most critical exchanges is in the look. *Betrayed* is replete with long shots of the characters gazing at each other or gazing into an off-screen space, their eyes unblinking. Jens watches Anna; Anna watches Jens watching her; their dialogue is punctuated by long periods of silence in which the camera focuses on eyes that gaze offscreen.

Finally, Farocki remarks that Bresson's films are replete with figures on society's margins who don't fit in. Anna is an outsider who cannot conform to bourgeois life and considers Jens's apartment a prison. She frequently runs away and is most at "home" with other transients in bars and nightclubs. In the penultimate sequence of *Betrayed*, a former male lover of Anna's encounters Edith, in the guise of Anna, and Jens in the bar where Anna used to perform. He immediately detects that something is out of place because she looks like "a housewife playing at being a whore." He condemns her for selling out and adopting a bourgeois lifestyle and reminds her of a blood pact that the two had made earlier to save each other if either became middle class. Finally, it is the most peripheral of all the characters, the half-mad Eddi, who plays the critical role and shatters the otherwise perfect illusion. Like the stock figure of the village idiot, he is the one able to see through the deception with a preternatural insight. Like in Bresson's films, the marginal characters function to signal the falsity and duplicity of standardized middle class norms, and West Germany's rush to embrace social conformity is condemned.

Betrayed is a Brecht/Bresson mixture, with highly stilted artificial performances in which characters play clichéd roles, in the well-worn narrative of the attempt to convert a sex worker with a heart of gold. From the "facts" of a newspaper article, Farocki creates a metaphor for the postwar West German "consumer society." In addition to the deliberate staginess of the performances and the disorienting delivery of lines by the actors, what seems to have irritated audiences and critics was a heavy-handedness and condescending spirit that suggested that Farocki's imagined spectators were stupid and couldn't reach their own conclusions. As Ronald Glomb observes, "The audience is more intelligent than the filmmaker thinks."[40] This sentiment is echoed by Andre Simonoviescz, who sees Farocki's deliberate slow placing and alienation effects as stemming from the worst kind of didacticism. He wonders why, "with such an abundance of ideas.... Farocki saw the need for slow motion pace and alienation. There is enough social reality that one can read from the pictures without having to draw attention to the social relevance through didactic pauses or underlining."[41]

When it was first released in 1985, *Betrayed* could be most closely aligned to the film movement New German Cinema (NGC), which had actually been over for at least three years—its "death" coincided with that of Fassbinder. NGC was a term made in America that applied to the West German film industry based in Munich and not Berlin. Farocki had always been an outsider of this group and a staunch critique of many of the filmmakers. In his writings as editor of *Filmkritik*, he disparages, for example, Fassbinder's *Lili Marleen* (1981). It is not surprising that Farocki attributes *Betrayed*'s poor reception to the NGC aficionados taking their "revenge." And yet, stylistically and thematically, *Betrayed* seems to be related to those films that Farocki so disdained. Farocki was filming by the rules of a type of independent European avantgarde cinema. Unfortunately for him, by the time *Betrayed* was released, its time was over. Audiences were used to that type of film and were tired of it. As astutely noted, "Farocki is not alone in German Cinema. Instead of a story, we keep seeing explanations of reality, as if the filmmakers didn't trust the audiences to be able to read their pictures."[42] By 1985 NGC was passé, and the Oberhausen Manifesto was under attack. Already by the beginning of the 1980s, a new type of film was in demand as evidenced by the international success of one of Farocki's former student colleagues at the DFFB, Wolfgang Petersen, and his film *Das Boot* (1981), and also the vastly popular television series *Heimat* (1984) by Edgar Reitz. National and international audiences were looking for a new product that embraced formal cinematic conventions and did not stress the viewer with an alienating and off-putting style. A new cinema that was brighter, more contemporary, and global in its appeal—in short, more Hollywood. In 1985 such a film was presented at festivals at the same time as Farocki's—Dorris Dörrie's "lighthearted" feminist comedy, *Men*. *Men*, a first feature film by a new generation of West German filmmakers, presented itself as the antidote to the gloom and doom of the immediate postwar era. It signaled that West Germany had overcome its past and was ready to move on and focus on contemporary concerns like other Western nations had.

And so Farocki, with his tail between his legs, returned to independent filmmaking and his signature brand of compilation essay films and observational documentaries. Immediately following *Betrayed*, he produced *As You See*, *Indoctrination* (1987), and *Images of the World and the Inscription of War* (1988). However, a decade later in 1995 two important events occurred that would affect his career. One of these was his entry into the art world with his first installation, *Interface*. The second was the beginning of his collaboration as screenwriter with feature film director Christian Petzold. Their partnership started that year with the film *Pilotinnen* and ended with his death and the post-humous film *Transit* (2018).

CHAPTER 4

War

For Europe, for ourselves, and for humanity, comrades, we must turn over a new leaf, we must work out new concepts, and try to set afoot a new man.
—Frantz Fanon, *The Wretched of the Earth*

Is war technology still the forerunner of civil technology such as radar, ultra-shortwave, computer, stereo sound, jet planes? And if so, must there be further wars so that advances in technology continue, or would the simulated wars produced in laboratories suffice? And, moreover, does war ever subordinate itself to other interests? Does war not always find—according to Brecht—a loophole?
—Harun Farocki, "Cross Influence/Soft Montage"

Student uprisings, political agitation, and mass demonstrations rocked West Berlin during the mid-1960s when Farocki attended the DFFB. Like much of the world, West Germany was then in turmoil, and the city was at the epicenter of anti-authoritarian protests. The country's protest level was higher than ever since the Weimar Republic. Struggles for women's rights and against imperialism, colonization, and foreign wars fomented a robust camaraderie, creativity, and an overflow of the "political" into all areas of culture. Farocki's production during these years reveals his full-throated support for many of these social movements. For example, his 1967 *The Words of the Chairman* is sharply critical of the recent visit to Berlin by the shah and empress of Iran. The highly stylized short features two figures wearing paper-bag masks representing the Iranian royals. A third figure assails them by throwing a paper-plane missile in their direction. Farocki's *The Campaign Volunteer* (1967), made that same year, tracks a young volunteer's electioneering. The film knits together an oblique narrative about the man's earlier life with documentary footage of Berlin's Kreuzberg neighborhood and interviews with local denizens. We learn that the man, who had an intimate relationship with an Algerian woman, studied "Third World" liberation movements. The production ends with his citing the final words of Frantz Fanon's *The Wretched of the Earth* (1961), which serves as one of this chapter's epigraphs. The necessities articulated in Fanon's directive guided Farocki's early films.

THE TELEVISION WAR

Although generally involved in protest and activism, Farocki honed his interests on the multiple ways the military-industrial complex, with its economic imperative and global network of connections, invaded all aspects of everyday life. One particular armed conflict preoccupied him: the U.S. war in Vietnam. That offensive, widely considered a Cold War-era proxy war, created an international solidarity movement united in condemnation of the United States as an imperial aggressor waging war against a militarily inferior country and its predominantly peasant population. Politicians, veterans, writers, artists, filmmakers, and cultural workers united in protesting the bloody and, for many, unjust confrontation. Writing in 1998, Farocki recalls, "The war which the United States waged against Vietnam was outrageous, first and foremost in its extreme cruelty. It assumed that civil society would regard it without interest or passion."[1] In 1968, Farocki made two shorts that directly addressed the Vietnam War: *White Christmas*, and *Their Newspapers*. He co-directed the latter with fellow DFFB student Helke Sander, and Skip Norman served as cinematographer for both.

In *White Christmas*, Farocki juxtaposes media images of Vietnam with the commercial "kitsch" of Christmas in North America and Europe. He scores the short film to Bing Crosby's eponymous 1942 hit. The production opens with a winter wonderland. White horses draw Santa Claus's sleigh through a snow-covered forest. A hand-scrawled intertitle interrupts the enchanted sequence to announce that many Americans will not be home for Christmas this year. The intertitle also notes that nine million copies of Crosby's recording have been sold in advance, which will help to remind the tens of thousands of U.S. soldiers serving abroad of the holiday back home. Farocki underscores the connection between sentimentality and commercial marketing strategies that manufacture emotion—a topic he returns to in *Remember Tomorrow Is the First Day of the Rest of Your Life* (1972) and *Some Day You Will Love Me Too* (1973).

The next scene occurs in a sparse living room where a mother and three children sit next to a Christmas tree awaiting Santa Claus. The legendary figure arrives bearing gifts. One child receives a shiny jet-airplane toy, and the other a Lincoln Logs set he uses to build a redwood cabin. Another intertitle ironically comments that the North Vietnamese will also receive Christmas gifts this year: the United States will drop many bombs on them. At this point, the redwood cabin explodes, and a rapid sequence of found-footage images of bombing raids flashes on the screen. While Crosby's silky voice croons, a bombing raid delivers a blizzard of missiles. The bomb deluge visually rhymes with a Christmas Day snowstorm. The next intertitle's sans-serif typeface is austere. It bears the refrain from a German Christmas psalm, "Today Our Holy Land Is Born." A photo of an anguished Vietnamese woman who, pieta-like, carries her dead child in her arms follows the refrain. Next appear the words "tortured" and "murdered," followed by *Auferstanden* (resurrection or resistance). The following images show

4.1 Harun Farocki, *White Christmas* (1968)

camouflaged Vietnamese engaging U.S. soldiers in battle. Though a mere three minutes long, *White Christmas* features tropes about war, technology, and media spectacle that recur throughout Farocki's oeuvre.

Their Newspapers is sixteen minutes long. The film addresses print journalism's complicity in the war, through the way it represents Vietnam. Specifically, Farocki and Sander target tabloid newspapers such as *Bild Zeitung* (*BZ*) that secure their readership through sensational stories. The filmmakers divide the production into two eight-minute parts. Part 1 directly confronts news media. Part 2 is subdivided into four sections, each addressing the question: "What is the difference between West Berlin and Vietnam?" The production opens with the typed words: "Problems of urban anti-authoritarian and anti-imperialist struggle with West Berlin as an example." Two alternating voice-overs spoken by Farocki and Sander follow this opening. The voices state: "As news," "As mangled news," and "Vietnam comes to Berlin." The voice duet continues throughout the film, undermining the authority traditionally ascribed to voice-over in documentaries.

As is well known, tabloid newspapers are particularly egregious. They disseminate fake news that distracts readers from real issues. They are also often complicit with state surveillance systems that monitor local citizenry. In *Their Newspapers*, Farocki and Sander focus particularly on the *BZ* tip hotline. The call center provides an outlet for citizens to report suspicious activities anonymously. The hotline's slogan promises a reward: "For every one of your reports that we print, you get 20 Marks. Berliners keep your eyes open." The film features a series of "Hallo BZ" calls. These range from a caller who reports a man putting up political posters on the street, to another who betrays student protesters, and yet another who relays the whereabouts of what he identifies as left-wing "riots." Instead of reporting news and making its public more knowledgeable, the media fosters spies and turns its public into informers—*Hilfssheriff*in* (assistant sheriffs)!

Farocki and Sander's film questions how to make the Vietnam War relevant to the West German citizenry, especially in Berlin. *Their Newspapers* dialogues with the French omnibus production *Loin du Vietnam* (Far from Vietnam, 1967), which underscores the war's relevance to Europeans through a series of tableaus.[2] Continuing the project begun by the omnibus film, Farocki and Sander's production takes up Ernesto "Che" Guevara's 1967 call to "create two, three, many Vietnams." Over shots of Vietnamese war causalities, the duet remarks, "The suffering of the Vietnamese, an image of its suffering, comes from Vietnam to Berlin." A similar pronouncement was made by the French precursor that called for bringing the war back to France. The final scene in that film represents Parisians running from an aerial bombing.

Their Newspapers' second part begins with the question, "What is the difference between West Berlin and Vietnam?" The same question repeats five times. The first scene comprises a U.S. military officer and a woman having a drink. Then, in a sequence that recalls the exploding cabin in *White Christmas*, the lighter blows up, bomb-like, as the officer lights the woman's cigarette. The second scenario features footage of Berlin mayor Klaus Schütz (who Farocki identifies as K. Schtz) addressing a large audience. The mayor asserts that the U.S. army is helping to bring order to Vietnam. His claim prompts jeers and whistles from the audience, and his entourage rapidly escorts him from the auditorium to safety. As he exits, the words "We are governed by idiots" scrawl across the screen.

In the film's third response to the question about the difference between West Berlin and Vietnam, a man stands reading a newspaper in an exterior passageway. Another man, played by Farocki, walks towards the first, turns around, scales a wall, crosses a terrace, jumps back to the street level, and attacks him from behind. The commentators pronounce, "The Vietnamese people use all supports, all ledges, windows, bricks, roofs, doors, paths, and the entire surface of their country to fight against aggressors and their lackeys." They conclude that "the surface of Vietnam is an ally of the Vietnamese people. The aggressors want to change the surface to their advantage," but to no avail. The film's final sequence, strongly reminiscent of the beginning of *Far from Vietnam*, begins with stock footage of jet bombers taking off from a warship in the China Sea and flying towards the East Asian mainland. As they drop a cascade of bombs on the Vietnamese countryside, Farocki and Sander intercut the footage with bundles of newspapers falling from the sky onto Berlin streets. City residents scurry to safety. To the questions, "How can we protect ourselves? What can we do?," the film responds: "We have to destroy the apparatus."

Farocki's understanding of an apparatus derives from Michel Foucault's definition of a *dispositif*: a "system of relations" established between the elements of a "heterogeneous ensemble" to produce norms, habits, practices, and subjectivity more generally.[3] Farocki lists several operative apparatuses such as the "apparatus of misery and poverty," the "war-apparatus," the "manipulation apparatus," "the anti-emancipation apparatus," and many more. Filmed sequences accompany the list. One takes place in a classroom-like setting similar to the study hall in *The Division of All Days* (1970). A woman at a desk reads from a text. She informs

4.2 Harun Farocki, *Their Newspapers* (1968)

the assembled group that "the combative collective needs a mobile apparatus [to add] new meaning to private communication." Two sets of images underscore this point. In the first, two cars slow down at a traffic light, and the passengers pass an envelope from one car to another. The second features an extreme close-up of Farocki passionately kissing a woman. As he and the woman part, he removes a clump of paper from his mouth. The implication is that the two figures have exchanged the wad during the kiss. Later, while sitting on a window ledge, Farocki flattens the mass and then folds it into a paper airplane. Then, in a gesture recalling the toy flyer scene in *The Words of the Chairman*, he throws the plane into the city from a window. The commentary remarks, "The combative collective launches news as a weapon." It continues with the assertion that all *BZ*'s articles "attack the working class and disrupt solidarity with the oppressed peoples of the Third World." The final sequence gives the children's game "Paper, Rock, Scissors" a political twist. Two dictums follow the observation that "paper dulls scissors, stone weighs down paper, and paper directs the stone's path": "No more stones without paper and no more paper without stones." On the soundtrack plays breaking glass as theory, practice, words, and action come together in an acoustic event.

The next year, for his final student project, Farocki's first feature, *Inextinguishable Fire* (1969), builds on these earlier investigations.[4] The production critiques the Vietnam War by investigating Dow Chemical Company's incendiary antipersonnel weapon: napalm. Farocki directly confronts Western audiences' tacit support of the U.S. military campaign in Indochina by demonstrating their passive consumption of media images about the conflict. He divided the film into three parts. In part 1, he appears in the guise of a television newscaster. The latter proceeds to read a detailed account of a napalm attack in Vietnam. Part 2 stages several fictional scenes set in a Dow Chemical Plant, and part 3 is a short skit featuring a worker, a student, and an engineer. The film fuses fact and fiction in a manner that eschews genre classification. The resulting production is a cinematic form that stands outside those three then dominant: the feature film, epitomized by classical Hollywood cinema; documentary film, and more specifically, Cinema Verité and American Direct Cinema; and avant-garde film, including abstract and structuralist experiments. Already, at this early stage, Farocki adopts the essay film format in *Inextinguishable Fire* to produce his negative critique. The essay structure's relative freedom and its legacy in the German language as the "form of critique par excellence" enable opportunities the other genres do not provide.[5]

In part 1, Farocki, formally attired in suit and tie, sits at a bare office desk. He reads a text in the role of a television news anchor. The text comes from the powerful testimony of Thai Bihn Dahn, a Vietnamese citizen who suffered the horrible effects of a napalm attack. "The flames and unbearable heat engulfed me," he recalls. "I lost consciousness. Napalm burned my face, both arms and legs.... For thirteen days I was unconscious." Farocki then looks directly into the camera and asks, "How can we show you the damage caused by napalm?" He notes that representations of napalm attacks usually rely on documentary images from which viewers close their eyes or look away. To avoid the documentary genre's pitfalls, he proposes a "demonstration of how napalm works." At this point, he burns his left forearm with a lit cigarette. As the cigarette singes his skin, he explains: "A cigarette burns at four hundred degrees. Napalm burns at three thousand degrees." With this act, which literalizes the idiomatic expression "to put one's hand in the fire," Farocki implicates the spectator in a novel way.[6] He refers to the performed act as a "weak demonstration" of anti-war protest in contrast to the self-immolations before the media that shocked television viewers worldwide in the 1960s, first that of Buddhist monk Thich Quang Duc in Saigon in 1963, and then two years later the U.S. Quaker Norman Morrison on the steps of the Pentagon. Farocki's act ignites a flash of media images in the spectator's imagination. The effect of napalm passes from those experiencing it to those reporting it and finally to those witnessing it from a safe distance in their living rooms. Strategies of how to restore initial shock value to mass mediatized images from the war circulated amongst many artists and cultural workers at the time. For example, the British theater director Peter Brook, in his play *US* (1966), burnt live butterflies on stage, and Martha Rosler collaged photographs from the war into glossy home design magazines in her series "House Beautiful: Bringing the War Home, 1967–1972."

Part 2 of *Inextinguishable Fire*, the longest of the three parts, stages a Dow chemical plant in Michigan. It includes experiments with rats and a series of fictional (albeit based on official Dow press releases) conversations about napalm between plant managers, scientists, engineers, U.S. State Department officials, and factory workers. The characters participate in complex economic and philosophical debates about the relation of the incendiary mixture of chemicals to the military-industrial complex.[7] In addition to the highly stylized philosophical rhetorical dialogues, Farocki employs intertitles and documentary footage of North American television news reports from Vietnam. If *Their Newspapers* targeted print media, *Inextinguishable Fire* puts television as a medium of production, transmission, and distribution under pressure. Farocki's camera closes in on the television set until the image on the screen merges with the receiver. A sequence that links the workers in factories that produced the atomic bomb to those at the Dow chemical plant follows. The progression establishes a direct link between Hiroshima and Vietnam.[8] The commentary notes that the workers that produced the atomic bomb realized their culpability "too late."[9] The film then cuts back to the Michigan plant, where the firm's managers argue that napalm saves lives. The scene's final shot focuses on the plant's chief chemist, who notes that Harvard University students are protesting Dow Chemical Company. What they do not realize, she says with a shrug as she enters her luxury car, is that napalm is only one of six hundred different valuable products the company makes.

Farocki set part 3 of *Inextinguishable Fire* in the lavatory of a vacuum cleaner factory. The first character, a worker, explains that since his wife wants a carpet sweeper, he has been regularly stealing components and attempting to assemble a device at home when he has all the necessary parts. However, in a punch line, he states that his efforts to put the pieces together have consistently realized submachine guns. The second character repeats the scene. But in this case, the character is a student convinced that the vacuum cleaner factory is manufacturing automatic weapons for export. He steals parts from the factory floor to expose the company's actual mission. However, when he reassembles the parts, the result is a vacuum cleaner. The third character, an engineer who works in the same factory, concludes that both the worker and the student are correct. He shows that the vacuum cleaner can operate as a powerful weapon, and the submachine gun can have significant domestic use. The functions are two sides of the same coin, a similarity reinforced by the fact that the same actor plays all three roles. Farocki actualizes the picture-puzzle concept in this final skit, metamorphosing the two-dimensional optical illusion into a three-dimensional conceptual trope. The film concludes with the statement that what the company manufactures "depends on the workers, the students, and the engineers," as they are all implicated in the military-industrial complex.

The year before he released *Inextinguishable Fire*, Farocki published "Staubsauger oder Maschinenpistolen: Ein Wanderkino für Technologen" (Vacuum Cleaners or Machine Guns: A Travelling Cinema for Technologists), where he outlines the three scenarios that eventually find their way into the third section of the film. The essay focuses on bringing political work and education together and

4.3 Harun Farocki, *Inextinguishable Fire* (1969)

finding a role for film within that conjunction. In the text, Farocki recounts his previous work in a working group focused on the burgeoning role of technology and cybernetics in different learning spheres, including philosophy, science, and education. The group organized a tour of technical high schools and trade schools. It conducted discussions and teach-ins and used an instructional film for its political agenda. The film remained untitled. The group projected it on small monitors instead of a large screen. In this way, it broke all associations with traditional cinema. Following a sequence in which four engineering students speak about their lives, the film ends with the three "agitational skits," all of which Farocki later used in *Inextinguishable Fire*.[10] "Vacuum Cleaners or Machine Guns" is the earliest example of a direct correlation between Farocki's written essays and his filmic work. It also anticipates Farocki and Antje Ehmann's traveling video production workshops, titled *Labour in A Single Shot* (2011–14), in which film plays a crucial role in the discussion between labor and work.

The production company "Harun Farocki, Berlin-West" produced *Inextinguishable Fire* for WDR Köln. Through his hyper-stylized imitation of a newscaster in part 1 and his images of broadcast television's war footage, Farocki self-reflexively critiques the institution that produced his work. He offers a formal and thematic alternative to the standard nightly fare. The feature is fictional. Nevertheless, it includes facts, documents, records, testimonials, and official pronouncements. The mode of delivery is striking. The news anchor's highly stylized monotone functions to heighten the alienation effect.[11] The production's intertitles, appropriated television footage, and theatrical staging remind spectators that they are watching highly mediated events. The reliance on found television footage to impart war images underscores the nightly news's spectacularization of the Vietnam War, referred to as the first "television war." In the post-World War II era, Western civilians experience war primarily through images. By focusing on a factory that produces both weaponry and domestic products, Farocki underscores the few degrees that separate domestic viewers in West Germany from the war in Indochina. *Inextinguishable Fire* highlights the extent to which Vietnam enters Western consciousness through consumer goods such as television, household cleaning supplies, and pesticides designed to improve the quality of everyday life.

A dozen years after *Inextinguishable Fire*, Farocki revisits Vietnam in his feature *Before Your Eyes—Vietnam* (1982) and its accompanying publication "Hund von der Autobahn" (Dog from the Freeway).[12] *Before Your Eyes—Vietnam* drops

Inextinguishable Fire's openly confrontational style in favor of a reflective, distanced, semi-fictional meditation on "real" war's codification as an image archive. The heady protests of the late-1960s gave way to resignation in the early 1980s as a Helmut Kohl-led West Germany ushered in the neoliberal era. Farocki recalls, "The [anti-war] protest was a flash in the pan, however, and the war had already been forgotten before it ended. Unlike World War I, whose outbreak seemed to confirm the theory of imperialist competition, the Vietnam War didn't serve to justify any theories. It was also not handed down as a tale of resistance like the Spanish Civil War. A shrug of the shoulders was all that was left."[13] Of course, the war in Indochina also left behind an enormous image archive. *Before Your Eyes—Vietnam* interrogates the role of media images, especially photographs, in identifying, conceptualizing, and recalling the Vietnam War for Western audiences. One of the film's characters concludes that the pictures of the war "revealed something new about the United States, [namely, that it operates like] a sadist, a murderous thief, a jealous man in rage . . . , an execution machine."

The main premise of the film is an enamored couple who ponders the intricate relationship between love, politics, and war. Farocki fashions this Gordian Knot out of filaments from the Vietnam War that the couple seeks to untangle as they consider photographs, newsreel footage, and other documents. Reenactments of famous prize-winning photographs and historical events punctuate the film. The two protagonists stare at their images in a mirror. The man declares, "It's like a trailer for a war film; an exciting love story against the background of war and genocide." The film challenges viewers to maintain their interest in and concern for Vietnam beyond the U.S. incursion. Although the war visualized something (*etwas wird Sichtbar*—something is made visible—as the German title underscores), the question of what is readable remains. Vietnam takes the form of an old love affair struggling to remain relevant. Representation of the conflict became a Hollywood genre. Classics like Hal Ashby's *Coming Home* (1978), Michael Cimino's *Deer Hunter* (1978), and Francis Ford's Coppola's *Apocalypse Now* (1979) were instant box office hits. The transformation of war into entertainment impelled Farocki to revisit the genre.

Farocki's noir-style black-and-white film opens with the couple noted above walking down a street at night. The male figure tells his companion that he finds her beautiful. She responds by asking why beauty is important. He replies philosophically: "Because beauty means the possibility of ending horror." The film then cuts to a brightly lit modern hotel, which recalls the establishment in Jean-Luc

War 151

4.4 Harun Farocki, *Before Your Eyes Vietnam* (1982)

Godard's *Alphaville* (1965). A left-wing activist disguised as a sex worker confronts a U.S. intelligence operative. She reviews his brief but active career, which began in Algeria a decade earlier, then moved to North Vietnam, Venezuela, and back to Vietnam, culminating in a U.S. university professorship, and accuses him of crimes against humanity. He shrugs off the account of his heinous deeds and tells her that her (and, by extension, our) knowledge of Vietnam is wholly a by-product of the war: "Americans bombed Vietnam to make it larger and more visible." While he says this, the hotel television plays a newsreel broadcast reporting on the evacuation of Danang in April 1975. Farocki intercuts these sequences with scenes of a protestor in Berlin, who requests from a butcher a liter of blood from a freshly slaughtered animal to fill an empty bottle. "It's for a film," he explains nonchalantly. In a staged action as part of a protest against the war in Vietnam, he pours the liquid over his head. There is also a sign bearing the words: "Coventry, Dresden, Hanoi," that makes a problematic elision between Hitler's blitz bombing of a city in the UK, the allied response in Dresden, and the U.S. bombing raids in Vietnam.

Farocki then cuts to a staged reenactment of waterboarding torture. The actors are Western, and their movements and Brechtian delivery of lines reinforce the

4.5 Harun Farocki, *Before Your Eyes Vietnam* (1982)

tableau's theatrical nature. Other reenactments include characters carefully defusing and disassembling a hand grenade and recycling spent bullets and cartridges. A striking sequence acted out by children restages Eddie Adams's 1968 Pulitzer prize-winning photograph of Nguyễn Văn Lém's execution. One child pantomimes shooting his friend while another crouches on the ground, taking the picture. The child's game amplifies the act's initial horror, and reinforces the absurd dictum that to be photographed, even at the moment of death, is to be made real. Vietnam's afterlife exists in spectacularized photographs of life at its termination. The lives of victims who were not pictured pass as if they never existed.[14]

Throughout the film, Farocki draws analogies and through his characters delivers maxims such as "The U.S. is a machine and Vietnam a tool. The machine cannot break the tool." At one point, prompted by a photograph of a U.S. soldier listening to the ground with a stethoscope, Farocki states, "The Vietcong is a disease that runs through Vietnam and the U.S. has assumed the role of the doctor that seeks to heal it." Farocki also obliquely references German atrocities in World War II, drawing a connection between the horrors the United States inflicted on the Vietnamese and those committed by the Germans at mid-century. A picture of a hanged man appears among photographs from Vietnam. An actor reads a caption that explains that the man was a prison guard lynched by inmates upon their liberation. However, he reveals that the photographer did not take the picture in Vietnam but in Europe upon the liberation of a concentration camp in 1945. At this point, another voice interjects, "The text is correct, but it is not true" (*Es ist wichtig, aber nicht wahr*), riffing on Godard's 1967 pronouncement, "*Une image juste! Juste une image?*" (A just image, or just an image?) He concludes, "It is less important what an image shows than what is behind it." Farocki ends with the observation that "images are often shown as proof of things that cannot be proven." Later, citing from Frances Fitzgerald's book *Fire in the Lake*, the woman repeats, "Vietnam becomes visible [*Sichtbar*], we still don't get the real picture but something becomes visible [*etwas wird Sichtbar*]."

Film's ability to render events visible remains in question. Unless a director shoots the production in a single take, the editing process contrives narrative order and visual segues. Farocki invokes the montage process in *Before Your Eyes—Vietnam* through phrases such as "Two things can be closely related but separate, or far apart but closely related," and "One begins an investigation by connecting ideas and ends by separating them." Editing visualizes things, relating them, and assembling arguments. Although Farocki primarily focused *Before Your Eyes* on Vietnam, he uses the film to make more significant claims about the interconnectivity of images, media, and world events. The Vietnam War, as the first television war, initiated a seismic change in how politics both forms and *is formed by* images. Visual media at once represents and co-produces war. Farocki questions how images circulate. He probes the platforms that distribute images for consumption. He also questions the afterlife of images. If the primary medium for disseminating information is now television, then what role can his films serve? Can film, with its reliance on theatrical release, play an active role in contemporary politics?

Farocki formulated an active guerilla-like strategy to market *Before Your Eyes—Vietnam*, much as he had with *Between Two Wars* (1978). He carried out tactics that promoted the film well beyond conventional marketing techniques.[15] He drove a VW van marked with the production's title below an enlarged film still through the streets of West Berlin. He steered the vehicle along streets he knew pedestrians and automobiles traveled frequently. He also graffitied *Etwas Wird Sichtbar* with bright paint on several city walls. Farocki began the publicity campaign with the title only. As the release date approached, he started to include his name. High visibility was key. He recalls, "I wrote [graffiti] on a pedestrian bridge over the urban freeway in the Berlin district of Halensee because I had read that it is the most-traveled road in Germany. It wasn't easy to bend over the railing and write the upside-down letters."[16] Then, several days before the film's premiere, Farocki and actor Ronny Tanner staged a live performance (titled *Ronny and Harun Act Up*) in the lobby of the Delphi Theater foyer.

Farocki also distributed an eight-page pamphlet to the audience at *Before Your Eyes—Vietnam*'s premier. The printout included stills from the film, a list of credits, excerpts from the screenplay, and a quotation from Susan Sontag's memoir *Trip to Hanoi*. The quotation begins, "What I'd been creating and enduring for the last four years was a Vietnam inside my head, under my skin, in the pit of my stomach." The pamphlet also included a newspaper editorial by Pier Paolo Pasolini, "Has Vietnam Gone Out of Fashion?," and a fictitious interview between Farocki and "Rosa Mercedes." As an independent auteur filmmaker, Farocki assumed the role of promoting his productions. Recognizing the extent to which paratextual formulations shape and affect reception, he developed a calculated paratextual structure around *Before Your Eyes—Vietnam*.[17]

Complementing the release of *Before Your Eyes—Vietnam*, Farocki published "Dog from the Freeway," whose title cites Carl Schmitt's characterization of a partisan at the end of *Before Your Eyes—Vietnam*. Both "Dog from the Freeway" and *Before Your Eyes—Vietnam* are composed mainly of quotations by writers. Besides Schmidt, Farocki extensively references sources, including Sontag's *Trip to Hanoi*, Frances FitzGerald's *Fire in the Lake*, and John le Carré's *The Honourable Schoolboy*. There are strong parallels to Godard, who adopts a similar tactic in *One + One* (1968). Farocki is quite open in his admiration for Godard and cites Sontag's praise for the Franco-Swiss filmmaker: "In his brilliant episode from the film *Far From Vietnam*, Godard reflects (as we hear his voice, we see him sitting behind an idle movie camera) on how good it would be if each one of us made a Vietnam inside ourselves."[18] Such indirection works differently in the print essay than in the film. The text's comprehensive footnotes allow readers to track down sources and encourage further research. The citation tactic is part of Farocki's *Verbundsystem* in which reference materials and found footage are recycled into the montage of the film.

Here, Walter Benjamin's "hardware" aphorism in *One-Way Street* (1928), where he illuminates his bricolage technique of citation, is instructive in comprehending Farocki's method: "Quotations in my work are like wayside robbers who leap out, armed, and relieve the idle stroller of his conviction."[19] For Benjamin, as for Farocki, quotations are pre-composed building blocks that stand out from the rest of the text. Their redeployment defamiliarizes both the source text and the new text in which they now operate. *Before Your Eyes—Vietnam* features extensive dialogue about media images' role in forming opinions and producing shared (false) histories that reduce complicated networked relations to singular perspectives. "Dog from the Freeway" is far more discursive and theoretical. Farocki includes historical details and critical analyses that would not be possible in a cinematic mode. The essay complements the film; it serves as the backstory, the footnotes, and the invisible scaffolding upon which Farocki builds his sounds and images. The relationship between film essays and written texts is like an expanded juxtaposition of image and text. The two function separately and together. The hinge between them recalls the edit between sequences. As Farocki explains a few years later, in "Reality Would Have to Begin," "Texts should make images accessible, and images should make texts imaginable."[20]

Farocki published "Dog from the Freeway" in *Filmkritik*, tapping into the journal's readership and guaranteeing an archived print afterlife. The text allowed people to access an account of the film following its limited run in theaters. This ability was crucial given that Farocki made *Before Your Eyes—Vietnam* before the widespread use and circulation of videotapes. At the time, if one missed the initial theatrical release, the only way to access the film and others like it was on television or through a private screening at a film archive.[21] Farocki's translation from one medium to another was at once a multi-pronged interventionist strategy and a canny study of the different conditions that apply when making a film, staging a live performance, or writing a text. Each mode transforms thought in different ways.

According to the published minutes of a discussion of *Before Your Eyes—Vietnam* at the sixth Duisburg Film Week in November 1982, "Harun Farocki answered the question as to his specific interest in making this film by saying that the film was not due to one particular interest, but rather that it stood in the continuum of his work and resulted from the multi-polar contiguities of his other activities."[22] Accordingly, Farocki made the film to continue his ongoing investigation of how images work and how best to integrate political engagement and practice with his role as an intellectual and cultural worker. His primary concern was to develop forms that could aid in the struggle against state-sponsored capitalism in the West.

To support this goal, Farocki turned to Schmitt's "Theory of the Partisan," where the Nazi political theorist claims that a new type of combatant emerged during the Spanish Civil War: the guerilla. Schmitt argues that this partisan, the guerilla fighter, does not follow conventional rules of warfare but develops novel tactics that are difficult for their adversaries to predict. The new tactics place the "enemy" *within*—rather than external to—the system. Following this model, Farocki suggests a new type of filmmaker who attacks the system from within, in unanticipated and unexpected ways.

That Farocki would find Schmitt's theory of the partisan productive is not surprising. After all, Schmitt's concept related as well to the RAF and the guerilla fighters in Vietnam as to the revolutionaries fighting colonialism and imperialism in Latin America and worldwide. Both *Before Your Eyes—Vietnam* and "Dog from the Freeway" end with Schmitt's 1963 pronouncement: "If the inner and, according to optimistic opinion, immanent rationality of the technically organized world is implemented completely, then the partisan will perhaps cease to be a valid troublemaker. He will vanish of his own accord in the frictionless performance of technical-functional processes, no different from the disappearance of a dog from the freeway."[23] Schmitt's forecast that technologized society will put an end to resistance, action, and subterfuge resonates with Farocki's prognosis of what the proliferation of surveillance technology might do to the existing social order.

MINING THE ARCHIVE, FORENSICS AS METHODOLOGY

In addition to Vilém Flusser's and Friedrich Kittler's theories of image production and technologies of vision, Paul Virilio's *War and Cinema: The Logistics of Perception* captured Farocki's imagination. Virilio's volume, which Farocki read upon its German translation in 1986, relates war to how vision organizes, identifies, and interprets information. The media theorist observes that "alongside the 'war machine,' there has always existed an ocular (and later optical and electro-optical) 'watching machine' capable of providing soldiers, and particularly commanders with a visual perspective on the military action under way."[24] He begins his study in the early twentieth century with observations linking the technologies of photography, film, and radio to war. In particular, Virilio focuses on cameras placed on World War II bombers. Airforce commanders installed the imaging devices on the warplanes to assess the sorties' success rate. Farocki's first film to achieve broad international distribution and acclaim, *Images of the World and the Inscription of War* (1989), tracks this nexus of war, technology, and imaging. His decision to release the film in video format with an English voice-over partly facilitated its success. The year before he made *Images of the World*, Farocki completed *Images-War* (1987), a related, though much shorter, compilation film. This production laid the groundwork for *Images of the World*. Many of its images resurface in the later film, including photographs from an Auschwitz album, aerial pictures of the Auschwitz camp, and mugshots of Algerian women. Both investigate how wars produce, generate, record, document, and archive images.

Several wars are depicted in *Images of the World*, predominantly World War II, the Cold War, and the Algerian War of Independence. If Farocki's earlier conundrum fixated on how to filmically render an abstract concept like capital, now the Cold War constitutes a challenge for him. How to represent a conflict that primarily takes an ideological form? *Images of the World* articulates the formal and aesthetic with the historical and political context of contemporary mass media and technological warfare. The dense, multi-layered essay film contemplates the relationship between vision and the increasingly technologically bound nature of representation and truth. It interrogates the photographic process and the disciplines that use its resultant images: engineering, military science, architecture, urban planning, and the fine arts. As with *Inextinguishable Fire*, *Images of the World* demonstrates that all systems are interrelated. There is no outside to the military-industrial complex. Not even a nation such as West Germany during times of relative "peace" is free from this dynamic.

Like *As You See* (1986) and *Images-War*, *Images of the World* is a compilation film. Farocki constructed it entirely from archival sources, including photographs, industrial films, commercial records, training films, and his own past work. The building blocks' multiplicity and heterogeneity enabled Farocki to structure the film visually and rhythmically, and for the montage to follow a musical compositional structure based on Dziga Vertov's theory of "the interval." Concomitantly he adopted Artavazd Peleshyan's theory of "distance montage," which organizes a film according to "blocks" of images and phrases. Farocki was reading Peleshyan at the time and takes from his text that "one should not only edit two connecting shots. Even images that are far apart comment on one another. That means again: to find a kind of composition for images."[25] But while these blocks schematically repeat throughout the production, the context in which they appear is different each time, which shifts their meaning and alters the overall composition. Peleshyan's distance montage loosely combines Lev Kuleshov's notion, that what immediately precedes and follows an image determines its meaning, with those of Vertov. As Peleshyan explains, "The viewer constructs a montage connection not only between the repeated elements but also between their respective surroundings."[26]

According to Peleshyan, as a *spatial* art, film coalesces totalities from the recurring fragments the director sets in motion. Like a kaleidoscope, which produces different images from the same pieces at every twist, when film editors reshape one piece of the production, they alter the whole.[27] In contrast to classical montage that brings together two elements, Peleshyan's montage disentangles "them by means of inserting a third, a fifth, a tenth piece between them."[28] Insofar as film is also a *temporal* medium that operates as "a progression of details that can only be combined by using our memory," sound, too, plays a key role in its makeup. Sound forms its own montage blocks that work with the image track. In distance montage, the same images and sounds repeat throughout the film rhythmically at regular intervals—sometimes the two together, sometimes separately. A firm believer in post-production sound, Peleshyan underscores that the meaning of an image block changes according to the sounds that accompany it. When the same sounds or images appear in different contexts and settings, the conceptual concretion changes. "The most important thing," Peleshyan writes, "is the montage of the contexts."[29]

Farocki employs a variant of distance montage in much of his work from *As You See* onwards. Identical images and sounds punctuate the filmic texts, returning throughout single works and a multitude of productions. The image blocks that repeat in *Images of the World* include footage from a Hannover water-research laboratory; aerial photographs of the I. G. Farben factory in Auschwitz; photogrammetric studies by civil engineer Albrecht Meydenbauer; pictures taken by SS officers in the Auschwitz concentration camp; portraits of unveiled Algerian women made in the 1960s by French soldier Marc Garanger; drawings of the Auschwitz camp by Alfred Kantor, one of its inmates; the Serge Lutens model (recycled footage from *Make-up* [1973]); an art school class; and relatively high-tech, computer-generated images of robotized industrial production lines and flight simulators. Farocki arranges these blocks into patterns and variations to build his filmic essay. He suggests that photography's historical purpose in the scientific, military, forensic, and aesthetic realms has been not only to record and preserve but also to mislead, deceive, and even destroy that which it images. Photography, in other words, has often functioned to obfuscate vision. In *Images of the World*, Farocki uncovers a dimension of the political unconscious of photography. As it addresses what photography images but remains invisible to its viewers, *Images of the World* self-reflexively creates, in Farocki's words, its own "film puzzle."[30] It shows that which hides in plain sight.

Farocki devotes a significant part of *Images of the World* to analyzing 1944 Allied aerial photographs of the I. G. Farben plant. The images reveal that the photographers unwittingly pictured the Auschwitz concentration camp. Farocki points out the gas chambers, the lines of victims, and the crematorium. He explains that because reconnaissance personnel were not looking for death camps but for the layout of the munitions factory, they did not see the evidence of mass extermination captured in their photographs. Farocki's project highlights what remains in/visible. If, following Theodor W. Adorno's theory of the picture puzzle, ideology obscures some representations and foregrounds others, then in *Images of the World*, both the image-maker's and the viewer's ideologies determine how war is documented.

Three of Farocki's image sequences are notable for how they draw attention to women. The first is the picture of a woman who has just arrived at Auschwitz. Farocki describes her as beautiful. The second is Garanger's photographs of Berber women. The photographer, Farocki points out, pictured these women because authorities suspected them of criminality. The third is a photo of a smiling female prisoner in Auschwitz. About the latter, the commentary states, "In Auschwitz, apart from death and work, there was a black market, there were love stories and resistance groups." In addition to the two photographs of female prisoners, the same image of handwritten numbers on a slip of paper repeats three times haphazardly throughout the work. Finally, near the end of the film at the fourth and fifth instances of its inclusion, the narrator explains that the numbers are "coded messages from Auschwitz prisoners who belonged to a resistance group. They set a date for an uprising.... They set fire to the crematorium with explosive devices made from powder that women had smuggled out from the Union Munitions factory." Once again, the theme of a guerilla fighter who forms part of a secret resistance from within emerges. It is worth noting that in 1975, Farocki wrote an essay for *Filmkritik*, "Geschichte" (History), that focused on resistance groups and sabotage against the German occupation of the Czech Republic during World War II.[31]

Except for the voice-over commentary by Cynthia Beatt, *Images of the World*'s soundtrack is almost entirely silent. Beatt's measured delivery is carefully choreographed to the *défilement* of images. At times there is a barely audible tinkling of piano keys. The piano plays skeleton renditions of Beethoven's *Razumovsky Quartets* and Bach's *English Suites*. The sparsity of notes immediately attracts attention. The notes serve as signals, alerting us that something significant is happening on screen. Yet, they are not part of the diegesis. Instead, their isolated sound recalls a horn in an enveloping fog, which may represent the density of visual stimuli, documents, and images that threaten to overwhelm the viewer. When thinking about the placement and interaction of sound and image blocks, Peleshyan stresses that while "the visuals function in the state of a changed soundtrack, ... the latter functions in the state of changed visuals."[32] In other words, the music prompts the spectator to examine the images closely, which in turn aids in recognizing patterns and decoding messages.

Farocki weaves these multiple-image sequences combined with a female voice-over, subtly punctuated by musical notes, into a previously unknown history of women resistance fighters. However, *Images of the World* is also deeply concerned with the present. Just as Farocki rigorously probes archival images, his film beckons contemporary viewers to do the same with his assembled material. Given that the production centers on blind spots, one wonders what Farocki's film might be concealing. Are we missing something when viewing the film? In the penultimate image sequence, the commentary summons German-Austrian philosopher Günther Anders as it notes the following: "In 1983, as the number of atomic weapons in the Federal Republic of Germany was to be increased again, Günther Anders recalled 'the failure to bomb Auschwitz,' and demanded that the reality must now begin.... This reality means blocking the entrances to all murder institutions [in our society].... Let us destroy the possibility of access to these weapons." Farocki inserts one of Kantor's drawings of Auschwitz over which the artist had scrawled the words: "Block the access." Kantor, originally from Prague, managed to survive the Holocaust after having been imprisoned in Theresienstadt and Auschwitz. During his incarceration he produced hundreds of sketches and watercolors detailing life in the camps. These works constitute both a record of what was happening as well as messages suggesting possible paths of resistance. By inserting this image by Kantor, within the context of Anders's proclamation, Farocki links the plea to block the train tracks bringing prisoners to Auschwitz to the contemporary context.

4.6 Harun Farocki, *Images of the World and the Inscription of War* (1988)

In his essay "Reality Would Have to Begin," Farocki considers Anders's text more extensively than in the film. In this deliberation, he includes a lengthy quotation from Anders's tract that ends with, "This idea is not new. It reminds me of an action—or rather a non-action—more than forty years ago, when the Allies learned the truth about the extermination camps in Poland. The proposal was immediately made to block access to the camps, which meant bombing the railroad tracks."[33] From this perspective, *Images of the World* functions as a highly coded message at the height of the Cold War. The directive calls for the disruption of train lines leading to bases where the military had installed atomic weapons in West Germany. Made two years after the Chernobyl nuclear disaster, Farocki's project, both text and film, continues his agit-prop agenda of the 1960s and early 1970s. But whereas the earlier calls for direct action were overt, those in *Images of the World* are much more subtle. Recall his question at the end of *Interface* (1995): "Is it about decoding a secret, or keeping it?" By the late 1980s, Farocki's guerilla-style filmmaking of the 1960s had gone underground.

The differences between the *Images of the World*'s filmic and written renditions deserve mention. Farocki's film is a montage work that brings together myriad conceptual threads and image sequences, many of which remain disconnected. However, his written essay follows a narrower and more rational path. The author centers the text on World War II and the failure of the allies to "see" what they had imaged. This failure prevented them from liberating the camps earlier and saving many lives. Farocki fleshes out the history of two prisoners, Rudolf Vrba and Alfred Wetzler, who escaped from Auschwitz and filed reports with various officials announcing the mass extermination in the camps. He also includes detailed information about former inmate Lili Jacob's discovery of a Nazi photo album after liberation. Farocki analyzes the photographs, supplementing the images with archival information about everyday horror in the camps. The last part of the written text recounts an incinerator's destruction by the now-freed prisoners. The cinematic essay manifests greater liberty and more unrestricted association. Unlike the written rendition, which unfolds linearly and discourages digressions, the film's image constellations offer alternative paths and models of thought.

Another recurring sequence in *Images of the World* that merits mention are the shots of proto-virtual reality military training programs. These "second hand" shots of technologically manufactured vision recall those of television screens in *Inextinguishable Fire*. However, whereas camera operators in Vietnam made the images that appeared on television screens worldwide in the 1960s, computers in North American and Western European studios created these military scenes twenty years later. The new "operative images" present—rather than *represent*—material objects and events. Scientific, medical, military, and surveillance sources generate them. They are not meant to be viewed aesthetically, and it is only their repurposing by Farocki that reframes them as art.

Operational images lack the human touch of images produced for entertainment, advertising, and education industries. Instead, programmed machines make them. Farocki purposefully appropriates operative images in *Images of the World* and reinscribes them into a cultural, aesthetic, and philosophical system. His tactics rely on techniques that require spectators to locate meaning in the gaps between images and other free-play spaces, such as breaks, reiterations, prolapses, misdirections, and verbal or visual puns. Farocki builds dynamic constellations where images communicate as a "form of intelligence" out of jumbles of recycled images. "Montage," he insists, "must hold together with invisible forces the things that otherwise become muddled."[34]

With *Respite* (2007), Farocki resumes his forensic method of investigating life in the Nazi death camps begun in *Images-War*. The film meticulously analyzes 16 mm film footage shot in 1944 by Rudolf Breslauer, then an inmate at the Westerbork Transit Camp in the northeastern Netherlands. Like Breslaur's film, *Respite* is silent. Its black-and-white images unroll before our eyes. Some images are recognizable, having served as visual testimony in countless fictional and nonfictional films about the Holocaust. But much of the footage Farocki uses was little known. His use of these unfamiliar images generates an uncanny feeling. Camp Westerbork commander Albert Gemmeker ordered Breslauer to document life in the prison. The images the latter rendered are the opposite of "operational images." The cameraman's identity is known, as are the horrific conditions under which the Nazis forced him to work. Farocki reveals that upon Breslauer completing his task in October 1944 the Westerbork camp's authorities deported him to the Auschwitz concentration camp, where he soon perished. However, the footage he left behind today serves as an invaluable documentary record of everyday life in the prison camp, and of individuals the Nazis soon obliterated. The recurring shot of a child, perhaps two and a half, waving goodbye from the boxcar

4.7 Harun Farocki, *Respite* (2007)

window of a train headed toward Auschwitz underscores the enduring horror of this footage. The images "grip" the viewer, refusing to let go.

Farocki refers to this horrific footage as "respite," which he also uses to title the piece. *Respite* suggests an interlude, an interruption, and a rest between imprisonment and death. Farocki's intertitles and graphic markings on the print comment on the display. The images trouble conventional representations of the camps. They are nothing short of shocking, but not how one might expect: spectators are left to wonder how to process images of camp inmates engaged in seemingly "fun" activities. In one scene, a group of young women standing in a circle outdoors laugh. The film is much less formally experimental than Farocki's Gulf War installations. The single-channel work respects the linear montage determined by the archival footage. Farocki carefully analyzes the frames of footage like a forensic scientist and, in one case at least, restores a prisoner's identity before the Nazis annihilate her.[35] By comparing the barely legible name on a suitcase with a list of prisoners deported to Auschwitz, Farocki determines that an elderly disabled woman was Frauke Kroon, born in 1882 and sent to the death camp on May 19, 1944, on the same train as the young child. The absolute silence in which Farocki presents the material makes the procession of historical footage even more powerful. The production is devoid of commentary, music, and archival audio. It confronts the spectator with a void. Farocki explains that whereas commentary often serves to reassure the spectator, "enforced silence has an oppressive effect." This result is because, in a perfectly silent film, one can "hear reaction from the audience that would otherwise have been lost behind the film score and sound effects."[36] In other words, silence is at once accusatory and strategic for Farocki in *Respite*. It beckons voices and encourages social communication. It is, in a word, political.

VIRTUAL WARS

Farocki made *Images of the World* just as the Cold War order collapsed and digital media began to proliferate. Many of the production's images reference the increased role of simulation in digital production. The film also questions how images without negatives might be archived and retrieved in the future. Farocki mulls over this question in "Reality Would Have to Begin," where he observes the following: "If one considers an image as a measuring device, then one should ignore chance and subjectivity. To conceive of a photographic image as a measuring device is to insist on mathematicality, calculability, and finally the 'computability' of the image-world." He explicitly references Flusser in these comments. The media theorist, he remarks, has shown the significant extent to which "digital technology is already an embryonic form in photography, because the photographic image is built out of dots of information. The human eye synthesizes these dots into an image. This leads one to activate the code and create new images. Hence, images without originals become possible and are generated."[37]

The fall of the Berlin Wall, the collapse of the former Soviet Union, and the former "Second World"'s turn to a capitalist economy were as significant to the end of the twentieth century as the transition to digital media. Farocki and Andrei Ujica obliquely document these transformations in *Videograms of a Revolution* (1992). While the capitalist "revolution" was peaceful in most of Eastern Europe, it was relatively violent in Romania and the Balkans. Insurgents summarily executed President Nicolae Ceausescu, his family, and accomplices, and a genocidal war broke out in Yugoslavia. Farocki and Ujica compiled *Videograms of a Revolution* from over 125 hours of amateur footage, news footage, and excerpts from the Bucharest television station overtaken by demonstrators as part of the 1989 Romanian uprising. The filmmakers distill a reconstruction of the revolution from this vast diversity of perspectives. They assemble amateur video footage from between December 21 and 26, 1989, recording Ceausescu's last days. *Videograms of a Revolution* constructs a history of that moment through video recordings of events as they unfolded in "real/reel time." They show that for many, the revolution only became real when television broadcasted it—that by the late twentieth century, *pace* Flusser, technology not only records but makes events real.[38]

Strikingly, however, Farocki did not address the horrific events that transpired with the breakup of Yugoslavia. Unlike many of his politically committed peers, including Godard, Chris Marker, and Marcel Ophuls, Farocki seemingly ignored this atrocity that took place so close to home. He also remained relatively silent about the Rwandan genocide and even the massive bombing raids of the 1990s Gulf War. Instead, the 1990s constituted a centripetal repositioning for Farocki. His production increasingly focused on the changes in film and video production brought about by the technological shift from analog to digital. As a result, Farocki put war and global politics on the back burner. At the same time, he learned how to reconfigure his filmmaking practice intended for television, video, and theatrical distribution to art exhibition venues.

In the late twentieth century, the digital turn affected every aspect of image production, from cameras, sound, and editing equipment, to distribution and storage possibilities. Access to a vast virtual archive and desktop digital editing systems profoundly affected Farocki's working method. Furthermore, the European Union's formation in 1993 initiated a restructuring of funding opportunities in the arts. Politicians reduced the revenues of regional public television stations, and film projects ceased to be economically supported unless they had trans-European connections. Concomitant with the decrease in resources, two other developments affected independent filmmakers like Farocki. First, new state-of-the-art projectors facilitated gallery projections, and museums finally began to exhibit film and video works. Moving images proliferated in the art world in the 1990s, which generated new funding sources for production, exhibition, and distribution. There followed a radical rethinking of image-making processes that, with few exceptions, had been conceived of as single-channel projections. For Farocki, who had been producing work primarily for television for the past quarter of a century, this meant recasting his mode of production. He began to make films and videos for gallery display. Film installations encouraged multiple channel productions, numerous screens, innovative looping techniques, and creative ways of thinking about cinematic time and space. They rendered film audiences mobile, as well as able to navigate projection sites relatively unrestrictedly and have more control of a film's sequential and temporal orders. Spectators could process multiple screens and projections simultaneously. They could also conduct conversations about the productions while they experienced them. This novel form of spectatorship contrasts sharply with the more conventional ritual of quietly sitting in a dark theater focused on a single set of images for a prescribed period. It also differs from the practice of watching films on a television screen in the privacy of a home setting. From the mid-1990s onward, formal and institutional changes framed Farocki's work in a dramatically new way.

After the turn of the new millennium, Farocki resumed investigating the relationship between war and media as the U.S. military engaged in a second Gulf War. Prior to this, the decisive year was 1991, during the first Gulf War in Iraq, when the way warfare was conducted and publicly represented dramatically changed. Farocki recalls that "the images from the head of a projectile in 1991, together with the expression 'intelligent weapons,' were both terrifying and fascinating because they revealed that from this moment onwards bullets could no longer be considered blind."[39] In response to this new military landscape, Farocki made the three-part double-channel video installation *Eye/Machine I* (2000), *Eye/Machine II* (2001), and *Eye/Machine III* (2003), and the companion single-channel *Erkennen und Verfolgen* (War at a Distance, 2003) which was for theatrical screenings. These productions examine the new type of imagery taken from cameras mounted on bombs—what the U.S. military described as "suicide cameras." The film and the installations remix some of the same footage. For Farocki, these new operational images produced entirely by machines changed the constitution of shots.[40] They also profoundly impacted the ontology of the image. As he observes in "War Always Finds A Way," "Since 1920 in the USA, shots filmed from a position normally not taken by a person have been called *phantom shots*.... Images taken from the point of view of a person are called *subjectives*. We can therefore regard the shot from the perspective of a bomb as a *phantom subjective*."[41]

Both *War at a Distance* and the *Eye/Machine* triptych include extensive sequences of black-and-white images captured by suicide cameras. The images are fortuitous, abstract, and silent. Their drama plays out through the condensed burst of white mass emitted as the bombs hit their targets, terminating the pictures' resolution. Fascinated by the proliferation of these highly aestheticized images on television news broadcasts, Farocki remarks, "Showing something in art that comes close to the unconsciously visible was outperformed in 1991 by the U.S. military when it made surveillance images the main images of war reporting."[42] The viewing public found these machine-made operative images much more alluring than footage shot by war journalists.

Farocki tackles different aspects of the new computerized warfare's recording mechanism in the *Eye/Machine* series. He employs the suicide camera images to comment on transformations in knowledge production in the digital age. Each part of the series relies on the same basic set of image sequences, rearranged or reshuffled into different constellations according to the focus. In this respect, he evokes Max Bense's understanding of the essay as a kaleidoscopic form in which, following a turn of the device, the same shards can produce infinitely different narratives.[43]

Images made by suicide cameras mounted on bombs play on two screens in *Eye/Machine I* (twenty-three minutes). Occasionally, on alternating screens, Farocki replaces the operative images with a black screen on which he inserts a text theorizing about the nature of these images, and how visual regimes of recognition are changing. These texts are necessary because of the images' abstract and indecipherable quality to the untrained eye. As one intertitle

168   War

explains, "Without references to everyday experience the images fail to grip." Farocki follows operative images with footage taken by movement recognition cameras. He juxtaposes these sequences with the same archival footage he uses in *As You See*, of factory workers operating hole-punching machines. Then, a succession of images from blast furnaces and individuals monitoring various live-feed screens follows a text that reads, "Industrial production soon replaced manual work [...] ." The sentence completes a minute later: "[...] and visual work." Another series, this time of machine-made images of computers performing tasks seemingly without human intervention, follows. Succinct phrases

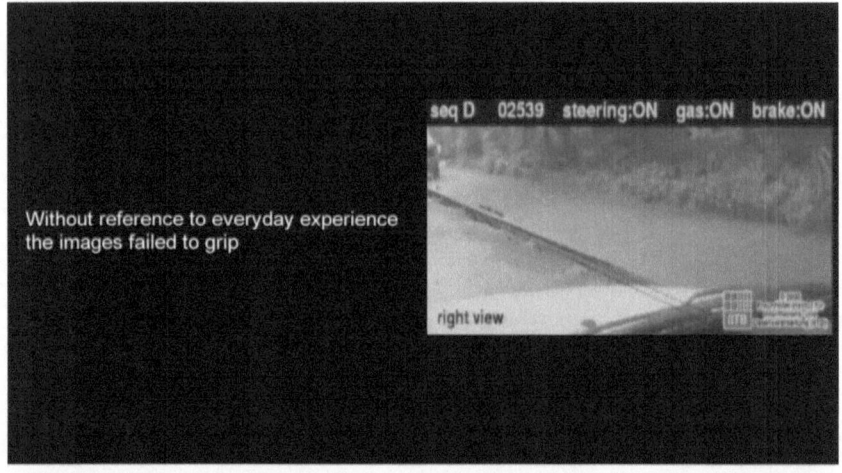

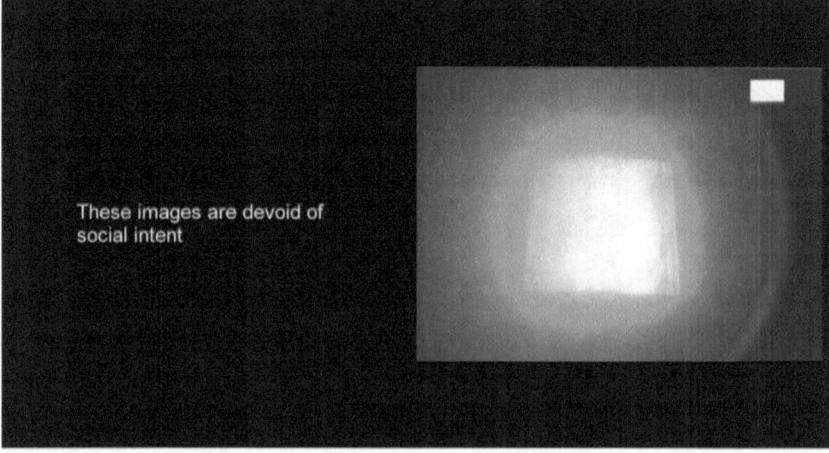

4.8 Harun Farocki, *Eye/Machine I* (2000)

reflect on the images produced by computerized cameras including bomb detectors, mobile surveillance machines, factory robots, and medical cameras. Farocki underscores the dialectical nature of these "camera eyes." Medical professionals may utilize these images benevolently to perform minimally invasive surgery, but military personnel employ the same images in much more malevolent ways. The military uses them to wage highly lethal "surgical strikes." His tone is neutral as he links the images produced by these technologies with a series of statements: "The machines perform the tasks blindly"; "These images are devoid of social intent"; "In an age of flow, production images monitor the predetermined"; and "An image of the world to be processed." Farocki thus establishes connections and forges bonds out of seemingly disparate elements.

At the end of *Eye/Machine I*, Farocki replays the footage taken by the suicide cameras and states, "We saw images like these during the war in Iraq." Immediately following another statement—"Operational images and not propaganda"—he underlines the following in red: "Not propaganda, yet an ad for *intelligence machines*." The suggestion is that the circulation of operational images in news media promotes the new technology in the same way that the American Forces Network in Berlin promoted the United States' superior way of life through high-fidelity radio broadcasting. *Eye/Machine I*'s concluding text reads: "For machines no longer performing their tasks repetitively or blindly—but rather independently, *autonomously*. Imagine a war with *autonomous machines*—without soldiers—like factories without workers." Farocki stresses the words autonomous and machines, emphasizing the military ambition of rendering humans as redundant in war production as they increasingly are in factory production.

Eye/Machine II (fifteen minutes) begins with the familiar footage of the punch-hole operator on the left-hand screen and a missile on the right. A text proclaims: "There must be a connection between production and war." Farocki then introduces footage from a 1943 German military documentary. Next, he presents images of a simulated tracking system for aircraft developed during World War II. To make the simulator, engineers glued model ships onto a conveyor belt. They then installed a chamber above the belt into which a person climbs to operate a camera. They aimed to simulate the perspective of a bomber pilot in flight. Farocki follows this sequence with other images of simulation devices, including a scuba diving chamber and a fighter aircraft. Finally, he pauses over an image-processing system that both guides warheads and records their destruction. The intertitle muses that this marks "the end of the single purpose machine" and "the announcement of flexible automation."

Eye/Machine II traces a history from the hole-punching machine to the automated missile that performs multiple tasks. Farocki strengthens the connection between labor and war industries that he began with *Inextinguishable Fire* and continued in *Between Two Wars*. He includes archival footage from 1942 of the first bomb to include a television camera. The camera transmitted images from the bomb to a nearby aircraft. Mostly unrecognizable footage plays on the left-hand screen, and a text explains the images on view on the right. As it turns out, the images depict a bomber narrowing in on a targeted ship. The text informs viewers that this technology was deployed much more successfully in 1991 when bomb-tracking images became part of war. Images featured in *Eye/Machine I*, taken from suicide cameras, follow. Farocki then returns to the hole-punching machine accompanied by the text: "Eyes and hands sense location and position of the work piece. There must be a connection between war and production. Does the next rationalization need a next war?" The film ends with two soldiers with VR equipment guiding missiles through a simulated environment.

Eye/Machine III (seventeen minutes) begins with a hand that sets the pattern for motion sensors scanning for aircraft. Farocki then includes a spectacular military advertisement created in the early 1970s by Paveway, a producer of high-tech incendiary devices. The advert publicizes a new type of smart bomb. Richard Wagner's "Ride of the Valkyries" provides the musical soundtrack, leading one to suspect that Francis Ford Coppola must have seen this clip before making *Apocalypse Now* (1979). A sequence from a 1942 film on the V1 guided missile follows this. *Eye/Machine III* includes less text and more spectacular computer-generated images than the previous iterations. In one moment, visually reminiscent of images from the explosion of the atomic bomb, the text announces that the image track's beauty is uncalculated. Machines design the cinematographic techniques, and assembly robots record the images. The latter are not meant for the lay public. Their target viewers are war technicians. In response to a series of clips ending in explosions, an intertext reads: "In 1991, these images were shown on television, as if the television viewers were to be turned into war technicians [who could empathize with] the technology of war."[44] The advertisement for Paveway repeats, including the statement that the need for bombs decreases in proportion to their improved precision. The gist is that economic imperative calls for high-precision weapons. Advanced guidance systems are economically advantageous. Paveway's products save money in the end. They also minimize collateral damage. Wars fought with them are more "humanitarian" than previous military conflicts.

Farocki conceived *Eye/Machine I* as a double projection with the two videotapes in a continuous loop cast onto a single large screen in the exhibition space. The pithy intertitles spaced at regular intervals allow spectators to enter the diegesis at any point in the loop. As with so many of his earlier productions, understanding Farocki's *Eye/Machine* trilogy does not require following a teleologically structured narrative. Instead, spectators are encouraged to glean clusters of meaning and apprehend constellations. Farocki uses two separate screens in both *Eye/Machine II* and *III*, increasing the distance between images. These installations transform the content of the videotapes in several ways. First, the continuous loop at once recalls the constant replay of media images on television and satellite surveillance cameras that continuously record visual matter. Second, the installations' positioning puts spectators in the place of information surveyors or gamers. Third, the effect of two discrete images simultaneously playing increases the information before the viewer. As Farocki explains about *Interface*, "One image doesn't take the place of the previous one, but supplements it, re-evaluates it, balances it."[45] For example, the effect of the double projection with the worker on the left and the rocket on the right is, as Farocki elucidates, that "the worker turns his back to the rocket, the rocket flies away from the worker—a negative shot/reverse shot—a connection that holds its own.... I was struck by the horizontal connection of meaning, the connection between productive force and destructive force."[46] In double-screen projections, soft montage creates a mediated space between images. Unexpected associations emerge. Farocki interrupts the mechanized image-making systems and restores natural vision in the gap between the tracks. In contrast to a single-channel projection's monocular vision regime, the two-channel projection in an installation context opens up more space for thought, interpretation, and reflection. The associations viewers construct form the historical narrative.

In the single-channel *War at a Distance*, Farocki arranges two image frames set at a diagonal. One frame features in the upper left-hand quadrant, and the other in the lower right-hand corner. The two images overlap in the center. As he explains in "Cross Influence/Soft Montage," "I produced a so-called single channel version of all double projections, a video that shows both images in one, diagonally transposed and slightly overlapping to make the best use of the frame.

This allows the work to be shown on television and elsewhere, an inconsistency arising from financial and political reasons."[47] Although employing a different formal gesture, the goal of *War at a Distance* is the same as *Inextinguishable Fire*'s: to activate the spectator. Farocki's montage use, whether linear or spatial, recalls Adorno's advice on finding a film form that "neither lapses into arts-and-crafts, nor slips into mere documentary." That film form is "*montage*, which does not interfere with things but rather arranges them in *a constellation* akin to that of writing."[48]

In each *Eye/Machine*, Farocki makes arguments out of image sets that he mobilizes in different ways. He produces new meanings and constellations by changing the montage and the data's order. Like a DJ, he bases his *Verbundsystem* practice on remixing found material and creating new versions. The single-channel *War at a Distance* (fifty-four minutes) weaves together disparate threads from all three *Eye/Machines* to develop a new production. The original German title, *Erkennen und verfolgen* (To Recognize and to Follow), suggests the process whereby the computer identifies a target and then pursues it. The voice-over that takes the place of the written text in this film is the most striking difference between the two productions. Beatt's carefully modulated tone, cadence, and meter are reminiscent of *Images of the World*. A sound bridge between the two projects forges a link across time and space. Beatt begins: "Images like these were shown in 1991 of the Gulf War . . . , images from the missile head, from cameras hurtling towards their targets." Further on, the commentary states that "the war was soon forgotten."

The single-channel film begins with the footage taken from the suicide cameras mounted onto bombs in the first Gulf War, followed by a military computer training program, the punch-hole operator, World War II German documentaries on recognition systems, various weapons commercials, myriad computer-generated images, and virtual reality games. Sometimes, Farocki expands the clips. For instance, he inserts the 1972 Paveway commercial, including its pitch: "Previously it took two hundred bombs to destroy a target. With a computer, this number can be reduced to forty. With Paveway, it's one bomb one target!" Although *War at a Distance* progresses as a single-channel film, sometimes two image frames occupy the screen juxtaposed diagonally. Towards the conclusion, over recurring images of the manually operated punch-hole machine and a red missile flying against a green forested backdrop, the commentary observes a connection between war and technology: "War promotes technological development." The narration continues, "The Second World War generated the impulse that led to the development of computers, jet planes, shortwave broadcasting, stereo sound, and more besides." A spectacular image of an atomic bomb explosion gives way to computer graphics of missiles. The commentary resumes: "Will the next developments depend on there being a next war, or will computer battlefields be enough?" The same diagonally juxtaposed images reappear as the narrator notes another connection: "Manual work is being abolished here, and at the same time being displaced to poorer countries. Today, too, wars are more likely to take place in poorer countries than in rich ones."

In both the *Eye/Machine* installations and the *War at a Distance* film, Farocki anticipates the viewer's alienation when confronted by "operational images." The commentary declares that the images fail to grip if they do not connect to everyday experiences. Indeed, except for the analog footage, none of the images are the product of a human eye looking through a camera. Instead, computer-programmed machines produce them. The result is a proliferation of images "of the world to be processed," as technological vision wholly supplants natural vision. Images generated by war evolve across Farocki's oeuvre, from the television sequences captured in *Inextinguishable Fire* to the simulated computer-training program in *Images of the World*. For Farocki, operational images "do not portray a process but are themselves part of a process."[49] Yet, what evidence or historical trace these images leave behind remains in question. Can one construct a memory from images that humans have not taken? For most viewers, the images of the first Gulf War were indecipherable. With no connection to the real, the images failed to "grip," unlike photographs taken during World War II. War increasingly resembles a computer game; it is hard to imagine a less dramatic representation. The images transform history into a simulation, which perfectly befits the digital medium.[50]

Farocki relied entirely on operational images to make *War at a Distance* and the *Eye/Machine* series. The makers of this footage did not intend it to be part of an art project. Instead, it was highly functional; cameras took most of it on location. Even if the footage's perspective was from that of a falling bomb, the images transmitted back to base operations in the United States gave the impression that the view "over there" was being transported back to "over here." However, Farocki observes that in the second Gulf War, "images shot from the heads of projectiles were hardly shown at all. We also didn't hear anything more about 'intelligent weapons,' only about *precision guided weapons*."[51] U.S. Army personnel commanding computers carried out the war from North America, processing and acting on the images they received, making the war even more remote.

Following the U.S.-led coalition's invasion of Iraq and the start of the protracted armed conflict, Farocki addressed the unprecedented technology used by the U.S. military in his four-part installation *Serious Games I–IV*. The piece comprised "I: Watson Is Down" (2010), "II: Three Dead" (2010), "III: Immersion" (2009), and "IV: A Sun with No Shadow" (2010). *Serious Games* makes clear that the United States was fighting a significant part of the Iraq War from home. Parts I, III, and IV comprise double-channel looped video projections. Only part II, *Three Dead*, is a single-screen production. The footage is taken from two military bases: Twenty-Nine Palms, California, and Fort Lewis, Washington. In the former, sophisticated *Virtual Battle Space* gaming programs prepare soldiers for war abroad. The soldiers maneuver tanks, go out on forays, engage in firefights, and kill enemy "combatants" in a virtual environment. They also learn to read the desert's subtle signs and the ways of its inhabitants to avoid ambushes. The soldiers train in this digital environment for months before deployment.[52] Farocki observes that the soldiers, sitting at computer terminals "immersed" in virtual games, look more like gamers or IT specialists than military combatants.[53] Twenty-Nine Palms functions as both a virtual training site and a real departure terminal. The single-screen format simulates the single-minded focus of the soldiers preparing for war; it does not allow multiple perspectives or space for critique.

Farocki depicts the Fort Lewis camp, in contrast to Twenty-Nine Palms, as a site of post-production. Here, soldiers reassemble and analyze footage and other data from the battlefield. Farocki also films educational seminars at Fort Lewis, where private industry peddles computer software to military therapists treating veterans. One of these programs, *Virtual Iraq*, helps soldiers suffering from post-traumatic stress disorder (PTSD) process and address their injuries. In one scene, a therapist sets up a program based on details provided by a soldier about his traumatic injury. The soldier wears a camouflage uniform and sophisticated headgear that recreates sounds, images, and smells. As he recollects his traumatic experience and describes it to the therapist, the latter alters the VR environment accordingly.

In the third part of *Serious Games*, "Immersion," Farocki records another training session between a therapist and a soldier in a manner reminiscent of his Direct Cinema documentaries. Images of the soldier play on the right-hand screen while computer images intermingle with shots of the psychologist on the left.

Farocki explains that he decided to present images on two separate screens to "create a very obvious off-space." Audiences, he states, are "always in the 'off,'" and the use of images playing on two screens is the best way to engage them.[54] The VR headgear and goggles engulf the head of the soldier, depersonalizing him for the viewer. The dialogue, however, seems very "real." As the soldier recounts the events that led to his traumatic injury, he becomes agitated and ever more silent, and sweats profusely. Upon prodding by the psychologist, he reveals the terror he experienced when seeing the blown-up body of a fellow combatant. The soldier, now hysterical, cries out: "—and there's flesh, and there's blood, and there's bits of uniforms, and it's... it was... and I'm like, shit! So, at this point, I'm completely freaking out. I'm convinced I'm going to die." The scene abruptly ends as the soldier removes his VR goggles: it becomes apparent that he is acting for marketing purposes. Farocki's recording of these role-playing exercises evokes *How to Live in the FRG* (1990). He recalls that during this sequence's filming, "the Air Force psychologists were thoroughly uninspired—they just rattled through their scripted role-play." However, "the psychologist who was not working for the Air Force (but rather trying to sell something to it) was a different kettle of fish entirely. He plays the role of a traumatized patient so well that nearly anyone watching would think he must have actually experienced what he is talking about."[55]

Farocki learned through conversations with veterans at Fort White who had undergone, or were planning to undergo, trauma therapy that virtual video games made the treatment more acceptable to them. The soldiers revealed that they would rather tell their friends that they were playing virtual reality games than that they were receiving psychological aid. Farocki also found that the programs'

4.9 Harun Farocki, *Immersion* (2009)

image quality was significantly inferior to comparable games on the commercial market because the gaming industry's budget is approximately tenfold that devoted to injured veterans. This realization led him to compare the software and image quality of *Virtual Iraq* to *Virtual Battle Space*. He finds that the latter develops the "reality" in far more detail. The designers constructed the scenes based on cinematographic principles of staging, montage, and visual effects. One *Virtual Battle Space* scenario, for instance, includes a flock of birds to enhance the "reality effect." Directors often employ this tactic in fictional films where they insert secondary scenes not crucial to the narrative to make the diegetic world more believable.[56]

Farocki discovers that the gross disparity in image quality between commercial video games and therapeutic technology is even greater between military preparatory games and immersion technology. The military spares no expense when developing software that trains soldiers to kill but takes significant shortcuts when treating wounded veterans. Farocki addresses this disparity in part IV of *Serious Games*, "A Sun with No Shadow." Once again, he draws attention to the many details designers embedded in the settings of virtual scenes created for training. For instance, he shows that whereas the training scene's software designers keyed perfectly depicted shadows to the movement of the sun, they did not even bother to program shadows in the software made for therapy. Accordingly, Farocki exposes the discrepancy between computer games that prepare soldiers for action and those that adjust them back to civilian life. He reveals that the war's palpable effects transcend the removal of an unwieldy VR helmet. Actual war is very different from what video games simulate. Real war is interminable—it does not end when soldiers return home. In this manner, *Serious Games* recalls the last part of *Inextinguishable Fire* that demonstrates how war today seeps into all spheres of life. As Farocki and Ehmann summarize in their text "Serious Games," "The boundary between war and non-war is no longer distinct."[57]

Farocki's *Serious Games I–IV* installation differs significantly from his other war pieces. Whereas he projected *Inextinguishable Fire* and *Images of the World* on a single screen affixed to a surface and mounted the two channels of *Eye/Machine* on a wall, he rendered *Serious Games* sculptural. He installed screens in the middle of the exhibition space where visitors could view them from both sides. The sculptural installation requires spectators to ambulate around the four parts, taking in the projections from multiple vantage points. All the while, the bodies of other spectators move freely, with some obstructing the view.

Furthermore, the transition from stationary to mobile spectator further affects the montage in *Serious Games*. If, as Farocki argues, in soft montage the space between the two fixed elements or images produces thought and generates meaning, then in *Serious Games*, an additional montage occurs in the space between the body of the viewer and that of the screen. In sharp contrast to a VR world in which artificially constructed landscapes generate simulations of movement, the spectators phenomenologically *sense* the reality of war in works such as *Serious Games*. The documentary "real" emerges in the gallery where the installation's active engagement with its public is in direct contrast to the remote way military planners use virtual weapons to wage war.

The call for action and increasing frustration with the perpetual state of war that has permeated the globe in the twenty-first century prompted Farocki and Ehmann to curate an international exhibition focusing on war. Upon receiving the Wilhelm Loth Prize from the city of Darmstadt in 2009, Farocki proposed curating a show rather than making a new work. The exposition, "War-Media-Art," featured work by approximately two dozen artists, including Peggy Ahwesh, Alice Creischer, Allan Sekula, Andreas Siekmann, Hito Steyerl, and Martha Rosler. Farocki and Ehmann expand on Brecht's proclamation that "war is inventive. When none of the customary reasons for waging war applies, it finds new ones. When all the resources from which war draws sustenance are exhausted, it shifts to a new mode of existence and taps a new resource."[58] Their exhibition and its accompanying catalog brought together disparate works united only by the fact that they all protested the proliferation of war in the twenty-first century. Formally, the contributions each stood on their own. The artists left it to the viewer to make connections, draw conclusions, and create meaning. Not surprisingly, given Farocki's long-standing exploration of montage, he and Ehmann pivoted to this technique when explaining their reason for eschewing an overarching narrative in the catalogue: "It is better to assemble montages than to interpret. This introduction suggests establishing changing relationships between elements and fragments. That is what we do in our exhibition project, and this book is attempting to achieve the same thing: a text montage on war-media-art."[59] For their contribution to the show, the artist-curators examined hundreds of war films, searching for recurring patterns in the genre. The final product of this research consists of an archive of moving-image sequences that span over a century of filmmaking.[60] Aptly titled *War Tropes* (2011), the production identifies five motifs employed in most surveyed films. These include "Gazes," which capture the protagonist in close-up looking thoughtfully and ponderously out over the horizon; "Attention," which represents soldiers maneuvering across a difficult terrain on high alert; "Souvenir," composed of shots of the protagonist reflecting on a photograph or a letter from a loved one back home; "Connection," which gathers images of media technologies like radios, walkie talkies, and more modern devices that enable communications between troops and commanding headquarters; and "Where is Elbe 14?" which features stunning sequences of fighter aircraft in flight. The result is a cinematographic thesaurus of war films built from the genre's most emblematic forms.

Spanning half a century, Farocki's extensive body of work on war and technology employs a contrapuntal cadence and an associative use of fragments to uncover a history of war's mediatization that corresponds to the history of images. The filmmaker-videographer-artist wed images, sound, and text into productions that demonstrate the extent to which the North Atlantic military complex's war machine intertwines with the image sphere. His films, videos, and artworks draw upon a bevy of critical and literary texts as much as the histories of photography, cinema, and modern art to highlight the parallel between the development of media technology and cultural techniques and the steady extension of the battlefront. Dialectically, they cast technological progress as the world's worst nightmare.

CHAPTER 5

An Image Lexicon, or Towards a Media Archeology

In an appendix, one can select the conversation in its entirety, just as in a book. In my contributions to a collection of filmic terminology I would also like to include the film from which I quoted in its entirety in the appendix. It is always in the interest of the reader to be able to check whether the quote captures the spirit of the film in general, or indeed what the relationship between the quotation and the film is as a whole.

—Harun Farocki, "A Cinematographic Thesaurus"

Allow me to conclude with two early pronouncements by Farocki in his critique of television. The first, from "About Working with Images for Television," explains the similarity between how producers select visual tracks in made-for-television documentaries and how mediocre poets compose verse using "rhyme lexicons." Farocki underscores that even if the message's intention is progressive, the cookie-cutter production process ensures that "resistance will consist of a heap of mannerisms."[1] He makes the second pronouncement in "Images from Television," and in the film *The Trouble with Images* (1973). In both, he presents two image sequences representing leisure time and the service industry. The first is of a rollercoaster, and the second of a hand that serves cake. Farocki explains that "the roller coaster image has been specifically selected by the docu-director to express, clarify, and make vivid the concept of leisure, and the image of the hand serving cake... to illustrate the concept of service.... The docu-director reaches into an imaginary lexicon."[2]

The term "lexicon" surfaces multiple times in Farocki's writings. However, instead of relating the term to words, Farocki applies it to images. As he explains much later, "I am a lover of dictionaries. I get great pleasure out of looking up words and their etymological sources in specialized and obscure lexica.... In searching for order in my collection of material, I have to think of dictionaries because of the way they document the usage of a word or expression chronologically, through the decades or centuries." He continues, "It occurred to me that there is nothing comparable to a dictionary in the realm of cinema. How might one even name such a thing? One could call it an 'illustrated book,' a 'thesaurus' or a 'treasure trove of images,' or perhaps even an 'archive of filmic expressions.'"[3] Farocki regrets that, unlike the writer, who has access to many word definitions, etymologies, and synonyms, the makers of television documentaries must rely on a limited range of well-worn stock images and sequences. The patterns, compositions, and gestures that these images render are familiar. Television documentaries regularly repeat them. Accordingly, stock images of rollercoaster rides or servings of cake become typical representations of leisure. Decades later, Farocki laments that the poverty of images extends to art filmmaking as well: "Television documentaries have become formulaic, something that isn't necessarily lost in the transition from television to the art world."[4]

Farocki's *The Division of All Days* (1970) and *Something Self-Explanatory (15x)* (1971) translate Marx's economic theory into filmic language. In a related work, *The Language of Revolution* (1972), Farocki explores how cinema depicts revolutionary speech. He asks how media reproduces live rhetorical performances that actively seek to move people. We can trace his interest in revolutionary language to his review of Roland Barthes's *Mythologies*. Barthes writes, "There is one language which is not mythical, it is the language of man as a producer: whenever man speaks in order to transform reality and no longer to preserve it as an image, wherever he links his language to the making of things . . . , myth is impossible. This is why revolutionary language proper cannot be mythical. . . . The bourgeoisie hides the fact that it is the bourgeoisie and thereby produces myth; revolution announces itself openly as revolution and thereby abolishes myth."[5] Like "operational language," "revolutionary language" stands outside of the bounds of myth. How, then, can a filmmaker, whose craft mobilizes images, make a film that centers on a type of language that eschews myth?

Farocki takes up this challenge in *The Language of Revolution*. The film focuses on five memorable revolutionary speeches. Part 1 opens with iconic images from the French Revolution and speeches by Georges Danton and Louis Antoine de

Saint-Just drawn from Fritz Umgelter's film *Danton's Tod* (Danton's Death) (1963). Part 2 shifts to late 1960s Cuba. It features newsreel footage of Fidel Castro's television address on the economic importance of sugar production. Part 3 centers on the U.S. civil rights movement, contrasting talks by Jesse Jackson ("I am Somebody") and Malcolm X ("The Ballot or the Bullet"). Part 4 examines a monologue by Vladimir Lenin following the Russian Revolution. Farocki's film concludes with a late-1960s speech by Berlin-based political activist Rudi Dutschke.[6] Like in *Inextinguishable Fire* (1969), Farocki intersperses Brechtian-style sequences, including one of a news commentator and several skits, between these five major sections.

In *The Language of Revolution*, Farocki addresses the change that occurs when cultural producers channel speech through new media. How is the dynamism of a live performance transformed? Is it possible for words to keep their initial unique revolutionary impetus and urgency once cultural producers record them? Can media effectively record the language of revolution, or does recording transform revolutionary language into myth? For Farocki, the revolutionary movement, the movement of words, and that of the film must correspond. He mediates Danton's and Saint-Just's words through the German playwright Georg Büchner's *Danton's Tod* (Danton's Death) (1835). In his drama, Büchner transcribed and translated the speeches from the original 1794 trial in France. Farocki does not film a live performance of Büchner's play; instead, he turns to Umgelter's cinematic version. By drawing from a film source, he underscores the speeches' mediation and journey through history—from court records to written drama, to live theatrical performance, to feature film.

Moving forward approximately 170 years from the eighteenth-century court records and 135 years from Büchner's dramatic adaptation, both time periods before technological recording, Farocki shifts to an era dominated by broadcast television. Castro delivered his speech in front of live cameras; he intended it for mass transmission. The Cuban leader often strategically employed television as the revolution's broadcast medium. Decades later, Farocki shows how video assumes that function in *Videograms of a Revolution* (1992). Lenin's 1919 speech presents Farocki with an interesting technological challenge: it predates television and synchronized-sound film recording. Lenin's speech exists only as an audial recording. However, instead of playing it over a blank screen, Farocki matches stock historical footage of Lenin to sound recordings of his voice. Additionally,

The Language of Revolution features a commentator analyzing Lenin's rhetoric. The expert concludes that Lenin improvised a great deal; he did not draft his speeches beforehand but developed them while speaking. This delivery technique, the professional argues, impresses on audiences that they are taking part in the arguments' formulation.

In contrast to the oral deliveries from the French Revolution courtroom, then first reenacted on the theatrical stage, cinema mobilized sound and image in the early twentieth century to help speeches reach the public.[7] Forty-five years later, filmmakers used synch systems to make simultaneous audiovisual recordings. Farocki employs a 1963 clip of Jesse Jackson addressing a crowd to make this point. He avoids found footage of Malcolm X. Instead, he presents a 1964 speech by X through the medium of the record album "Ballots and Bullets." A record is a technology on which sound, usually music, is inscribed but a record is also a legal account. Farocki sets up a turntable before a camera and drops the needle as X's speech begins. X's disembodied voice resounds powerfully without visual distractions. An image of X's face from the album cover fills the screen. Farocki

5.1 Harun Farocki, *The Language of Revolution* (1972)

plays with the double meaning of "revolution" as the overthrow of an order from below and vinyl records' measure of rotation: revolutions per minute.

The Language of Revolution offers distinct possibilities for representing social revolution. The extreme reaction revolutionary language generates attests to its power. The words of several figures Farocki focuses on—Danton, X, and Dutschke—led to violence against them. Farocki includes counter speeches by Saint-Just, who condemns Danton to death, and Jesse Jackson, who represents the civil rights movement's non-violent wing. Whereas Jackson rouses crowds to sing, X urges them to "swing" (their fists). Farocki follows Jackson's and X's contrasting speeches with an unusual (for him) avalanche of montaged images of violence against black bodies, set to the soundtrack of Lena Horne's "Now!" The montage is not dialectical; rather, it is associative and cumulative as it assembles a plethora of images of acts of racist brutality. Within this rapid succession of images, Farocki slips in a photograph of the martyred Nazi propaganda hero Horst Wessel, composer of the Third Reich's national anthem. The photograph forges a link between Nazi crimes and U.S. racism. The sequence ends with the word "NOW" spelled out on a bullet-ridden screen.

The language of revolution is formula-less. Each example stands alone. At the film's end, Farocki cautions, "To assess a speech or a text, one has to ask: Who is speaking? Who is the audience? When and where did its members live? To which class do they belong? What is the audience's situation?" The media that record words and images and the platforms that disseminate them are as important as the words and images themselves. To achieve maximum effect, cultural producers must carefully calibrate language and, by extension, images to their target audiences. Speeches are words and sentences that combine to form a sort of movement, similar to how single images together compose moving-shot sequences in films. Like a filmmaker's relation to images, the speechmaker must select words from various possibilities and deploy them with utmost precision. Farocki stresses that a cinematographic lexicon should include moving-shot sequences, gestures, expressions, and concepts instead of static images. Media theorist Wolfgang Ernst underscores this sentiment in a collaborative essay written with Farocki, "Given that the moving image is the first medium that can 'store' time, one of the greatest challenges now is how to 'sort' this time. Within film, time enters the pictorial archive."[8] Speechmakers deliver speeches for publics to hear. However, once recorded, the moment of reception can vary. Recording devices preserve oratorical performances in time. In *The Language of Revolution*, Farocki studies what happens to revolutionary language when it is translated into audiovisual media. Are certain tropes recognizable across space and time? The film comprises the first entry in his cinematographic lexicon.

A concern that Farocki returns to throughout his practice first emerges in *The Language of Revolution*: How does the technology that nests the grammar and style of image production determine the latter? Farocki notes, "The technological revolution has also seen the rise of particular effects that are made possible by those devices, indeed they are part of the programmes of these machines.... Today there are technical advances nearly every year, which produce, in turn, stylistic proclivities."[9] Farocki again addresses the correlation between a revolution, its expression, and the media that transmits it in *Videograms of a Revolution*.[10] Working with Andrei Ujica, Farocki found that in the collected amateur video footage from Nicolae Ceaucescu's last days, there were repetitions of the angles, shots, gestures, and images. A certain homogeneity of style emerged. Recalling Vilém Flusser, Farocki remarks, "Flusser emphasizes the manner in which any individual photograph or filmic expression is a product of programming."[11] The video anticipates the Internet's ever growing audiovisual archive and database, made increasingly accessible by advanced search engines. The result is a potentially unlimited and readily available virtual treasure trove of information and images, however, often with the outcome of a search repeating the ever same.

In contrast to *Videograms of a Revolution*, compiled primarily of non-professional media images, *Die führende Rolle* (The Leading Role) (1994) shows how professional media shape and produce political events. Farocki created a montage film from footage of the "Fall of the Wall" and German reunification featured on public news broadcasts in former East and West Germany. He refuses the Western rhetoric heralding the "end of Communism" and the "triumph of Capitalism." His voice-over complains about the difficulties of putting "a revolution into images." The film begins with footage of Deutsche Demokratische Republik (DDR) dignitaries, including General Secretary Erich Honecker, visiting a workers' celebration. Following his usual method of media analysis, Farocki repeats this footage at regular intervals throughout the production in order that new meanings might emerge. This is followed by a clip from a DDR news report from October 19, 1989, the first day Egon Krenz (the DDR's last communist leader) assumed power. The clip, which repeats several times in the film, shows Krenz visiting a factory and speaking with workers. Farocki uses these two sequences to muse on the factory as a "historic site" in East Germany, where the keyword was "work."

In West Germany, factories only enter the news when their owners shut them down or accidents occur—they are not part of everyday life. The next set of news clips follows events after the "Fall of the Wall." They show East Germans crowding the shopping streets of West Berlin, visibly startled by the abundance of commodities and fresh produce stalls. People go on shopping sprees, exchange currency, and sell personal possessions. Farocki notes that the black market that emerged at the Cold War's end resembled the one in the aftermath of World War II. The many media images that celebrated the "Fall of the Wall" failed to capture how the end of communism ushered in the beginnings of consumerism. They failed to recount the importance of work and the dignity of the worker in the former DDR. Farocki produces a view that differs from the standard narrative of capitalism's triumphal march touted by dominant news broadcasts. His final words in the film, "a revolution buried in images instead of emanating from them," underscore how broadcast media produces a history that conforms to and confirms dominant ideology (Western capitalism) through repetition of the ever same. They overlap with Flusser's claim that today's world is made of images.

Farocki pursues how communication media (press, radio, television, film—that is, *mass* media) translates, performs, and creates politically transformative events in *The Language of Revolution*, *Videograms of a Revolution*, and *The Leading Role*. In these productions, Farocki explores how communication media encodes revolutionary words and actions into new modes, and he subsequently decodes them as images of revolution. The productions repeat common rhetorical, gestural, stylistic, or movement-based characteristics for each event. They implement the real. The revolutions live on as media myths. Myths that will obscure other histories and truths.

Farocki articulates his conception of a media archive or library in an early unpublished text, "What Ought to Be Done" (1975/76).[12] Here, he imagines a research institute for nonfiction films that would include a "national image library" (*nationale Bilderbibliothek*) that filmmakers and documentarians could access. The concept of an image library evokes Aby Warburg's never completed project Mnemosyne Atlas. Whereas Warburg centered on still images from antiquity to the present, Farocki's proposal considers an image bank of moving-media sequences and nonfiction images. Farocki was aware of the conundrum faced by filmmakers who rely on present-day images that will soon be out-of-date. He writes, "What one calls documentation, that shows the world as if it was known, has the effect that in a few years, we can no longer experience what it really looked like. Images must be made with which today's strange world can be discovered and the present becomes history. We need to produce building blocks. First, we need to develop them, then we have to assemble and dissemble them."[13] Depictions filmmakers make of historical events can function as building blocks for other filmmakers to assemble their projects. Moving images, like bricks, form the architectural structure of a film. However, filmmakers must ensure that these stored image blocks are neither standardized nor clichéd to avoid prefabricated future constructions.

The idea of a storage system image or archive for moving images that intrigued Farocki extended beyond documentary footage. In a 1982 review of John Cassavetes's *Too Late Blues* (1961), Farocki focused on a baseball game scene: "I am a collector of such scenes and images. If I wanted to make a book with them, I'd write to the publisher requesting images that resemble *Moments musicaux* (musical moments). These images should function like picture headlines: the chalk mark on the shoulder, the large shadow cast by the balloon seller in *The Third Man*," and so on.[14] Farocki, in a cinephiliac gesture like Jean Epstein's theory of photogenie, identifies and collects remarkable shots from film history that resonate long after the plot and narrative fade. Productions such as *Workers Leaving the Factory* (1995) bring together some of these shot sequences. As Farocki describes it, "A new archive system is thus on its way, a future library for moving images, in which one can search for and retrieve elements of pictures. Up to now, the dynamic and compositional definitions of a sequence of images—those things that are the decisive factor in the editing process of converting a sequence of images into film—have not been classified nor included."[15]

In the essay film *The Expression of Hands* (1997), made two years after the release of *Workers Leaving the Factory*, Farocki studied body techniques to actualize a "moving image archive."[16] The short begins with an analysis of the opening scene of Sam Fuller's *Pickup on South Street* (1953). In this sequence, Fuller films the hands of a thief in a crowded subway as the latter deftly opens a woman's purse and removes her wallet. A rapid shot/counter-shot series between the hands and the woman's face ensues, with her expression inexplicably suggesting erotic arousal. Farocki observes, "The hands do something different than the face." *The Expression of Hands* analyzes shots of hands and hand gestures from film history. The influence of Vilém Flusser is again apparent as Farocki, to a certain extent, actualizes in an audiovisual format theories proposed by the philosopher in his 1991 study on gestures.[17] In his investigation into the language and science of gestures,

Flusser focuses on hands as a means of expression. For his part, Farocki creates a filmic archive that in its entirety spans from an early 1908 film featuring a close-up shot of the hands of a female thief, who hides jewels in a bar of soap, to myriad sequences from labor, propaganda, horror, music, and contemporary war films. In one instance, he plays sequences from a U.S. New Deal documentary focusing on labor between 1934-1937. In another, he uncovers how propagandists mobilized the same images from the New Deal documentary for a pro-war film in 1944. As in *The Trouble with Images*, Farocki deploys the same stockpile of footage for different aims.

Farocki's 1980 essay on editing has a section entitled: "Gestic Thinking." For Farocki, edited sections of a film, those image blocks put together to build a production, must contain the equivalent of a "gestus"—a clear character gesture or movement included within each edited sequence. Unlike still images that express emotions, or staged poses in photographs or paintings, *gestus* is a technique of acting. It depends on movement. Gestus codifies cinematographic gestures across time and space. It operates synecdochically and must contain something of the whole within its form. The hermeneutic circle reemerges in Farocki's gestic regime as part of the social expression, which contains within it a whole. Concomitantly, the whole comprises gestic thinking.[18]

Farocki includes clips from classic silent films such as Robert Wiene's *The Hands of Orlac* (1924) and Louis Buñuel and Salvador Dalí's *Un Chien Andalou* (An Andalusian Dog, 1929), along with the scene from *Pickup on South Street*. Indeed, the silent film era holds a particular significance for Farocki because the absence of sound gives visual expressions greater meaning—it helps images to develop their own language. Leafing through an old textbook on sign language, Farocki wonders if filmmakers would have developed a cinematic language of visual signs if engineers had not discovered sound technology. A few minutes later, as if responding to his question, he presents a 1927 book on gestural acting in cinema: Dyk Rudenski's *Gestologie und Filmspielerei* (Gestures and Filmacting). He pauses over sections of this tome that explain the subtle nuances of the expression of hands. These include the difference between the fingers of a clenched fist facing the hand owner or away from that person, or between a slap delivered with the palm or the back of the hand. Hands, Farocki observes, are the only part of the body that one can see from every angle. A sequence of frozen fingers that cannot light a match and clips of maimed hands point to this delicate body part's vulnerability. Hands are crucial for labor, whether it be a skilled craft or a factory assembly line. Farocki presents a 1944 Nazi propaganda film about making a violin as an example of handcraft. The featured artisan gently bends and joins the pieces of wood. The film also highlights clips of hands shooting guns or strangling people. However, according to Farocki, piano players' hands are the most beloved in cinema. Perhaps this has to do with the likeness between the operation of a piano player's hands and audiovisual images. Like the process of the piano player, whose hands play two distinct lines of music at once, counterpoint in film creates multiple narratives and meanings.

In *The Expression of Hands*, two hands in particular appear more frequently throughout the production. Sometimes they frame an image; other times, they sketch on paper, illustrating a concept. Occasionally, the production depicts the hands at rest. Their long brown, slender fingers and delicate structure identify them as Farocki's. Many of his films feature them. They represent the craft, labor, and artistry that goes into his works. Farocki was transitioning from analog to digital editing systems when he made *The Expression of Hands*. With the transfer to digital came a loss of films' indexical nature. Also lost was film's tactile dimension, with the filmmaker's operation of passing a celluloid strip between fingers replaced by computer strokes. Digital technology streamlines dexterity from the hand to the fingertip. Computer programs replace manual labor, all that remains is the root word.

The Expression of Hands is one of Farocki's most intimate films. He made it shortly after the death of Ursula Lefkes, his wife of thirty years and mother of his daughters. His distinctive voice guides spectators through the text, punctuating significant moments. Early in the film, Farocki reveals a distorted reflection of his face on the editing screen. At another moment, he illustrates Rudenski's argument that unlike the palm, which evokes emotion, the hand's back signifies intellectual expression. Following Rudenski's example of the courteous hand kiss, Farocki films himself first lowering his mouth to kiss the back of his hand formally and then bringing his lips to kiss his open palm more intimately. At the end of the film, he concentrates on hands that bring or depict death. The final example features a close-up of the last gestures of a dying man's hand. Farocki's face appears on screen as the man's hand stops moving. He speaks the film's last words: "The essence of life is freed." And here we recall Flusser on the gesture of freedom, who writes, "Freedom is actually indivisible: it is the way we recognize that others are in the world with us."[19]

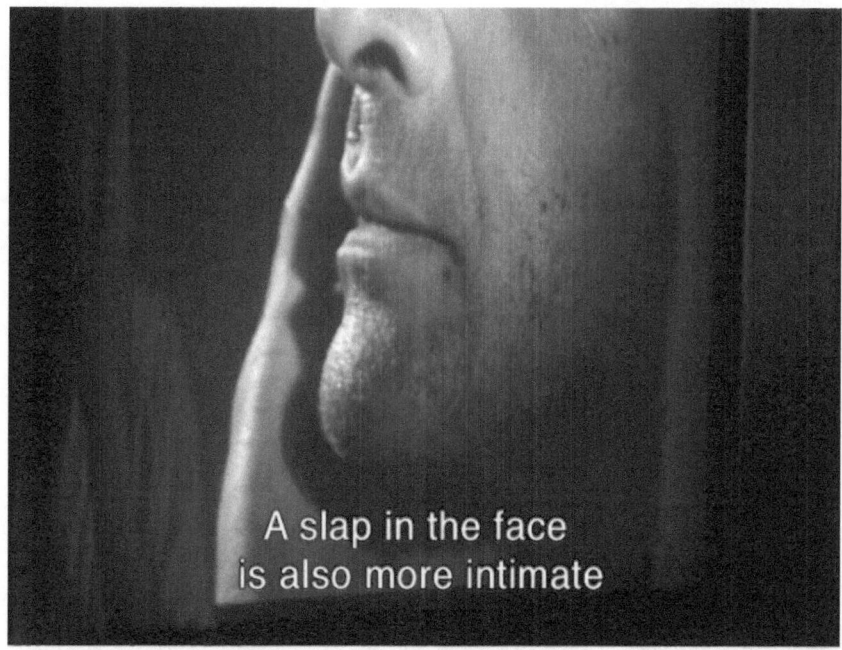

5.2 Harun Farocki, *The Expression of Hands* (1997)

In *The Expression of Hands*, Farocki writes three words on his hand: Papier Bühne Bildschirm (paper stage screen). Thirty years after the ending of *Their Newspapers* (1968) that features the game "paper rock scissors," Farocki exchanges the political tools of rocks and scissors for stages and screens. Each stands for a different expressive medium. Writing words, performing gestures, and making images translate thought into tangible and visible signs. The commentary explains that cinema is a medium based on seeing, not touching; it converts touch into the gaze, just as acting expresses social attitudes on stage. By focusing on hands, Farocki shows how these appendages encode, convey, and transmit attitudes; their range of expression is seemingly unlimited. However, once we codify their structure into a lexicon, we can read gestures like a language, with their movements acting like signifiers.

Not only can techniques of the body be indexed and made readily available for reference, retrieval, and reuse, but so too can the backgrounds, settings, and geographies in which filmmakers stage them. In his review of Volker Vogeler's *Das Tal der tanzenden Witwen* (Valley of the Dancing Widows, 1975), a German/Spanish Western-comedy, Farocki describes the generic character of the Western landscape. He notes filmmakers typically depict the Western landscape in a way that makes it impossible to grasp in its totality. The way filmmakers angle their shots of characters against the sky makes specific locales unrecognizable. The result is a familiar visual patterning that becomes the signature trope of the Western genre: "The valley is never visible. You can't get an idea of the layout of the (Western) town.... You can't imagine that a particular landscape surrounds the town. Filmmakers typically shoot the exterior shots against the sky. I was told that this film town in Spain was on a hill, so that filmmakers could do everything without background localization."[20] This production process is based on genre formulas that generate form and content like the made-for-television documentaries that Farocki decried earlier. Filmmakers suspend the resulting films in an artificial world that avoids pointers or markers of specificity and the real. As will later be the case with video games, players in this false world move through interchangeable virtual landscapes.

Forty years after Vogeler's *Valley of the Dancing Widows*, Farocki delivers an almost identical desert-valley landscape in *Parallel II* (2014), the second of the four in the series. However, the scene has been digitally manufactured and it serves as the backdrop for the video game *Red Dead Redemption*. Furthermore, Farocki offers up another game in a non-specific 1950s film noir Hollywood set and yet another

An Image Lexicon, or Towards a Media Archeology 191

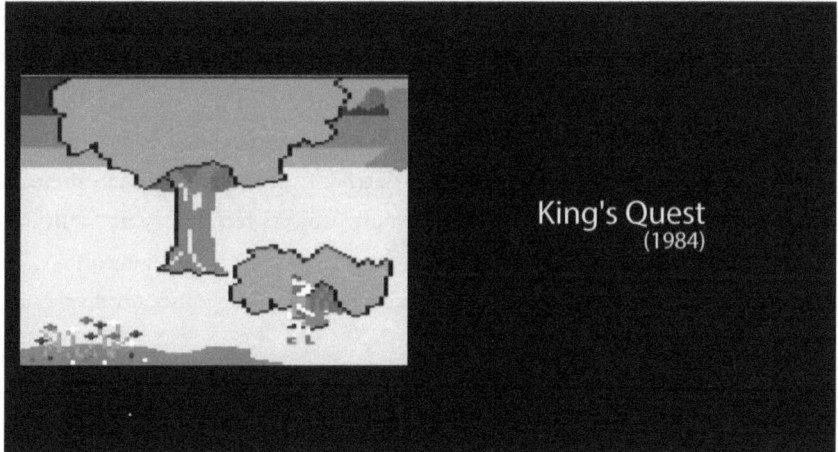

5.3 Harun Farocki, *Parallel I* (2014)

in a generic war zone. *Parallel I–IV* (2012–2014), Farocki's final work, completed shortly before his death, is a four-channel video installation. When first exhibited at New York City's Greene Naftali Gallery in September 2014, the work comprised four screens suspended in the middle of the gallery. The screens formed a cube-like space that viewers circumnavigated as they watched the looping sequences. Two screens comprise double-channel videos (I and III); the other two (II and IV) are single-channel projections.

Farocki produces a media archeology of the video game for the *Parallel* series. He begins with a visual history of video games' development from crude single-line graphics to denser images that start to proximate analog reality. He uses a tree to show the incremental complexity of CGI (computer-generated imagery) technology. "A tree is a tree," Barthes writes towards the beginning of "Myth Today." But he continues, "A tree as expressed by Minou Drouet is no longer quite a tree, it is a tree which is decorated, adapted to a certain type of consumption, laden with literary self-indulgence, revolt, images, in short with a type of social *usage* which is added to pure matter."[21] Later in this essay, Barthes returns to the tree and woodcutter to distinguish between language-object and metalanguage. Farocki, in "War Always Finds a Way," traces his use of the term "operational" to Barthes. He refers explicitly to Barthes's reflection on trees in "Myth Today" as crucial to his understanding of the term. Thus, Farocki's decision to begin *Parallel* by drawing attention to a tree beside a house and tracking the "historical representation of the tree in computer games" is a further nod to his indebtedness to Barthes. The tree develops historically from serving as a non-functional (operative) component to becoming the image equivalent of meta-language in games. Yet, if Barthes granted priority to culture over techniques, extending the sovereignty of culture into the domain of technology, Farocki now begins to grant priority to techniques, thereby reversing Barthes's thrust. Rather than projecting notions of culture into technology, he now projects technology into culture. He recognizes that the materiality and technicity of digital media technologies have thoroughly permeated the cultural techniques so obviously on display in video games.

In the early games of the 1980s, such as *Mystery House* (1984), *Pitfall* (1982), and *King's Quest* (1984), trees operated as props without a function. However, by decade's end, computer programmers added functionality to the trees, and they became an integral part of the narrative and game strategy. From lines to pixilated squares to more densely developed images, programmers transformed simple trees into blossoming flora whose wind-swept leaves sway uniformly and predictably. Farocki programs and controls everything in *Parallel I*; the glitch or "zero-day" do not exist.

For Farocki, computer games were the natural outcome of the film studio set. *Parallel I* depicts the four essential elements—fire, water, earth, and air—in the new game world. This first segment of the *Parallel* series is a dual-channel projection, with the computer game playing on one screen and informational titles on the other. Farocki juxtaposes a series of contrasting images. One of these compares analog film clips of a field of grass (earth) swaying in the wind to CGI of a sky with clouds (air). As the commentary notes, there are two types of wind in cinema, natural and machine-produced. In contrast, there is only one type of wind in computer graphics. The CGI's flickering connotes the indexical "reality" of the analog clips. The commentary muses, "Maybe computer-generated images will assume functions previously held by film; maybe that will liberate them for other things." The segment ends with the pronouncement: "The computer images try to achieve the effect of the film images. They want to surpass them, leave them far behind. They don't want to attract birds but creatures of their own design." Infinite representational possibilities open up once a metaverse moves beyond indexically imitating the natural world.

Parallel II investigates *Mindcraft*, a game where players build their worlds. *Mindcraft*'s programmers actualized a new community of spectators alongside active gamers, followers who watch the games and identify with players, following their actions. *Parallel II*'s opening evokes the solipsistic viewpoint of a child who believes that all that passes by the window on a long train or car ride has been placed there specifically for them. The narrator asks: "Does the world exist if I am not watching it?" A stark virtual reality appears out of nothingness and disappears just as quickly. The narrator continues: "Where does this world end? This world appears infinite, generated by the gaze that falls upon it." The suggestion is that vision determines existence but changes with technology.[22]

The existence of walls and invisible borders for players to transgress is a key feature of video games. Programmers of these virtual worlds inscribe ideology into them. The popularity of the U.S. myth of the West in these games has much to do with the way the myth nostalgically appeals to a previous Hollywood era that celebrated Manifest Destiny's expansion of territory and turned a blind eye to the genocidal bloodshed accompanying it. Though Hollywood has reconsidered this popular film genre, its earlier glory and much of its ideology thrives within the gaming industry, propelled by the endless drive for conquest, frontier crossing, and colonizing new virtual territories. *Parallel II* captures video games' evocation of unfettered freedom in a striking scene where a player breaks through the program's borders and virtually tumbles into an unbuilt environment. With nowhere to go, the player is caught in a forever time loop.

Parallel III continues the earlier segments' investigations of borders, thresholds, and realities in a virtual environment the narrator says "ends like a board game." This production focuses on the objects and props that furnish these environments. "Objects have no existence by themselves; by themselves, they are nothing," states the narrator. The objects in these environments require a game character to make them signify. Farocki draws parallels between the film camera's movement and the gaze that animates elements in the virtual worlds. A representation of a body of water in one of these worlds does not signify until a character, with whom the gamer is closely aligned, touches its surface. Even then, the water's surface seems hollow, with no water below. It appears to float on its own like an island in a primeval ocean—all simulation.

Parallel IV focuses on creating the actants. This last segment of the series opens with the declaration that heroes are figures thrown into the world without parents or teachers to instruct them. Instead, they must learn the game's rules through trial and error. Again, Farocki bases figures on archetypes; these include medieval figures on quests who develop through their adventures. Figures perform according to set codes and morphologies. Farocki presents the video game as a modern-day *Bildungsroman*. Participants learn the actions and gestures video game figures perform, such as pushing, bumping, resisting, and handling firearms. Farocki studies how this coded technology enables the participant, in the form of a virtual protagonist, to acquire additional skill sets that determine future behavior and advancement through the narrative. Farocki thus anticipates the learning potential of artificial intelligence (AI). The segment's final sequence centers on a male character violently threatening a female Asian store-clerk figure.

5.4 Harun Farocki, *Parallel I* (2014)

Although the clerk flees the shop, the videogame designers have not programmed her to *learn* and therefore be able to escape completely (she is not the hero of this game). Instead, she too is caught in a time loop, repeatedly returning to the scene of the crime. The commentary's final words attest to "the limitations of human freedom of action" within these built environments and underscore the clerk's repetitive behavior. In the end, agency is purely ideological, the product of programming. Programmers write players into fully encoded worlds. Survival is the primary goal in these worlds, and to survive necessitates eliminating as many adversaries as possible. The players must knock off even potential adversaries. It is, therefore, no surprise that programmers develop gaming and war industries in tandem and that the two technologies seamlessly converge. Their alliance is uncomfortable in its natural comfortableness.

While programmers use algorithms to generate new products, they also recognize that computer processes have an enormous potential to identify, classify, and archive vast media banks of sounds and images. In a speech at the 3rd International Flusser conference in 1999, Farocki acknowledges how digital technology allows him to realize his earlier dream of a moving-image lexicon. Citing Ernst, with whom he collaborated on the *Suchbilder* (Search Images) project, he states: "In principle, images (and their soundtracks) can be made accessible, sorted and archived by adequate algorithms of pattern recognition in a way that was previously inconceivable in the context of analog human image and motif associations." Ernst continues, "The digital image archive is thus able to identify image and sequence similarities that lie beyond the iconological fixation of the human gaze on content, on semantics, and to literally excavate a media-archaeological image knowledge, an 'optical unconscious' (Walter Benjamin), such as only technical media are able to generate."[23] As Farocki shows in *Parallel I–IV*, despite enormous technological advances, the backgrounds, structures, characters, and plots of moving-image productions remain the same. Algorithms identify *gestic* moments of expression, such as avoiding obstacles and pulling guns in video games. *Gestus* has thus migrated across media from live theater to film, television, and now CGI. Accordingly, the virtual world of the gaming industry provides yet another platform for Farocki's lifelong dismantling of image production into its constituent parts. What began with television producers creating formulaic sounds and images has metamorphosed into computer-generated algorithms that seem to take on a life of their own. And just as AI can generate characters and stories, one wonders if, in the future, makers will produce entire films through algorithms—productions that will stand as quintessential operational films.[24]

Farocki began as a writer who used words to decode, analyze, and critique contemporary society. With the same goal in mind, he moved on to film, video, and digital technologies over the years. Whatever his media, he rigorously and unrelentingly interrogated the translation of thought into language, never losing sight of the fact that media function according to the repetition of specific codes in the form of words, phrases, gestures, body techniques, pictures, images, and shot sequences. Similar to how critical writers use words in their analyses, Farocki consistently sought to employ images to make arguments. His filmic essays operate as forms of intelligence.

Notes

INTRODUCTION: FAROCKI THROUGH TIME

The epigraph is from Harun Farocki, "Reality Would Have to Begin," in *Nachdruck / Imprint: Texte / Writings*, ed. Susanne Gaensheimer and Nicolaus Schafhausen (New York: Lukas & Sternberg, 2001), 194.

1. Thomas Elsaesser, "Making the World Superfluous: An Interview with Harun Farocki" [1993], in *Harun Farocki: Working on the Sight-Lines*, ed. Thomas Elsaesser (Amsterdam: Amsterdam University Press, 2004), 177.
2. Harun Farocki, *Zehn, zwanzig, dreißig, vierzig: Fragment einer Autobiographie* (Berlin: Harun Farocki Institut/n.b.k., 2017), 88. (Unless otherwise noted all translations from German are my own.)
3. Harun Farocki, "*Bilderschatz*" (3rd International Flusser Lecture, December 7, 1999). For an English-language published version, see Harun Farocki and Wolfgang Ernst, "Towards an Archive for Visual Concepts, Part 2 'A Cinematographic Thesaurus,'" in Elsaesser, *Harun Farocki*, 279.
4. Because it was nearly impossible to change one's name in Germany, Farocki's passport and other legal documents list his birth name. His daughters, Larissa Lu and Annabelle Lee Faroqhi, retain the original spelling.
5. Many countries, including Germany, have naming laws in which a name must be submitted to the local registration office and officially approved. During the Third Reich, when Farocki was born, there was an approved list of names to which all citizens had to comply. Most likely, given his father's foreign status, he was given an exemption.
6. Thomas Meaney recently observed in the *Süddeutsche Zeitung* that Farocki, alongside Rainer Werner Fassbinder and Brigitte Reimann, was one of the oppositional voices during the Cold War period whose critique was recognized more outside of Germany than within it. Meaney, "Deutschland war lange das Land, das sowohl das amerikanische Imperium als auch das sowjetische Imperium einer intelligenten Kritik unterzogen hat, weil ihm beide Systeme fremdartig und synthetisch und falsch erschienen sind. Aber wenn es so weitergeht, werden Ihre wertvollsten oppositionellen Künstler—Rainer Werner Fassbinder, Brigitte Reimann, Harun Farocki—in der Anglosphäre bald intelligenter diskutiert als in ihrem Heimatland." *Siddeutsche Zeitung*, January 12, 2024.

7. Harun Farocki, "Written Trailers," in *Harun Farocki: Against What? Against Whom?*, ed. Antje Ehmann and Kodwo Eshun (London: Koenig Books, 2009), 221.
8. During the period of the Cold War until the Berlin Wall came down in 1989, there was very little economic or industrial investment in West Berlin. There were significant expenditures made in the sphere of culture, however. These include the well-known DAAD Artist-in-Residence program, started under the auspices of the Ford Foundation; the establishment of the Berlin Philharmoniker, Haus der Kulturen der Welt; and the support of educational institutions such as the Free University, Technical University, Akadamie der Künste, the DFFB and similar institutions.
9. Farocki, *Zehn, zwanzig, dreißig, vierzig*, 15.
10. Raymond Bellour, "Pourquoi Harun nous était si précieux," *Trafic* 93 (Spring 2015): 66.
11. During the 1960s and 1970s the most common misidentification would have been as Turkish due to the influx of *Gastarbeiter* ("guest workers") from Turkey to West Germany.
12. Norbert Thomma and Christiane Peitz, "Uuuuuh, This Won't Only Be Pleasant" [2014], in *Christian Petzold: Interviews*, ed. Marco Abel, Aylin Bademsoy, and Jaimey Fisher (Jackson: University Press of Mississippi, 2023), 166.
13. Aktion, "Endlich. Jetzt können Sie Harun Farocki treffen." The verb *treffen* means to meet as well as to hit a target. From the personal archives of Harun Farocki, located in Berlin, Germany.
14. Both the terms "Negro's Kiss" and "Moor's head" were in common usage until 2005 when "Schokoküß" was substituted.
15. Throughout this book, where applicable, I will first provide the original German language title followed by its English translation.
16. Ednei de Genaro and Hermano Callou, "'Keep the Horizon Open': An Interview with Harun Farocki" [2014], *Senses of Cinema* 79 (July 2016): n.p.
17. See Jill Godmilow's *What Farocki Taught* (1998) and Filipa César's *Spell Reel* (2017). In the latter, César adopts Farocki's formal strategy of soft montage as a means by which to highlight archival footage and place it in a dynamic relationship with contemporary footage.
18. Most prominent amongst these films were *The State I Am In* (2000), *Yella* (2007), *Jericho* (2008), *Barbara* (2012), and *Phoenix* (2014). The screenplay for Petzold's *Transit* (2018) was co-written by Farocki who originally wanted to adapt Anna Segher's eponymous 1942 novel.
19. See Gerd Conradt, *Starbuck: Holger Meins; Ein Porträt als Zeitbild* (Berlin: Espresso, 2001), 51.
20. On June 2, 1967, a peaceful protestor, Benno Ohnesorg, was killed by the Berlin police during a demonstration against the visit of the shah of Iran. Farocki was not in Berlin at the time.
21. See Tilman Baumgärtel, *Vom Guerrillakino zum Essayfilm: Harun Farocki* (Berlin: b_books, 1998).
22. Harun Farocki interview with Philip Goll, "Harun Farocki Interview" [2014], in *Harun Farocki: Another Kind of Empathy*, ed. Antje Ehmann and Carles Guerra (Barcelona: Fundació Antoni Tàpies, 2016), 57.

23. Harun Farocki, "Risking His Life: Images of Holger Meins" [1998], in *Harun Forocki*. Gaensheimer, *Nachdruck / Imprint*, 270.
24. See Michael Cramer, *Utopian Television: Rossellini, Watkins, and Godard Beyond Cinema* (Minneapolis: University of Minnesota Press, 2017).
25. See Volker Pantenburg, "TV Essay Dossier, 1: The Case of Westdeutscher Rundfunk (WDR)," *Critical Studies in Television* 14, no. 1 (March 2019): 106–138.
26. Farocki, *Zehn, zwanzig, dreißig, vierzig*, 159.
27. Harun Farocki and Hito Steyerl, "A Magical Imitation of Reality," *Cahier #2* (Milan: Kaleidoscope Press, 2011), 1–30.
28. The significance of Werner Dütsch in promoting and supporting independent filmmakers cannot be underestimated. As Antje Ehmann recalls, Dütsch "gave a kind of *carte blanche* to these amazing filmmakers who wanted to do cinema, but who couldn't find the money for it. . . . Dütsch gave money to James Benning, to Hartmut Bitomsky, to Harun. There was a group of maybe ten filmmakers that survived just because of this constellation." Flavia Dima, "In Conversation with Antje Ehmann, on the Legacy of Harun Farocki," Mubi, published February 23, 2021, https://mubi.com/en/notebook/posts/in-conversation-with-antje-ehmann-on-the-legacy-of-harun-farocki. Recent publications have brought attention to the vital role Dütsch played. See Volker Pantenburg, ed., *Werner Dütsch: WDR: Wie man sieht: Lola Montez* (Potsdam: Harun Farocki Institut, 2019).
29. Farocki as cited on dustjacket for Antje Ehmann and Carles Guerra, ed., *Harun Farocki: Another Kind of Empathy* (London: Koenig Books, 2016).
30. Volker Pantenburg, "Visibilities: Harun Farocki between Image and Text," in Gaensheimer, *Nachdruck / Imprint*, 16.
31. This label is confusing for an English speaker. What in English is a "feature" is in German a "Spielfilm." The closest proximation would be made-for-TV documentaries.
32. Harun Farocki, "Drückebergerei vor der Wirklichkeit: Das Fernsehfeature/Der Ärger mit den Bildern" [1973], in *Harun Farocki: Meine Nächte mit den Linken; Texte, 1964–1975*, ed. Volker Pantenburg (Berlin: Harun Farocki Institut/n.b.k., 2018), 132.
33. Farocki, "Drückebergerei vor der Wirklichkeit," 132.
34. Farocki, 138.
35. For a comprehensive study on the genre of the essay film see Nora M. Alter, *The Essay Film After Fact and Fiction* (New York: Columbia University Press, 2018) and Timothy Corrigan, *The Essay Film: From Montaigne, After Marker* (Oxford: Oxford University Press, 2011).
36. Harun Farocki, "Über *Bilder der Welt und Inschrift des Krieges*, Pressematerial des Basis-Film Verleih, 1988," in *Harun Farocki: Unregelmäßig, nicht regellos; Texte, 1986–2000*, ed. Tom Holert (Berlin: Harun Farocki Institut, 2021), 134.
37. The conference took place in Vienna, Austria, in May 1991. See the resulting publication, Christa Blümlinger and Constantin Wulff, ed., *Schreiben Bilder Sprechen: Texte zum essayistischen Film* (Vienna: Sonderzahl, 1992). The volume includes Farocki's contribution. Harun Farocki, "*Unregelmäßig, nicht regellos*" (Uncontrolled, but Not Without Rules), 145-155.
38. Theodor W. Adorno, "The Essay as Form" [1958], in *Essays on the Essay Film*, ed. Nora M. Alter and Timothy Corrigan (New York: Columbia University Press, 2017), 60–81.

39. Harun Farocki and Christa Blümlinger, "The ABCs of the Film Essay" [2015], in Alter, *Essay Film*, 297-98.
40. Harun Farocki, "Notwendige Abwechselung und Vielfahlt" [1975], in Pantenburg, *Harun Farocki*, 225. For an English version, see Harun Farocki and Ted Fendt, "Necessary Variation and Variety," *Grey Room* 79 (Spring 2020): 106-118.
41. Kaja Silverman and Harun Farocki, *Speaking About Godard* (New York: NYU Press, 1998), 142.
42. Adorno, "Essay as Form," 71.
43. Tom Holert posits that Farocki's shift to soft montage is part of his broader conception to view editing and montage as systems of "navigational sensing and modelling." Tom Holert, "Archive, Montage, Navigation: The Function of Knowledge in the Work of Harun Farocki," unpublished paper.
44. In his teaching materials for the University of Florida in 2002, Farocki included Peleshyan's essay, "Distance Montage, or the Theory of Distance." And in "ABCs of the Film Essay," he notes, "I got acquainted with his [Peleshyan's] work late, not until the late 1980s. I read his text about distance montage frequently. I inferred from this label that one should not only edit two connecting shots. Even images that are far apart comment on one another." Farocki, "ABCs of the Film," 300; Artavazd Peleshyan, "Distance Montage, or the Theory of Distance" [1971/72], in *Documentary Films of the Armenian Soviet Republic*, ed. Erika and Moritz de Hadeln, Garegin Sakojan, Hans Joachim Schlegel (self-published, 1989), 79-100.
45. Peleshyan, "Theory of Distance," 88.
46. For an analysis of culture and its currency as a class marker in society, see Pierre Bourdieu's *Distinction: A Social Critique of Social Judgement and Taste*.
47. Harun Farocki, "Cross Influence/Soft Montage" [2002], in Ehmann, *Harun Farocki*, 73.
48. "Film Funding Application. Working Title: On the History of Labor. Author/Producer: Harun Farocki, 1986." As reprinted in "Harun Farocki: On the History of Labor," ed. Volker Pantenburg (Berlin: Harun Farocki Institut, 2020), 3.
49. The entirety of Farocki's collected writing has been published by the Harun Farocki Institut/n.b.k. The first volume is the autobiography: Farocki, *Zehn, zwanzig, dreißig, vierzig*; followed by *Harun Farocki: Meine Nächte mit den Linken; Texte, 1964–1975*, ed. Volker Pantenburg (Berlin: Harun Farocki Institut/n.b.k., 2018); *Harun Farocki: Ich habe Genug!: Texte, 1976–1985* (2019); *Harun Farocki: Unregelmäßig, nicht regellos: Texte, 1986–2000* (2021); and *Harun Farocki: Lerne das Einfachste! Texte, 2001–2014* (2022).
50. Harun Faroqhi, "Unser Schnurre" [1964], in Pantenburg, *Harun Farocki*, 18.
51. Harun Faroqhi, "Manipulierte Wahrheiten" [1964], in Pantenburg, *Harun Farocki*, 21.
52. Harun Faroqhi, "Der tägliche Mythos" [1965], in Pantenburg, *Harun Farocki*, 26-27. For an English translation, see Harun Farocki and Ted Fendt, "Everyday Myth," *Grey Room* 79 (Spring 2020): 90-92.
53. Roland Barthes, *Mythologies* [1957] (London: Vintage Books, 1993), 8.
54. Barthes, *Mythologies*, 121.
55. Barthes, 11.
56. Barthes, 109.
57. Harun Farocki, "War Always Finds a Way," in *HF/RG*, Chantal Pontbriand et al. (Paris: Jeu de Paume/BlackJack éditions, 2009), 107.

Introduction   201

58. The board consisted of Bitomsky, M. Blank, R. Gansera, E. Ludwig, S. Röckel, M. Watz, and H. Zischler.
59. In 2018 "Rosa Mercedes" was adopted as the title of the Harun Farocki Institute's online journal for media critique. See https://www.harun-farocki-institut.org/de/category/rosa-mercedes/01/.
60. Harun Farocki interview with Georg Alexander, "*Minimale Variation*," WDR broadcast, July 27, 1969.
61. Harun Farocki, "Über das Wannseeheim für Jugendarbeit" [1971], in Pantenburg, *Harun Farocki*, 118.
62. As cited by Tom Holert, "Tabular Images: On *The Division of all Days* (1970) and *Something Self Explanatory (15x)* (1971)," in Ehmann, *Harun Farocki*, 89.
63. Holert, "Tabular Images," 87.
64. Volker Pantenburg has extensively researched Farocki's shifting pedagogical strategies.
65. Christian Petzold interview with Volker Pantenburg and Michael Baute, "To Truly See: Christian Petzold at the dffb" [2015], in Abel, *Christian Petzold*, 170.
66. It is interesting to note that critics often disassociate filmmakers-turned-artists who used to work in collectives such as Isaac Julien or John Akomfrah.
67. Dima, "Conversation with Antje Ehmann."
68. Christian Petzold interview with Ulrich Kriest, "In Hinterland of Nihilism" [2001], in Abel, *Christian Petzold*, 18.
69. Christian Petzold interview with Nicolas Wackerbarth and Christoph Hochhäusler, "Interview Christian Petzold" [2003], in Abel, *Christian Petzold*, 48; As Petzold reminisces: "Sometimes I really did write nonsense, and then would sit with him in his kitchen, and he would make an espresso—always overcooked, by the way, for twenty-five years in his stove-top espresso maker, the coffee was totally burned! And then the rubber seals not really put on so that brown stuff would flow out of it onto the stove. Harun was also king of putting the coffee spoon in the sugar, so it was all clumped up." "The Cinema Is a Warehouse of Memory: A Conversation among Christian Petzold, Robert Fischer, and Jaimey Fisher" [2016], in Abel, *Christian Petzold*, 188.
70. Christian Petzold interview with Jaimey Fisher, "An Interview with Christian Petzold" [2011], in Abel, *Christian Petzold*, 130.
71. Allan Sekula, "Reading an Archive: Photography Between Labor and Capital" [1983], in *The Photography Reader*, ed. Liz Well (London: Routledge, 2003), 443-452.
72. Roland Barthes, "Myth Today," 123-24.
73. Theodor W. Adorno, *Aesthetic Theory* [1969], ed. Gretel Adorno and Rolf Tiedeman, trans. Robert Hullot-Kentor (Minneapolis: University of Minnesota Press, 1997), 121.
74. Theodor W. Adorno, *Minima Moralia: Reflections from Damaged Life* [1951], trans. E. F. N. Jephcott (London: Verso, 1987), 194.
75. Farocki, "Cinematographic Thesaurus," 273.
76. Farocki, 280.
77. Farocki, 283.
78. Harun Farocki, "The Industrialization of Thought," *Discourse: The Journal for Theoretical Studies in Media and Culture* 15, no. 3 (1993).
79. In the late 1970s, in an advertisement for *Filmkritik*, Farocki organized the top filmmakers according to three leagues of soccer teams—for a total of thirty-three filmmakers.

As a sign of the times, except for Barbara Loden all were male, and aside from Yasujirō Ozu and Kenji Mizoguchi, white Western. It was only much later that Farocki admitted the importance of Straub's partner, Danièle Huillet.

80. Farocki, "Cross Influence/Soft Montage," 70.

1. CRITIQUE AND MONTAGE

1. Harun Faroqhi, "Der tägliche Mythos" [1965], in *Harun Farocki: Meine Nächte mit den Linken; Texte, 1964–1975*, ed. Volker Pantenburg (Berlin: Harun Farocki Institut/n.b.k., 2018), 27.
2. Walter Benjamin, *One-Way Street and Other Writings* [1928] (New York: Verso, 1997).
3. Harun Farocki interview with Rolf Aurich and Ulrich Kriest, "Werkstattgespräch mit Harun Farocki" [1998], in *Der Ärger mit den Bildern: Die Filme von Harun Farocki*, ed. Rolf Aurich and Ulrich Kriest (Constance: UVK Medien, 1998), 346–347.
4. Harun Farocki, "Selbstmord" [1964], in Pantenburg, *Harun Farocki*, 14.
5. Farocki writes about this suicide attempt, "I wanted to leave life the way one wants to leave a party that one doesn't like." Harun Farocki, *Zehn, zwanzig, dreißig, vierzig: Fragment einer Autobiographie* (Berlin: Harun Farocki Institut/n.b.k., 2017), 84.
6. Farocki, "Selbstmord," 14.
7. Harun Farocki, "Difficult Questions" [1989], in *Nachdruck / Imprint: Texte / Writings*, ed. Susanne Gaensheimer and Nicolaus Schafhausen (New York: Lukas & Sternberg, 2001), 218.
8. As cited by Volker Pantenburg, "TV Essay Dossier, 1: The Case of Westdeutscher Rundfunk (WDR)," *Critical Studies in Television* 14, no. 1 (March 2019): 116.
9. Harun Farocki, "Über die Arbeit mit Bildern im Fernsehen" [1974], in Pantenburg, *Harun Farocki*, 167.
10. Harun Farocki, "Drückebergerei vor der Wirklichkeit: Das Fernsehfeature/Der Ärger mit den Bildern" [1973], in Pantenburg, *Harun Farocki*, 138.
11. Farocki, "Drückebergerei vor der Wirklichkeit," 139.
12. Farocki, 139.
13. On the affinities between Farocki and Godard, see Volker Pantenburg, *Farocki/Godard: Film as Theory* (Amsterdam: Amsterdam University Press, 2015).
14. Farocki, "Drückebergerei vor der Wirklichkeit," 139.
15. See Alexander Kluge, Thomas Y. Levin, and Miriam B. Hansen, "On Film and the Public Sphere" [1979], *New German Critique*, no. 24/25 (Autumn-Winter 1981-1982): 206–220.
16. Ednei de Genaro and Hermano Callou, "'Keep the Horizon Open': An Interview with Harun Farocki" [2014], *Senses of Cinema* 79 (July 2016).
17. Gerhard Richter, *Thought-Images: Frankfurt School Writers' Reflections on a Damaged Life* (Palo Alto, CA: Stanford University Press, 2007), 20.
18. Theodor W. Adorno, "Benjamin's *Einbahnstrasse*" [1968], in *Notes to Literature*, vol. 2, ed. Rolf Tiedemann, trans. Shierry Weber Nicholsen (New York: Columbia University Press, 1992), 323.
19. Richter, *Thought-Images*, 13.

1. Critique and Montage 203

20. Roland Barthes, "The Reality Effect" [1968], in *The Rustle of Language*, trans. Richard Howard, ed. François Wahl (Berkeley: University of California Press, 1989), 141-148.
21. Harun Farocki, "Bilder aus dem Fernsehen" [1973], in Pantenburg, *Harun Farocki*, 146.
22. Harun Farocki and Hito Steyerl, *Cahier #2: A Magical Imitation of Reality* (Milan: Kaleidoscope Press, 2011), 16.
23. Bertolt Brecht, "Writing the Truth: Five Difficulties," *Pariser Tageblatt* (December 12, 1934).
24. Farocki, "Arbeit mit Bildern," 164. The translation of *Aufsätze* to "assignments" is limiting as the German encompasses written essays, compositions, and assignments.
25. Farocki, "Magical Imitation of Reality," 7. As such, Farocki follows in the footsteps of artists such as Christian Phillip Müller, Hans Haacke, and Andrea Fraser. On institutional critique, see Alexander Alberro, ed., *Institutional Critique: An Anthology of Artists' Writings* (Cambridge: MIT Press, 2009).
26. Farocki, "Arbeit mit Bildern," 164.
27. Farocki, "Bilder aus dem Fernsehen," 146.
28. Farocki, 147.
29. Farocki, "Drückebergerei vor der Wirklichkeit," 139.
30. Farocki, "Bilder aus dem Fernsehen," 146.
31. Harun Farocki, "Arbeiten–beim Fernsehen" [1975], in Pantenburg, *Harun Farocki*, 194.
32. Farocki, "Arbeit mit Bildern," 171. Emphasis mine.
33. Farocki, 171.
34. During the silent film era, the tedious job of "cutter" was performed mainly by working-class women. For more on this topic, see Kristen Hatch, "Cutting Women: Margaret Booth and Hollywood's Pioneering Female Film Editors," Women Film Pioneers Project, Columbia University, 2013, https://wfpp.columbia.edu/essay/cutting-women/.
35. Farocki, "Arbeiten–beim Fernsehen," 194.
36. Farocki, "Arbeit mit Bildern," 173. Emphasis mine.
37. Farocki, "Arbeiten–beim Fernsehen," 195.
38. Farocki, 194.
39. See Bertolt Brecht, "Radio as a Means of Communication: A Talk on the Function of Radio" [1926], *Screen* 20, no. 3-4 (Winter 1979): 24-28.
40. Farocki, "Arbeit mit Bildern," 173.
41. Farocki, 166.
42. Harun Farocki, "What an Editing Room Is" [1980], in Gaensheimer, *Nachdruck / Imprint*, 82.
43. Farocki, "Arbeit mit Bildern," 167.
44. Farocki, "Editing Room," 78.
45. Farocki, 80.
46. Farocki, "Magical Imitation of Reality," 16.
47. Farocki as cited by Volker Pantenburg, "Visibilities: Harun Farocki Between Image and Text," in Gaensheimer, *Nachdruck / Imprint*, 40.
48. Farocki, "Editing Room," 80.
49. These include *Die Sprache der Revolution* (The Language of Revolution) (1972), *As You See* (1986), *Images of the World and the Inscription of War* (1988/1989), *A Day in the Life of a Consumer* (1993), and many others.

1. Critique and Montage

50. On the reproduction of photographs in nonfiction film, see Roger Hallas, *A Medium Seen Otherwise: Photography in Documentary Film* (Oxford: Oxford University Press, 2023).
51. In their focus on ruins, Saeger and Seidenstücker contributed to a genre that came to be called *"Ruinenphotographie."*
52. See Keiko Ishida, "Albert Speer's 'Theory of Ruin Value,'" special issue, *Art Research* 1 (February 2020): 35-43.
53. On *Interface*, see Christa Blümlinger, "Harun Farocki, circuit d'images," *Trafic* 21 (Spring 1997): 44-49. English translation: Christa Blümlinger, "Image(circum)volution: On the Installation *Schnittstelle (Interface)*," *Senses of Cinema* 21 (July 2002), https://www.sensesofcinema.com/2002/harun-farocki/farocki_blumlinger.
54. Rembert Hüser, "Nine Minutes in the Yard: A Conversation with Harun Farocki," in *Harun Farocki: Working on the Sight-Lines*, ed. Thomas Elsaesser (Amsterdam: Amsterdam University Press, 2004), 302.
55. Theodor W. Adorno, "The Essay as Form" [1958], in *Essays on the Essay Film*, ed. Nora M. Alter and Timothy Corrigan (New York: Columbia University Press, 2017), 71.

2. Labor

The epigraphs to this chapter are sourced from: Jean-Louis Comolli and Annette Michelson, "Mechanical Bodies, Ever More Heavenly," *October* 83 (Winter 1998): 19; Harun Farocki, "Workers Leaving the Factory" [1995], in *Nachdruck / Imprint: Texte / Writings*, ed. Susanne Gaensheimer and Nicolaus Schafhausen (New York: Lukas & Sternberg, 2001), 232; and Harun Farocki, "Notwendige Abwechslung und Vielfalt" [1975], in *Harun Farocki: Meine Nächte mit den Linken; Texte, 1964–1975*, ed. Volker Pantenburg (Harun Farocki Institut/n.b.k.: Berlin, 2018), 225. English translation: Harun Farocki and Ted Fendt, "Necessary Variation and Variety," *Grey Room* 79 (Spring 2020): 106-118.

1. Farocki continues, "I must be sure of the future, while I work, I must assure myself of the future again and again, I always call to confirm that there is a future, without this there is no present." Farocki, "Notwendige Abwechslung und Vielfalt," 226.
2. For a comprehensive study, see Roy Grundmann, Peter J. Schwartz, and Gregory H. Williams, ed., *Labour in a Single Shot: Critical Perspectives on Antje Ehmann and Harun Farocki's Global Video Project* (Amsterdam: University of Amsterdam Press, 2021).
3. Antje Ehmann, https://www.labour-in-a-single-shot.net/en/films/, accessed July 28, 2023.
4. According to Brecht, "A photograph of Krupps or the AEG yields hardly anything about those industries." Bertolt Brecht, "Der Dreigroschprozeß" [1931], reprinted in *Bertolt Brecht—Große kommentierte Berliner und Frankfurter Ausgabe [GBA]* (Berlin, Weimar, and Frankfurt: Aufbau Verlag and Suhrkamp Verlag, 1992), vol. 21, 496.
5. Bertolt Brecht, "Questions from a Worker Who Reads" [1935], ed. John Willet and Ralph Manheim with Eric Fried, *Bertolt Brecht: Poems, 1913–1956* (New York: Methuen, 1976), 251-2.
6. Harun Faroqhi, "Glanz und Elend auf vier Rädern: Der Schrott in unser Landschaft" [1964], in Pantenburg, *Harun Farocki*, 17.
7. Faroqhi, "Glanz und Elend," 17. Interestingly the car cemetery is used as one of the settings in Godard's *One + One* (1968) and scrap metal sites recur in the films of Kluge.

8. Harun Farocki, "die agitation verwissenschaftlichen und die wissenschaft politisieren" [1969], in Pantenburg, *Harun Farocki*, 63-75.
9. Farocki, "agitation verwissenschaftlichen," 66.
10. Harun Farocki and Hartmut Bitomsky, "Zu den Filmen: H. Farocki und Gemeinschaftsproduktionen Farocki-Bitomsky," unpublished typescript, 1971, cited by Tom Holert in "Tabular Images: On *The Division of All Days* (1970) and *Something Self-Explanatory (15x)* (1971)," in *Harun Farocki: Against What? Against Whom?* ed. Antje Ehmann and Kodwo Eshun (London: Koenig Books, 2009), 82.
11. Farocki, "agitation verwissenschaftlichen," 71.
12. For example, Brecht-influenced writer Paolo Freire, author of *Pedagogy of the Oppressed* (1968), was a key figure in the reconceptualization of education. For an excellent global overview of new educational initiatives, see Tom Holert, *Politics of Learning, Politics of Space: Architecture and the Education Shock of the 1960s and 1970s* (Berlin: De Gruyter, 2021).
13. Farocki, "agitation verwissenschaftlichen," 72.
14. Farocki, 72.
15. For an insightful discussion of Farocki's pedagogical theories and their implementation in these two films, see Holert, "Tabular Images," in Ehmann, *Harun Farocki*, 75-92.
16. Harun Farocki, "Written Trailers," in Ehmann, *Harun Farock*, 222.
17. Farocki, "agitation verwissenschaftlichen," 63.
18. It is important to stress here that the theory of "operational language" that Farocki ascribes to Tretyakov was actually developed by his colleague Vinokur. I am indebted to Devin Fore's meticulous archival work tracing the emergence of the theory of operational language in the early Soviet theorists. As Fore writes, "Vinokur's analysis there furthermore revealed a new feature of this linguistic phylum, namely the mechanicity of the 'fixed and established form which has been determined beforehand.'" See Devin Fore, "The Operative Word in Soviet Factography," *October* 118 (Fall 2006): 127.
19. Fore, "Operative Word," 128.
20. Harun Farocki, "Die Rus und die Egs" [1969], in Pantenburg, *Harun Farocki*, 77. On the conundrum of filming abstraction, see Thomas Elsaesser, "Simulation and the Labour of Invisibility: Harun Farocki's Life Manuals," in "Life Remade: Critical Animation in the Digital Age," ed. Esther Leslie and Joel McKim, special issue, *Animation: An Interdisciplinary Journal* 12, no. 3 (November 2017): 214-229.
21. Sergei Eisenstein, "Notes for a Film of 'Capital,'" trans. Jay Leyda, *October* 2 (Summer 1976): 18.
22. Harmut Bitomsky and Harun Farocki, "Die Frage nach dem Kräfteverhältnis der Kämpfenden: Eine Art Lehrplan," *Internationales Forum des Jungen Films* Berlin (June 27–July 4, 1971), n.p., in Pantenburg, *Harun Farocki*, 98.
23. Karl Marx, *Capital: A Critique of Political Economy, Volume One* (1867).
24. Farocki, "Written Trailers," 223.
25. Harun Farocki, "Kapital im Klassenzimmer," in *Materialien zur Klassenschule* 2, nos. 1-2, Basis Reihe 1, Köln, 1970. Trans. Ted Fendt, "Capital in the Classroom," in *Cybernetics of the Poor*, ed. Diedrich Diederichsen and Oier Etzeberria (Berlin: Sternberg Press, 2020), 265-286.

26. This is a theme he will explore in more depth in the feature film *Betrayed*. The laws of chance and predictability as produced by shots and editing also find their way into Farocki's fictional short *Brunner is dran* (Brunner is next) (1973).
27. Production notes from the Harun Farocki website, accessed May 2021.
28. Farocki's cohort at the DFFB was populated with experimental and avantgarde filmmakers who challenged conventions. There was one exception: Wolfgang Petersen, who seemed to have learned his lessons well, entered the industry, and produced award-winning films like *Das Boot* (1981), *The Perfect Storm* (2000), *Never Ending Story* (1984), and *Troy* (2004).
29. Both Benjamin and Tretyakov developed theories that objects could carry history and memories. Already in *Something Self-Explanatory (15x)* Farocki explored the possibility of telling a story from the perspective of an object. Chapter 10 is titled "The Commodities Speak" and, amongst other narratives, provides the perspective of a piece of leather used for making the sole of a shoe.
30. See *Filmkritik*, no. 263 (November 1978). Essays include, "Das große Verbindungsrohr" (1976); "Zwischen zwei Kriegen, Filmentwurf" (*Between Two Wars*, film draft) (1977); "Zwischen zwei Kriegen, Outline" (*Between Two Wars*, Outline) (1978); "Zwischen zwei Kriegen (Anzeige)" (*Between Two Wars*, [advertisement], 1978); "Über *Zwischen Zwei Kriegen*" (About *Between Two Wars*, (1978); "Nicht nur die Zeit, auch die Erinnerung steht stille" (Not only Time but Memories Stay Quiet) (1978); "Notizen zu Alfred Sohn-Rethel, Franz Jung und Anderen" (Notes on Alfred Sohn-Rethel, Franz Jung, and Others) (1978); and "*Notiz zu zwischen zwei Kriegen*" (Notes on *Between Two Wars*) (1979).
31. Harun Farocki, *Filmkritik* [1978], in *Harun Farocki: Ich habe genug! Texte, 1976–1985*, ed. Volker Pantenburg (Berlin: Harun Farocki Institut/n.b.k., 2019), 149.
32. Harun Farocki, "Notizen zu Alfred Sohn-Rethel."
33. Harun Farocki, "*Zwischen Zwei Kriegen*."
34. See Alexander and Margerete Mitscherlich, *Unfähigkeit zu trauern* (Inability to Mourn, 1967) and Theodor W. Adorno, *What Does Coming to Terms with the Past Mean* (1967).
35. Farocki, "Written Trailers," 227. The difficulty that Germans have to discuss and debate issues related to Jewish people and to the state of Israel continues to this day. For example, in May 2019, Germany designated the Israel boycott movement (BDS) antisemitic. More recently, the terrorist attack on Israel by Hamas on October 7, 2023, has provoked Germany to censor and cancel individuals who either in the past or present support Palestinian rights, referred to the killing in Gaza as a "genocide," or have drawn parallels between the treatment of Palestinians today by the Israelis to the treatment of Jews by the Nazis. This has resulted in the cancellation of numerous art exhibitions, film screenings, prize ceremonies (when the recipient has indicated sympathy with Palestinians), and the dismissal of state employees such as professors, artists, and others. The irony is that many of those charged with antisemitism, such as artists Candice Breitz, Adam Broomberg, and 2023 Hannah Arendt prize recipient Masha Gessen, are Jewish.
36. On the explanation of and importance of Sohn-Rethel's economic theories on Farocki, see Tom Holert, "Archive, Montage, Navigation: The Function of Knowledge in the Work of Harun Farocki," unpublished lecture.
37. Harun Farocki, "*Über Zwischen Zwei Kriegen*" [1978], in Pantenburg, *Harun Farocki*, 164.

38. Farocki, "Über *Zwischen zwei Kriegen*," 165.
39. For a detailed explication of montage in *Kuhle Wampe*, see Nora M. Alter, "The Politics and Sounds of Everyday Life in *Kuhle Wampe*: Reconsidering Brecht's Film Theory," in *Sound Matters: Essays on the Acoustics of German Culture*, ed. Lutz Koepnick and Nora M. Alter (New York: Berghahn, 2004), 79-90.
40. In a subsequent full-length film on labor, *As You See* (1986), Farocki implements the concepts learned through his investigations of the *Verbundsystem*.
41. Bernd and Hilla Becher began photographing disappearing industrial architecture in the late 1950s. They exhibited their photos in a series of grids in which similar structures such as water towers, gas tanks, coal bunkers, silos, and the like are displayed, together forming a topology of structures. For a recent exhibition on the intersection between photography and industry, see *Fortschritt als Versprechen: Industriefotografie im geteilten Deutschland*, ed. Carola Jüllig and Stefanie Regina Dietzel for the Deutsches Historisches Museum, Berlin, 2023.
42. Farocki here picks up on Third Cinema theorist Julio García Espinosa, "For an Imperfect Cinema" (Cuba, 1969), who argues that meaning should be in showing the process and not trying to gloss things over with perfect images. Forty years later, Hito Steyerl updates Farocki and Espinosa: Hito Steyerl, "In Defense of the Poor Image," *e-flux journal*, no. 10 (November 2009).
43. See André Bazin, "The Ontology of the Photographic Image," *Film Quarterly* 13, no. 4 (Summer 1960): 4-9, and Philip Rosen, *Change Mummified: Cinema, Historicity, and Theory* (Minneapolis: University of Minnesota Press, 2001).
44. This, of course, is an occlusion that continues today as evidenced by Amazon's ban on filming within its warehouses.
45. Harun Farocki, "Projektbeschreibung Folder, 1983," in Pantenburg, *Harun Farocki*, 429-430. "Folder" was the working title of *An Image*.
46. Farocki, "Projektbeschreibung," 429.
47. Farocki learned a great deal about timing and pacing through his work with Straub and Huillet. This is reflected above all in the punctuated and modulated delivery of his voice-over commentaries.
48. Harun Farocki, https://www.harunfarocki.de/films/1980s/1986/as-you-see.html, accessed May 2021. Shortly before making *As You See*, Farocki wrote three reviews on the work of other filmmakers who made compilation films: "Unsichere Überprüfung" (1979) discusses Alberto Grifi and Gianfranco Baruchello's *La verifica incerta* (Uncertain Verification) (1964/1965) that is comprised entirely of footage from B films; "Geschichte der Nacht" (1979) critiques director Clemens Klopfenstein for being a "quotation Vampire," due to the reliance of quotations and citations from writers in his recent film; and most significantly, "Kamera in Aufsicht, 1983," in which Farocki reviews Michael Klier's *Der Riese* (The Giant) (1982), a film made entirely out of images from surveillance cameras.
49. Theodor W. Adorno, "The Essay as Form" [1958], in *Essays on the Essay Film*, ed. Nora M. Alter and Timothy Corrigan (New York: Columbia University Press, 2017), 70.
50. Harun Farocki, "What an Editing Room Is" [1980], in Gaensheimer, *Nachdruck / Imprint*, 82.
51. Farocki, "Editing Room," 82.

52. Theodor W. Adorno, *Theodor Adorno, Walter Benjamin, Ernst Bloch, Bertolt Brecht and Georg Lukacs: Aesthetics and Politics* (London: NLB, 1977), 129. Much has been made of this statement, including by film historian Robert B. Ray, who defines cinema as the "cross roads of magic and positivism," with film theory as a way to "break the spell." Robert B. Ray, *How a Film Theory Got Lost* (Bloomington: Indiana University Press, 2001).
53. Theodor W. Adorno, *Minima Moralia: Reflections from Damaged Life* [1951], trans. E. F. N. Jephcott (London: Verso, 1987), 94.
54. Petzold recalls that an "important book for Harun and myself was Georg K. Glaser's autobiography." Petzold models the protagonist in *Transit* on Glaser. See "Lives in Transit: An Interview with Christian Petzold" [2019], interview by Richard Porton, in *Christian Petzold Interviews*, ed. and trans. Marco Abel and Jaimey Fisher (Jackson: University Press of Mississippi, 2023), 236.
55. For a formal take on this genre, see Salomé Aguilera Skvirsky, *The Process Genre: Cinema and the Aesthetic of Labor* (Durham: Duke University Press, 2020).
56. Michael Renov, "New Subjectivities: Documentary and Self-Representation in the Post-verité Age," in *The Subject of Documentary* (Minneapolis: University of Minnesota Press, 2004), 174.
57. Farocki, "Editing Room," 80.
58. During negotiations, it emerges that NTCE workers all own shares in the company, protecting their interests.
59. "Films," Harun Farocki, Antje Ehmann, https://www.harunfarocki.de/films/2000s.html.
60. Petzold interview with Marco Abel, "'The Cinema of Identification Gets on My Nerves': An Interview with Christian Petzold" [2006], in *Christian Petzold: Interviews*, ed. Marco Abel, Aylin Bademsoy, and Jaimey Fisher (Jackson: University Press of Mississippi, 2023), 90–91.
61. In subsequent versions, Silverman's voice was substituted by that of another narrator.
62. Harun Farocki, "Workers Leaving the Factory," 232.
63. Farocki, 232.
64. Farocki, 246.
65. For a fascinating firsthand account into Farocki's research process for this film see Matthias Rajmann, *Aus der Recherche für Zum Vergleich* (Berlin: Harun Farocki Institut, 2021).
66. Dziga Vertov, "On Kino Pravda" [1924], in *Kino-Eye: The Writings of Dziga Vertov*, ed. Annette Michelson, trans. Kevin O'Brien (Berkeley: University of California Press, 1984), 45.

3. CRITIC AS FILMMAKER

The epigraph is from Harun Farocki, "'Keep the Horizon Open': An Interview with Harun Farocki" [2014], *Senses of Cinema*, no. 79 (July 2016).
1. *Filmkritik*, no. 2-4 (1984).
2. Robert Bresson, *Notes on the Cinematograph* [1975], trans. Jonathan Griffin (New York: New York Review of Books, 2016), 10.

3. *The Song of Ceylon* was directed by Basil Wright and produced under the auspices of the GPO (General Post Office), John Grierson's production unit housed within the Post Office in Britain during the 1930s. For an analysis of *The Song of Ceylon* as an essay film, see Nora M. Alter, *The Essay Film After Fact and Fiction* (New York: Columbia University Press, 2018).
4. Unpublished conversation between Harun Farocki, Michael Baute, and Stefan Pethke (October 10, 2008). I am grateful to Volker Pantenburg for this reference.
5. Harun Farocki, "Kamera in Aufsicht" [1983], in *Harun Farocki: Ich habe genug! Texte, 1976–1985*, ed. Volker Pantenburg (Berlin: Harun Farocki Institut/n.b.k., 2019), 432.
6. For a comprehensive tracking of Farocki's conceptualization of operational images, see Volker Pantenburg's "Working Images: Harun Farocki and the Operational Image," in *Image Operations: Visual Media and Political Conflict*, ed. Jens Eder and Charlotte Klunk (Manchester, UK: Manchester University Press, 2017), 49–61. See also Trevor Paglen, "Operational Images," e-flux, November 2014.
7. Gilles Deleuze, "Postscript on Control Societies" [1990], *October* 59 (Winter 1992): 3–7.
8. In his comments on Peter Lorre's acting in *Man Is Man*, Brecht writes, "For over and above the meaning of individual sentences a quite specific gest was being brought out here which admittedly depended on knowing what the individual sentences meant but at the same time used this meaning only as a means to an end." He continues, "The speeches' content was made up of contradictions, and the actor had not to make the spectator identify himself with individual sentences and so get caught up in contradictions, but to keep out of them." Bertolt Brecht, "The Question of Criteria for Judging Actors" [1931], in *Brecht on Theatre*, ed. and trans. John Willet (New York: Hill and Wang, 1964), 54.
9. In addition to Brecht's theory of *Gestus*, Farocki was influenced by Marcel Mauss's *Techniques, Technology and Civilisation* which discusses the impact of technology on human movement. Marcel Mauss, *Techniques, Technology and Civilisation* [1935] (New York: Durkheim Press/Berghahn Books, 2020); and Vilém Flusser, *Gestures*[1991], trans. Nancy Ann Roth (Minneapolis: Univeristy of Minnesota Press, 2014).
10. Heiner Müller, "Intelligence Without Experience: An Interview with Harun Farocki" [1981], in *Germania*, trans. Bernard and Caroline Schütze (New York: Semiotext(e), 1990), 163.
11. The full descriptive title reads: *Discourse on the Progress of the Prolonged War of Liberation in Viet Nam and the Events Leading Up to It as Illustration of the Necessity for Armed Resistance Against Oppression and on the Attempts of the United States of America to Destroy the Foundations of Revolution*. On a detailed analysis of the play and its placement within the larger context of protest theater against the Vietnam War, see Nora M. Alter, *Vietnam Protest Theatre: The Television War on Stage* (Bloomington: Indiana University Press, 1996).
12. In both *Taste for Life* and *On Display: Peter Weiss*, Rosa Merzedes (sic Farocki's pseudonym) is credited as cameraman and editor, respectively.
13. See Vilém Flusser, *Towards a Philosophy and Photography* (London: Reaktion Books, 2000); and Vilém Flusser, *Into the Universe of Technical Images* (Minneapolis: University of Minnesota Press, 2011).
14. Vilém Flusser, "Television, Image and Political Space in the light of the Romanian Revolution," April 7, 1990, Kunsthalle Budapest, 24:32, https://www.youtube.com/watch?v=QFTaY2u4NvI.

15. It should be noted that Flusser insists on the word "magicised" and not "*Entzauberung*" (disenchantment) which would lead us to Max Weber.
16. Harun Farocki, "Written Trailers," in *Harun Farocki: Against What? Against Whom?*, ed. Antje Ehmann and Kodwo Eshun (London: Koenig Books, 2009), 225.
17. Harun Farocki and Christa Blümlinger, "The ABCs of the Film Essay" [2015], in *Essays on the Essay Film*, ed. Nora M. Alter and Timothy Corrigan (New York: Columbia University Press, 2017), 304.
18. Wetzel situates Farocki's film as follows: "As if unintentionally taken from 'real life,' Harun Farocki's feature film, *Betrayed*, was for me another surprise of the film year 85.... The story comes from the last pages of a newspaper: a man kills his wife; her sister takes her place and nobody notices. Farocki writes that one can take this story both as a metaphor and as a simple plot. Similar to films by Hitchcock, Sirk and Lubitsch, *Betrayed*, is both deceptively self-evident and dizzyingly profound. One of the most amazing truths is that one only values what one loves." Kraft Wetzel, "Was antwortet der Neue Deutsche Film auf Zimmerman und Hollywood?," *Film*, no. 5 (1986): 18.
19. Harun Farocki, "Brief vom 8. November 1983," Johannes Beringer's private collection.
20. Wetzel, "Neue Deutsche Film," 18.
21. Harun Farocki, "Ich habe genug!" [1985], in Pantenburg, *Harun Farocki*, 446.
22. Katrin Bettina Müller, "Das Unaussprechliche," review of *Betrayed*, by Harun Farocki, *Die Tageszeitung*, February 15, 1990, https://taz.de/Archiv-Suche/!1780321&s/.
23. Ronald Glomb, *Volksblatt*, February 16, 1990.
24. Farocki would use fax technology for his most personal and intimate correspondence to ensure that there would always be a record.
25. Piero Scaruffi, "The 1,000 Best Films of All Time: The 1980s," Piero Scaruffi, https://www.scaruffi.com/cinema/chro980.html.
26. Harun Farocki, "Vertauschte Frauen" [1980], in Pantenburg, *Harun Farocki*, 261.
27. Farocki, "Vertauschte Frauen," 264. An earlier version of *Betrayed* exists in the form of Farocki's unpublished and undated screenplay *Zwei Schwestern* (Two Sisters).
28. Farocki, 264.
29. Farocki, 264.
30. As Petzold recollects, when he studied with Farocki they would watch many films, often with shots of naked women, "but the films that got us excited were always about the one who desires." James Lattimer, "'As If We Were Dreaming It': Christian Petzold's *Undine*" [2020], in *Christian Petzold: Interviews*, ed. and trans. Marco Abel and Jaimey Fisher (Jackson: University Press of Mississippi, 2023), 248.
31. Andre Simonoviescz, "Mord in Werbeblock," *Tip Berlin*, no. 4, February 1990, 53.
32. Harun Farocki, *Zehn, zwanzig, dreißig vierzig: Fragment einer Autobiographie* (Berlin: Harun Farocki Institut/n.b.k., 2017), 49.
33. Caillois observes, "A characteristic of play, in fact, is that it creates no wealth or goods, thus differing from work or art." Work should be "an occasion of pure waste." He continues, "As for the professionals—the boxers, cyclists, jockeys, or actors who earn their living in the ring, track or hippodrome or on the stage... It is clear they are not players but workers." Roger Caillois, *Man, Play, and Games* [1958] (Champagne Urbana: University of Illinois Press, 2001), 5-6.

34. Müller, "Das Unaussprechliche"; Ronald Glomb, *Volksblatt*, Feb 15, 1990.
35. Müller.
36. This insight may have been offered by Farocki, who tended to promote his films in the form of reviews, or interviews with himself, often using the alias Rosa Mercedes.
37. Simonoviescz, "Mord in Werbeblock," 53.
38. Simonoviescz.
39. Harun Farocki, "Bresson ein Stilist" [1984], in *Harun Farocki: Ich habe genug!*, 438. This was, incidentally, Farocki's last contribution to the journal, written before he resigned from the editorial board but published several months after.
40. Glomb, *Volksblatt*.
41. Simonoviescz, "Mord in Werbeblock," 53.
42. Simonoviescz.

4. WAR

The epigraphs for this chapter originate from Frantz Fanon, *The Wretched of the Earth* [1961] (New York: Grove Press, 1963); and Harun Farocki, "Cross Influence/Soft Montage" [2002], in *Harun Farocki: Against What? Against Whom?*, ed. Antje Ehmann and Kodwo Eshun (London: Koenig Books, 2009), 74.

1. Harun Farocki, "Risking His Life: Images of Holger Meins" [1998], in *Nachdruck / Imprint: Texte / Writings*, ed. Susanne Gaensheimer and Nicolaus Schafhausen (New York: Lukas & Sternberg, 2001), 272.
2. *Loin du Vietnam* (*Far from Vietnam*), dir. Jean-Luc Godard, Joris Ivens, William Klein, Claude Lelouch, Chris Marker, Alain Resnais, and Agnès Varda (1967). The film was conceived of and organized by Marker, who sought to bring like-minded filmmakers to the Democratic Republic of Vietnam to film the war. When the North Vietnamese government denied travel/filming visas to all but one of the members of the collective (Ivens), the filmmakers were forced to reconceptualize their project.
3. Michel Foucault, "The Confession of the Flesh: A Conversation with Alain Grosrichard, et al." [1977], in *Power/Knowledge: Selected Interviews & Other Writings, 1972–1977*, ed. Colin Gordon (New York: Pantheon Books, 1980), 194.
4. *Inextinguishable Fire* is one of Farocki's best-known films from his early period. It continues to have a vivid afterlife and is screened regularly in programs or installed alongside Farocki's contemporary work (most recently in his 2011 solo MoMA exhibition). It is also the source of filmmaker Jill Godmilow's *What Farocki Taught* (1998).
5. Theodor W. Adorno, "The Essay as Form" [1958], in *Essays on the Essay Film*, ed. Nora M. Alter and Timothy Corrigan (New York: Columbia University Press, 2017), 76.
6. About this film, Georges Didi-Huberman writes, "'Putting one's hand in the fire'—to signify a moral or political engagement, one's responsibility when faced with a truthful content. As though it had become necessary, in our current historic conditions, to truly dare 'to put (*legen*) one's hand in the fire' in order to better understand, to better read (*lesen*) this world from which we are suffering—which we must state, repeat, claim to be suffering from—yet which we refuse to suffer (*leiden*)." Georges Didi-Huberman, "How to Open Your Eyes," in Ehmann, *Harun Farocki*, 42-43.

7. For an excellent analysis, see Diedrich Diederichsen's *Napalm Death*. Diederichsen links Farocki's meditation on napalm to I. G. Farben's manufacture of Zyklon B Gas used in the concentration camps. He concludes: "The *tertium comparationis* between the Nazi regime and Vietnam War would therefore not be described from a perspective of geopolitics or culture war (Kulturkampf) but from a perspective critical of capitalism, one which specifies the roles of corporations and describes them according to the way they are organized under specific capitalist conditions." Diedrich Diederichsen, "Napalm Death," in Ehmann, *Harun Farocki*, 55.
8. In an interview three decades later, Farocki comments: "I'm ashamed that in my film I use examples of Hiroshima and Vietnam and *don't* say Auschwitz." "Jill Godmilow (and Harun Farocki)" [1998], in *A Critical Cinema 4: Interviews with Independent Filmmakers*, ed. Scott MacDonald (Berkeley: University of California Press, 2005), 154. In a slight variation in another discussion with the two filmmakers, Farocki explains, "Recently at a presentation it occurred to me that Hiroshima and Vietnam were mentioned but not Auschwitz. I tend to think that the monstrous war of the USA in Vietnam not only shocked but also unburdened us (the Germans). 'We are not the only barbarians.'" Jennifer Horne and Jonathan Kahana, "A Perfect Replica: An Interview with Harun Farocki and Jill Godmillow," *Afterimage* 26, no. 3 (November/December 1998): n.p. A similar sentiment is expressed in Georg Tabori's drama *Cannibals* (1968) in which a character exclaims, "I was happy because I realized that everybody is a murderer, not only me."
9. Farocki includes this oblique reference to Heinar Kipphardt's documentary play *In der Sache J. Robert Oppenheimer* (In the Matter of J. Robert Oppenheimer) (1964).
10. Farocki explains, "In the case of a film that is political by virtue of its context, the discussion about aesthetics becomes one about aesthetics of effect." Harun Faroqhi, "Staubsauger oder Maschinenpistolen: Ein Wanderkino für Technologen" [1968], in *Harun Farocki: Meine Nächte mit den Linken; Texte, 1964–1975*, ed. Volker Pantenburg (Berlin: Harun Farocki Institut/n.b.k., 2018), 59. For an English version, see Harun Farocki and Ted Fendt, "Vacuum Cleaner or Submachine Gun: A Traveling Cinema for Engineers," *Grey Room* 79 (Spring 2020): 93–95.
11. As Farocki recalls, "The producer at WDR, Reinhold W. Thiel, thought that the actors' way of speaking and acting was not stylized enough, or stylized in the wrong way and proposed that all the actors should be dubbed by two voices. Night after night I edited the working prints into synchronized loops." Harun Farocki, "Written Trailers," in Ehmann, *Harun Farocki*, 222.
12. Tom Holert has assembled an invaluable resource of material related in Tom Holert, ed., *Harun Farocki: Before Your Eyes—Vietnam; Commentary, Document, Material* (Berlin: Harun Farocki Institut and Motto Books, 2017).
13. Farocki, "Risking His Life," 272.
14. "Celebrated" photographs include Malcom Browne's 1963 photo of the self-immolation of Thich Quang Duc, Ron Haeberle's 1968 photographs of the My Lai Massacre, and Nick Ut's 1972 image of Kim Phuc running naked and burning from a napalm attack.
15. An overview of Farocki's guerrilla tactics and their relation to his cinematic practice may be found in Tilman Baumgärtel, *Vom Guerillakino zum Essay Film: Harun Farocki Werkmonographie eines Autorenfilmers* (Berlin: b_books, 1998); and more recently in Antje

Ehmann's "Megaphone, Chocolate Kisses, and Spray Cans: Harun Farocki's Guerilla Tactics," in *The Physiognomy of Power: Harun Farocki/Florentina Pakosta*, ed. Thorsten Sadowsky (Salzburg: Verlag für moderne Kunst, 2021), 166-168.

16. Harun Farocki, *Zehn, zwanzig, dreißig, vierzig: Fragment einer Autobiographie* (Berlin: Harun Farocki Institut/n.b.k., 2017), 189-190.
17. On the paratextual in literature, see Gérard Genette, *Paratexts: Thresholds of Interpretation* (Cambridge: Cambridge University Press, 1987).
18. Harun Farocki, "Dog from the Freeway," in Gaensheimer, *Nachdruck / Imprint*, 116.
19. Walter Benjamin, "Hardware" [1928], in *One-Way Street*, ed. Michael Jennings (Cambridge: Harvard University Press, 2016), 84.
20. Harun Farocki, "Reality Would Have to Begin" [1992], in *Harun Farocki: Working on the Sight-Lines*, ed. Thomas Elsaesser (Amsterdam: Amsterdam University Press, 2004), 193-201.
21. As the decade of the 1980s advanced, more filmmakers and artists had their films transferred to video to reach a broader public. German filmmakers such as Wim Wenders and Werner Herzog were quick to embrace video technology, whereas some filmmakers such as Ulrike Ottinger resisted due to the degradation of the formal aesthetic qualities of the medium. Farocki's *Images of the World and the Inscription of War* reached international audiences thanks to its video format that included English subtitles.
22. "Minutes of the Discussion on *Before Your Eyes—Vietnam* at the 6th Duisburg Film Week [1982]," in *Harun Farocki: Before Your Eyes—Vietnam; Commentary, Document, Material*, 19.
23. Farocki, "Dog from the Freeway," 160.
24. Paul Virilio, *War and Cinema: The Logistics of Perception* [1984], trans. Patrick Camiller (London: Verso, 1989), 4.
25. Harun Farocki, "The ABCs of the Film Essay" [2015], in Alter, *Essay Film*, 300.
26. Artavazd Peleshyan, "Distance Montage, or the Theory of Distance" [1971/72], in *Documentary Films of the Armenian Soviet Republic*, ed. Erika and Moritz de Hadeln, Garegin Sakojan, and Hans Joachim Schlegel (self-published, 1989), 89.
27. Peleshyan, "Distance Montage," 84.
28. Peleshyan, 88.
29. Peleshyan, 90.
30. Harun Farocki, "Über: *Bilder der Welt und Inschrift des Krieges*" [1988], in *Harun Farocki: Unregelmäßig, nicht regellos; Texte, 1986–2000*, ed. Tom Holert (Harun Farocki Institut/n.b.k., 2021), 134.
31. Harun Farocki, "Geschichte" [1975], in Pantenburg, *Harun Farocki*, 199-204.
32. Peleshyan, "Distance Montage," 97.
33. Farocki, 'Reality Would Have to Begin," 162.
34. Farocki, "Cross Influence/Soft Montage," 74.
35. Elsaesser provides a careful analysis of *Respite*, both its dialogue with Farocki's earlier anonymous depiction of camp inmates in *Images of the World* and as he works against an "epistemology of forgetting." Thomas Elsaesser, "Holocaust Memory as the Epistemology of Forgetting? Re-wind and Postponement in Respite," in Ehmann, *Harun Farocki*, 57-68. Farocki's careful mode of analysis here is clearly in dialogue with the research collective Forensic Architecture.

36. Harun Farocki and Hito Steyerl, "A Magical Imitation of Reality," *Cahier #2* (Milan: Kaleidoscope Press, 2011), 23.
37. Farocki, "Reality Would Have to Begin," 197.
38. As Klaus Kreimeier concludes in his observations on the film, "Like the revolutionaries of 1789 who wanted people to put their trust in the guillotine, the new power in Romania wants people to put their trust in the media." Klaus Kreimeier, "Enlargement of a View: About *Videograms of a Revolution*," in Ehmann, *Harun Farocki*, 185.
39. Harun Farocki, "War Always Finds a Way," in *HF/RG*, ed. Chantal Pontbriand (Paris: Jeu de Paume, 2009), 106.
40. On how operational images are transforming the media landscape, see Jussi Parikka, *Operational Images: From the Visual to the Invisual* (Minneapolis: University of Minnesota Press, 2023).
41. Farocki, "War Always Finds," 103.
42. Farocki, 108.
43. Max Bense, "On the Essay and Its Prose" [1948], trans. Margit Grieb, in Alter, *Essay Film*, 49-59.
44. The role of empathy in Farocki's works is explored in the 2016 Tàpies Foundation exhibition: "Harun Farocki: Another Kind of Empathy," curated by Antje Ehmann and Carles Guerre.
45. Rembert Hüser, "Nine Minutes in the Yard: A Conversation with Harun Farocki" [1999], in Elsaesser, *Harun Farocki*, 302.
46. Farocki, "Cross Influence/Soft Montage," 71.
47. Farocki, 73.
48. Theodor W. Adorno and Thomas Y. Levin, "Transparencies on Film" [1966], *New German Critique*, no. 24/25 (Autumn-Winter 1981-1982): 203.
49. Harun Farocki, "Eye/Machine III," https://www.harunfarocki.de/installations/2000s/2003/eye-machine-iii.html, accessed May 2021.
50. Early on in *Sans Soleil* (1982), Chris Marker contemplates the way in which computer imaging devices could change history by creating new images. More recently, filmmaker artist Hito Steyerl has explored the developing role of AI and the metaverse in recent works such as *SocialSim* (2020).
51. Farocki, "War Always Finds," 110.
52. Over four decades earlier, Armand Gatti conceived of a satirical play, *V comme Vietnam* (1967), set on the West Coast, involving a virtual war in Vietnam directed by a computer.
53. Harun Farocki, "Jeux sérieux," *Trafic* 78 (Summer 2011): 55-63.
54. Harun Farocki, "Anaesthetising the Image: *Immersion*, Harun Farocki," in *Killer Images: Documentary Film, Memory and the Performance of Violence*, ed. Joram Ten Brink and Joshua Oppenheimer (London: Wallflower Press, 2012), 73.
55. Farocki, "Magical Imitation," 21.
56. Farocki explains, "This has nothing to do with the fighting of war, rather, it is used to enhance a reality effect. It is the same as in a fictional film when secondary scenes are inserted that have nothing to do with the narrative." Farocki, "Jeux sérieux," 60.
57. Antje Ehmann and Harun Farocki, "Serious Games," in *Serious Games: War—Media—Art*, ed. Ralf Beil and Antje Ehmann (Berlin: Hatje Canz, 2011), 26.

58. Ehmann and Farocki, "Serious Games," 24.
59. Ehmann and Farocki, 27.
60. In their 2008 installation *Feasting or Flying*, Farocki and Ehmann apply a similar methodology to assemble a series of cinematic sequences depicting male suicide.

5. AN IMAGE LEXICON, OR TOWARDS A MEDIA ARCHEOLOGY

The chapter epigraph comes from Harun Farocki and Wolfgang Ernst, "Towards an Archive for Visual Concepts, Part 2: 'A Cinematographic Thesaurus," in *Harun Farocki: Working on the Sight-Lines*, ed. Thomas Elsaesser (Amsterdam: Amsterdam University Press, 2004), 281.

1. Harun Farocki, "Über die Arbeit mit Bildern im Fernsehen" [1974], in *Harun Farocki: Meine Nächte mit den Linken; Texte, 1964–1975*, ed. Volker Pantenburg (Berlin: Harun Farocki Institut/n.b.k., 2018), 173.
2. Harun Farocki, "Bilder aus dem Fernsehen" [1973], in Pantenburg, *Harun Farocki*, 144-45.
3. Farocki, in Ernst and Farocki, "Cinematographic Thesaurus," 273.
4. Harun Farocki and Hito Steyerl, "A Magical Imitation of Reality," *Cahier #2* (Milan: Kaleidoscope Press, 2011), 20.
5. Roland Barthes, "Myth Today," in *Mythologies* [1957] (London: Vintage Books, 1993), 146.
6. In 1968, a right-wing activist shot Dutschke in an assassination attempt. Farocki, with Sander, made the short *Drei Schüsse auf Rudi* (Three Shots at Rudi) (1968).
7. As Jonathan Sterne argues, records were initially intended for courtroom use to produce more accurate accounts of trial proceedings. Their use in musical reproduction was an unintended consequence. For a fascinating history of the development of recorded music, see Jonathan Sterne, *The Audible Past: Cultural Origins of Sound Reproduction* (Durham, NC: Duke University Press, 2003).
8. Ernst, in Ernst and Farocki, "Cinematographic Thesaurus," 265.
9. Farocki, in Ernst and Farocki, "Cinematographic Thesaurus," 279.
10. For an insightful essay on how Farocki and Ujica analyze media images, see Benjamin Young, "On Media and Democratic Politics: *Videograms of a Revolution*," in Elsaesser, *Harun Farocki*, 245-260.
11. Farocki, in Ernst and Farocki, "Cinematographic Thesaurus," 279.
12. Harun Farocki, "What Ought to Be Done" [1975-76], in *What Ought to Be Done: Document, Commentary, Material*, ed. Harun Farocki Institut, trans. Volker Pantenburg and Michael Turnbull (Berlin: Harun Farocki Institut/Motto Books, 2016), 3-8.
13. Farocki, "What Ought to Be Done," 4-5.
14. Harun Farocki, "John Cassavetes: *Too Late Blues*" [1982], in *Harun Farocki: Ich habe genug! Texte, 1976–1985*, ed. Volker Pantenburg (Berlin: Harun Farocki Institut/n.b.k., 2019), 375.
15. Harun Farocki, "Workers Leaving a Factory" [1995], in Elsaesser, *Harun Farocki*, 238.
16. In his poignant homage to Farocki, Raymond Bellour uses *Expression of Hands* as a touchstone to discuss Farocki's invaluable contribution to an understanding of cinema. See Raymond Bellour, "Pourquoi Harun nous était si précieux," *Trafic* 93 (Spring 2015): 66-74. For theorized body techniques, see Marcel Mauss, "Technology of the Body" [1934],

in *Incorporations*, ed. Jonathan Crary and Sanford Kwinter (New York: Zone Books, 1992), 454–477.

17. Vilém Flusser, *Gestures* [1991], trans. Nancy Ann Roth (Minneapolis: University of Minnesota Press, 2014).
18. In his laudatory review of Ingemo Engström's *Kampf um ein Kind* (Struggle Over a Child, 1975), Farocki praises her film because it "is one of the few, in which one sees that the pieces are assembled. This alone would not be enough; the pieces must be put together in a way that both piece and whole remain present in the reception." Harun Farocki, "Kampf un ein Kind" [1975], in Pantenburg, *Harun Farocki*, 227.
19. Flusser, *Gestures*, 70.
20. Harun Farocki, "Das Tal der tanzenden Witwen" [1975], in Pantenburg, *Harun Farocki*, 230.
21. Barthes, "Myth Today," 109.
22. For an insightful critique on how screen technology has changed natural vision see Jonathan Crary, *Scorched Earth: Beyond the Digital Age to a Post Capitalist World* (New York: Verso, 2022).
23. Farocki citing Ernst in Harun Farocki, "Bilderschatz" [1999], in *Harun Farocki: Lerne das Einfachste! Texte, 2001–2014*, ed. Volker Pantenburg (Berlin: Harun Farocki Institut/n.b.k., 2022), 26. Farocki's lengthy citation of Ernst takes place at the end of his lecture in response to a question from the audience. Farocki's answer is not included in the English reprints of "A Cinematographic Thesaurus."
24. Current research in AI suggests that this has already been achieved. A collaborative MIT project, *In Event of Moon Disaster* (2019), by Halsey Burgund and Francesca Panetta takes a contingency speech written for Nixon in the advent that the Apollo 13 space mission were to have been a failure and combines it with documentary footage of Nixon to produce an alternative history. See "In Event of Moon Disaster," MIT Center for Advanced Virtuality, https://moondisaster.org/.

Writings by Harun Farocki

MONOGRAPHS

Farocki, Harun. *Bilderschatz*. Cologne: Walther König, 2001.
—. *Critica de la mirada: Textos de Harun Farocki*. Ed. Inge Stache. Buenos Aires: Editorial Altamira, 2003.
—. *Desconfiar de las imágenes*. Buenos Aires: Caja Negra, 2013.
—. *Diagrams: Images from Ten Films*. Ed. Benedikt Reichenbach. Berlin: Verlag der Buchhandlung Walther König, 2014.
—. *Eine indexicalische Spur: Register und Nachträge, 1964–2014*. Ed. Volker Pantenburg. Berlin: Harun Farocki Institut, n.b.k., and Verlag der Buchhandlung Walther König, 2023.
—. *Films*. Trans. Bernard Rival, Monique Rival, Pierre Rusch, and Bénédicte Vilgrain. Courbevoie, France: Théâtre Typographique, 2007.
—. *Harun Farocki: Ich habe Genug! Texte, 1976–1985*. Ed. Volker Pantenburg. Berlin: Harun Farocki Institut, n.b.k., and Verlag der Buchhandlung Walther König, 2019.
—. *Harun Farocki: Lerne das Einfachste! Texte, 2001–2014*. Ed. Volker Pantenburg. Berlin: Harun Farocki Institut, n.b.k., and Verlag der Buchhandlung Walther König, 2023.
—. *Harun Farocki: Meine Nächte mit den Linken; Texte, 1964–1975*. Ed. Volker Pantenburg. Berlin: Harun Farocki Institut, n.b.k., and Verlag der Buchhandlung Walther König, 2018.
—. *Harun Farocki: Über Ici et ailleurs / On Ici et ailleurs*. Trans. Ted Fendt. Berlin: Harun Farocki Institut/Motto Books, 2018.
—. *Harun Farocki: Unregelmäßig, nicht regellos; Texte, 1986–2000*. Ed. Tom Holert. Berlin: Harun Farocki Institut, n.b.k., and Verlag der Buchhandlung Walther König, 2021.
—. *Nachdruck / Imprint: Texte / Writings*. Ed. Susanne Gaensheimer and Nicolaus Schafhausen. Berlin: Vorwerk 8/Lukas & Sternberg, 2001.
—. *Reconnaître et poursuivre*. Courbevoie, France: Théâtre Typographique, 2002.
—. *Reconnaître et poursuivre*. Courbevoie, France: Théâtre Typographique, 2017.
—. *Rote Berta Geht Ohne Liebe Wandern*. Cologne: Strzelecki Books, 2009.
—. *Zehn, zwanzig, dreißig, vierzig*. Ed. Marius Babias and Antje Ehmann. Berlin: Harun Farocki Institut, n.b.k., and Verlag der Buchhandlung Walther König, 2017.
Farocki, Harun, and Kaja Silverman. *Speaking About Godard*. New York: New York University Press, 1998.

ESSAYS IN ENGLISH

For a comprehensive list of individual writings in German, see Harun Farocki Institut, https://archiv.harun-farocki-institut.org/de/person/harun-farocki/.

Farocki, Harun. "American Framing: Notes for a Film about Malls." In *Nachdruck / Imprint: Texte / Writings*, ed. Susanne Gaensheimer and Nicolaus Schafhausen, 292–305. Berlin: Vorwerk 8/Lukas & Sternberg, 2001.
—. "Betrogen." In *Harun Farocki: A Retrospective*, ed. Goethe Institutes of the U.S. and Canada, 13. New York: Goethe House, 1991.
—. "Biographical Note." In *Harun Farocki: A Retrospective*, ed. Goethe Institutes of the U.S. and Canada, 3. New York: Goethe House, 1991.
—. "Bresson, a Stylist." In *Harun Farocki: A Retrospective*, ed. Goethe Institutes of the U.S. and Canada, 18–21. New York: Goethe House, 1991.
—. "A Cigarette End..." In *Nachdruck / Imprint: Texte / Writings*, ed. Susanne Gaensheimer and Nicolaus Schafhausen, 42–77. Berlin: Vorwerk 8/Lukas & Sternberg, 2001.
—. "Cinema of Shrinkage." In *Shrinking Cities, Volume 1: International Research*, ed. Philipp Oswalt, 348–359. Ostfildern, Germany: Hatje Cantz, 2005.
—. "Commentary from the Film 'Bilder der Welt und Inschrift des Krieges'." *Discourse* 15, no. 3 (Spring 1993): 78–92.
—. "Controlling Observation." In *Nachdruck / Imprint: Texte / Writings*, ed. Susanne Gaensheimer and Nicolaus Schafhausen, 306–322. Berlin: Vorwerk 8/Lukas & Sternberg, 2001.
—. "Cross Influence/Soft Montage." In *Harun Farocki: One Image Doesn't Take the Place of the Previous One*, ed. Michèle Thériault, 139–144. Montréal: Galerie Leonard & Bina Ellen Art Gallery, 2008. Catalogue of a traveling exhibition held first at the Leonard & Bina Ellen Art Gallery, Montréal, in 2007.
—. "A Cut, or Television-Makers' Revenge." In *Nachdruck / Imprint: Texte / Writings*, ed. Susanne Gaensheimer and Nicolaus Schafhausen, 214–217. Berlin: Vorwerk 8/Lukas & Sternberg, 2001.
—. "Diary: Buildings—Film and Exhibition of Audio-Visual Material." In *Harun Farocki: Weiche Montagen, Soft Montages*, ed. Yilmaz Dziewior, 94–97. Bregenz, Austria: Kunsthaus Bregenz, 2011.
—. "Diary: Immersion (Working Title)." In *Harun Farocki: Weiche Montagen, Soft Montages*, ed. Yilmaz Dziewior, 48–50. Bregenz, Austria: Kunsthaus Bregenz, 2011.
—. "Diary: War Diary." In *Harun Farocki: Weiche Montagen, Soft Montages*, ed. Yilmaz Dziewior, 62–80. Bregenz, Austria: Kunsthaus Bregenz, 2011.
—. "Difficult Questions." In *Nachdruck / Imprint: Texte / Writings*, ed. Susanne Gaensheimer and Nicolaus Schafhausen, 218–221. Berlin: Vorwerk 8/Lukas & Sternberg, 2001.
—. "Dog from the Freeway." In *Nachdruck / Imprint: Texte / Writings*, ed. Susanne Gaensheimer and Nicolaus Schafhausen, 112–170. Berlin: Vorwerk 8/Lukas & Sternberg, 2001.
—. "Everyday Myth." Trans. Ted Fendt. *Grey Room*, no. 79 (Spring 2020).
—. "Film Courses in Art Schools." Trans. Ted Fendt. *Grey Room*, no. 79 (Spring 2020).
—. "Hairline Cross." In *Serious Games: War–Media–Art*, ed. Ralf Beil and Antje Ehmann, 95–97. Ostfildern, Germany: Hatje Cantz, 2011.

———. "Harun Farocki on a New Kind of Cinematographic Thesaurus." *KW Magazine* 1 (2001), 14-15.
———. "History of Nothing, 1960-1962." *#Videotapes*, June 2014.
———. "How to Live in the FRG." In *Harun Farocki: Against What? Against Whom?*, ed. Antje Ehmann and Kodwo Eshun, 163-165. London: Koenig Books, 2009.
———. "I Believed to See Prisoners/Eye." In *CTRL [SPACE]: Rhetorics of Surveillance from Bentham to Big Brother*, ed. Ursula Frohne, Thomas Y. Levin, and Peter Weibel, 422-425. Cambridge, MA: MIT Press, 2002.
———. "The Images Should Testify Against Themselves." In *Harun Farocki: Another Kind of Empathy*, ed. Antje Ehmann and Carles Guerra, 86-103. London: Koenig Books, 2016.
———. "The Industrialization of Thought." *Discourse* 15, no. 3 (Spring 1993): 76-77.
———. "Kino wie noch nie/Cinema Like Never Before." In *Kino wie noch nie/Cinema Like Never Before*, ed. Antje Ehmann and Harun Farocki, 12-21. Cologne: Walther König/Generali Foundation, 2006.
———. "Music Rules." In *Nachdruck / Imprint: Texte / Writings*, ed. Susanne Gaensheimer and Nicolaus Schafhausen, 226-229. Berlin: Vorwerk 8/Lukas & Sternberg, 2001.
———. "Necessary Variation and Variety." Trans. Ted Fendt. *Grey Room*, no. 79 (Spring 2020).
———. "On Image Questions: Harun Farocki Responds to Texte zur Kunst." *Texte zur Kunst*, no. 95 (September 2014): 62-66.
———. "On the Documentary." *e-flux* (2015).
———. "Phantom Images." In *Public* 29 (2004), 12-24.
———. "Points and Topics." In *Nachdruck / Imprint: Texte / Writings*, ed. Susanne Gaensheimer and Nicolaus Schafhausen, 222-225. Berlin: Vorwerk 8/Lukas & Sternberg, 2001.
———. "Reality Would Have to Begin." *Documents*, nos. 1-2 (1992): 136-146.
———. *Rétrospective / Exposition 23 Novembre 2017–14 Janvier 2018*, 2-5. Paris: Centre Pompidou, 2017.
———. "Risking His Life: Images of Holger Meins." In *Nachdruck / Imprint: Texte / Writings*, ed. Susanne Gaensheimer and Nicolaus Schafhausen, 268-290. Berlin: Vorwerk 8/Lukas & Sternberg, 2001.
———. "Serious Games." In *Visibility Machines: Harun Farocki and Trevor Paglen*, ed. Niels van Tomme, 113-120. Baltimore, MD: Center for Art, Design and Visual Culture, 2014.
———. "Serious Games. An Introduction." In *Serious Games: War–Media–Art*, ed. Ralf Beil and Antje Ehmann, 24-27. Ostfildern, Germany: Hatje Cantz, 2011.
———. "Shot/Countershot: The Most Important Expression in Filmic Law of Value." In *Nachdruck / Imprint: Texte / Writings*, ed. Susanne Gaensheimer and Nicolaus Schafhausen, 86-111. Berlin: Vorwerk 8/Lukas & Sternberg, 2001.
———. "The Silver and the Cross." In *Das Potosí-Prinzip: Wie können wir das Lied des Herrn im fremden Land singen? Koloniale Bildproduktion in der globalen Ökonomie*, ed. Alice Creischer, Max Jorge Hinderer, and Andreas Siekmann, 37-39. Cologne: Walther König, 2010.
———. "Snowdrops Bloom in September." Trans. Ted Fendt. *Grey Room*, no. 79 (Spring 2020).
———. "Somewhere Over the Rainbow: Ariel." In *Aki Kaurusmäki*, ed. Ralph Eue and Linda Söffker, 49-61. Berlin: Bertz + Fischer Verlag, 2006.
———. "Stop Coughing!" In *Jean-Marie Straub and Danièle Huillet*, ed. Ted Fendt, 154-155. Vienna: Synema, 2016.
———. "Substandard." In *Nachdruck / Imprint: Texte / Writings*, ed. Susanne Gaensheimer and Nicolaus Schafhausen, 248-266. Berlin: Vorwerk 8/Lukas & Sternberg, 2001.

—. "Sursis–Respite–Aufschub." *Intermédialités/Intermediality*, no. 11 (Spring 2008), 97-122.
—. "To Love to Work and to Work to Love: A Conversation about 'Passion.'" *Discourse* 15, no. 3 (Spring 1993): 57-75.
—. "Untitled." In *Videogramme einer Revolution von Harun Farocki/Andrej Ujica*. Berlin: Basis-Film Verleih, 1992.
—. "Vacuum Cleaner or Submachine Gun: A Traveling Cinema for Engineers." Trans. Ted Fendt. *Grey Room*, no. 79 (Spring 2020).
—. "War Always Finds a Way." In *HF/RG*, ed. Chantal Pontbriand, 102-112. Paris: Jeu de Paume/BlackJack éditions, 2009.
—. "What an Editing Room Is." In *Nachdruck / Imprint: Texte / Writings*, ed. Susanne Gaensheimer and Nicolaus Schafhausen, 78-85. Berlin: Vorwerk 8/Lukas & Sternberg, 2001.
—. "What Ought to Be Done." In *What Ought to Be Done: Document, Commentary, Material*, ed. Harun Farocki Institut, trans. Volker Pantenburg and Michael Turnbull, 3-8. Berlin: Harun Farocki Institut/Motto Books, 2016.
—. "Workers Leaving the Factory." In *Nachdruck / Imprint: Texte / Writings*, ed. Susanne Gaensheimer and Nicolaus Schafhausen, 230-247. Berlin: Vorwerk 8/Lukas & Sternberg, 2001.
—. "Written Trailers." In *Harun Farocki: Against What? Against Whom?*, ed. Antje Ehmann and Kodwo Eshun, 220-241. London: Koenig Books, 2009.
Farocki, Harun, and Christa Blümlinger. "Conversation with Harun Farocki: ABCs of the Film Essay." In *Essays on the Essay Film*, ed. Nora M. Alter and Timothy Corrigan, 297-213. New York: Columbia University Press, 2017.

Filmography

For more detailed information in English and German, and short synopses, see https://www.harunfarocki.de/films.html.

1966
Jeder ein Berliner Kindl (Everybody a Berliner Kindl)
West Germany, 4 minutes
Director: Harun Farocki
Cinematographer: Gerd Delp

1966
Zwei Wege (Two Paths)
West Germany, 3 minutes
Director: Harun Farocki
Cinematographer: Horst Kandeler

1967
Der Wahlhelfer (The Campaign Volunteer)
West Germany, 14 minutes
Director: Harun Farocki
Cinematographer: Thomas Hartwig

1967
Die Worte des Vorsitzenden (The Words of the Chairman)
West Germany, 3 minutes
Director, scriptwriter: Harun Farocki
Assistant director: Helke Sander
Cinematographer: Holger Meins

1968
Ohne Titel oder Wanderkino für Ingenieurstudenten (Untitled or: The Wandering Cinema for Engineering Students)
West Germany, 40 minutes
Director: Harun Farocki

1968
Drei Schüsse auf Rudi (Three Shots at Rudi)
West Germany, 4 minutes
Director, scriptwriter, editor: Harun Farocki
Cinematographer: Skip Norman

1968
White Christmas
West Germany, 3 minutes
Director, scriptwriter, editor: Harun Farocki
Cinematographer: Skip Norman

1968
Ihre Zeitungen (Their Newspapers)
West Germany, 17 minutes
Director, scriptwriter, editor: Harun Farocki
Assistant director: Helke Sander
Cinematographer: Skip Norman

1969
Ohne Titel oder Nixon kommt nach Berlin (Untitled or: Nixon Comes to Berlin)
West Germany, 2 minutes
Director, scriptwriter: Harun Farocki

1969
Nicht löschbares Feuer (Inextinguishable Fire)
West Germany, 25 minutes
Director, scriptwriter, editor: Harun Farocki
Assistant director: Helke Sander
Cinematographer: Gert Konradt

1969
Anleitung, Polizisten den Helm abzureissen (Instructions on How to Pull Off Police Helmets)
West Germany, 2 minutes
Director, scriptwriter, editor: Harun Farocki
Cinematographer: Michael Geißler

1970
Die Teilung aller Tage (The Division of All Days)
West Germany, 65 minutes

Directors, scriptwriters, editors: Hartmut Bitomsky and Harun Farocki
Assistant directors: Petra Milhoffer and Ingrid Oppermann
Cinematographers: Carlos Bustamante and Adolf Winckelmann

1971
Eine Sache, die sich versteht (15x) (Something Self Explanatory [15x])
West Germany, 64 minutes
Directors, scriptwriters: Hartmut Bitomsky and Harun Farocki, based on texts by Karl Marx and Friedrich Engels
Editor: Hasso Nagel
Cinematographers: Carlos Bustamante and David Slama

1972
Remember Tomorrow Is the First Day of the Rest of Your Life
West Germany, 10 minutes
Director, scriptwriter, editor: Harun Farocki
Assistant director: Klaus Krahn
Cinematographer: Fitz Grosche

1972
Die Sprache der Revolution: Beispiele revolutionärer Rhetorik, untersucht von Hans Christoph Buch (The Language of Revolution: Examples of a Revolutionary Rhetoric, Examined by Hans Christoph Buch)
West Germany, 45 minutes
Director: Harun Farocki
Scriptwriter: Hans Christoph Buch
Cinematographers: Bernd Maus and Joachim Pritzel
Editors: Ulla Agne and Claudia Karsunke

1973
Der Ärger mit den Bildern: Eine Telekritik von Harun Farocki (The Trouble with Images: A Critique of Television)
West Germany, 48 minutes
Director, scriptwriter: Harun Farocki
Editor: Evelyn Reichert-Panitz

1973
Einmal wirst auch Du mich lieben: Über die Bedeutung von Heftromanen (Someday You Will Love Me Too: About the Meaning of Dimestore Novels)
West Germany, 44 minutes
Directors, scriptwriters: Hartmut Bitomsky and Harun Farocki
Assistant director: Walter Adler
Cinematographer: Karl Heinz Blöhm
Editor: Ursula Hermann

1973
Brunner ist dran (Brunner Is Next)
West Germany, 17 minutes
Director, scriptwriter: Harun Farocki, based on the story *Le mauvais vitrier* by Charles Baudelaire
Cinematographer: David Slama
Editor: Rolf Basedow

1973
Make Up
West Germany, 29 minutes
Director, scriptwriter: Harun Farocki
Assistant director: Tillmann Taube
Cinematographer: Carlos Bustamante
Editor: Rolf Basedow

1973
Sesamstrasse (Sesame Street)
West Germany, 29 minutes
Directors, scriptwriters: Hartmut Bitomsky and Harun Farocki
Cinematographer: Carlos Bustamante
Editor: Rolf Basedow

1974
Die Arbeit mit den Bildern: Eine Telekritik von Harun Farocki (The Struggle with Images: A Critique of Television)
West Germany, 44 minutes
Director, scriptwriter: Harun Farocki
Editor: Marion Zausch

1974
Plakatmaler (Poster Artists)
West Germany, 20 minutes
Director, scriptwriter, editor: Harun Farocki
Cinematographer: Rainer März

1974
Über "Gelegenheitsarbeit einer Sklavin" (About "Part-time Work of a Female Slave")
West Germany, 22 minutes
Director, scriptwriter: Harun Farocki

1974
Moderatoren im Fernsehen (Moderators)
West Germany, 22 minutes
Director, scriptwriter: Harun Farocki

1975
Erzählen (About Narration)
West Germany, 58 minutes
Directors, scriptwriters: Harun Farocki and Ingemo Engström
Cinematographer: Axel Block
Editors: Erika Kisters and Birgit Schuldt

1975
Über "Song of Ceylon" von Basil Wright (About "Song of Ceylon" by Basil Wright)
West Germany, 25 minutes
Director, scriptwriter: Harun Farocki
Editor: Marianna Müller-Kratsch

1976
Die Schlacht: Szenen aus Deutschland (The Battle: Scenes from Germany)
West Germany, 52 minutes
Directors: Harun Farocki and Hanns Zischler, television movie based on a stage play by Heiner Müller
Cinematographer: Jupp Steiof
Editor: Lilo Gieseler

1977
Sarah Schumann malt ein Bild (Sarah Schumann Paints an Image)
West Germany, 8 minutes
Director, scriptwriter: Harun Farocki
Cinematographer: Ingo Kratish
Editor: Rolf Basedow

1977
Einschlafgeschichten 1–5 (Bedtime Stories 1–5)
West Germany, 15 minutes
Director, scriptwriter: Harun Farocki
Cinematographers: Ingo Kratisch and David Slama

1978
Häuser 1–2 (Buildings 1-2)
West Germany, 10 minutes
Director, scriptwriter: Harun Farocki

1978
Zwischen Zwei Kriegen (Between Two Wars)
West Germany, 83 minutes
Director, editor: Harun Farocki
Assistant director: Jörg Papke
Cinematographers: Axel Block and Ingo Kratisch

1978
Ein Bild von Sarah Schumann (An Image by Sarah Schumann)
West Germany, 30 minutes
Director, scriptwriter: Harun Farocki
Cinematographer: Ingo Kratisch
Editor: Johannes Beringer

1979
Der Geschmack des Lebens (The Taste of Life)
West Germany, 29 minutes
Director, scriptwriter: Harun Farocki
Cinematographer: Rosa Mercedes (Harun Farocki)
Editor: Johannes Beringer

1979
Zur Ansicht: Peter Weiss (On Display: Peter Weiss)
West Germany, 44 minutes
Director, scriptwriter: Harun Farocki
Cinematographer: Gerd Braun
Editor: Rosa Mercedes (Harun Farocki)

1979
Single: Eine Schallplatte wird produziert (Single: A Record is Being Produced)
West Germany, 49 minutes
Director, scriptwriter: Harun Farocki
Cinematographers: Ingo Kratisch, David Slama, and Gert Braun
Editors: Gerd Braun, Gerrit Sommer, Helga Kohlmeier, Dorothea Haffner, and Brigitte Kurde

1979
Anna und Lara machen das Fernsehen vor und nach (Anna and Lara Are Playing Television)
West Germany, 18 minutes
Director, cinematographer, editor: Harun Farocki
Scriptwriters: Annabel Lee Faroqhi and Larissa Lu Faroqhi

1979
Industrie und Fotografie (Industry and Photography)
West Germany, 44 minutes
Director, scriptwriter: Harun Farocki
Cinematographers: Ingo Kratisch, Rosa Mercedes (Harun Farocki), and Rolf Silber
Editor: Hella Vietzke

1981
Stadtbild (View of the City)
West Germany, 44 minutes

Director, scriptwriter: Harun Farocki
Cinematographers: Ingo Kratisch and Ronny Tanner
Editor: Johannes Beringer

1982
Kurzfilme von Peter Weiss (Short Films by Peter Weiss)
West Germany, 44 minutes
Director, scriptwriter, commentary: Harun Farocki
Cinematographer: Rainer März

1982
Etwas wird sichtbar (Before your Eyes—Vietnam)
West Germany, 114 minutes
Director, scriptwriter: Harun Farocki
Assistant director: Ursula Lefkes
Cinematographer: Ingo Kratisch
Editor: Johannes Beringer

1983
"L'Argent" von Bresson ("L'Argent" by Bresson)
West Germany, 30 minutes
Directors: Hartmut Bitomsky, Manfred Blank, and Harun Farocki
Scriptwriters and commentary: Harun Farocki, Manfred Blank, Hartmut Bitomsky, Jürgen Ebert, Gaby Körner, Melanie Walz, and Barbara Schlungbaum
Cinematographers: Leo Borchard and Carlos Bustamante
Editor: Manfred Blank

1983
Interview: Heiner Müller
West Germany, 30 minutes
Director, scriptwriter, interviewer: Harun Farocki

1983
Jean-Marie Straub und Danièle Huillet bei der Arbeit an einem Film nach Franz Kafkas Romanfragment "Amerika" (Jean-Marie Straub and Danièle Huillet at Work on a Film Based on Franz Kafka's "Amerika")
West Germany, United Kingdom; 26 minutes
Director, scriptwriter, commentary: Harun Farocki
Cinematographer: Ingo Kratisch
Editor: Rosa Mercedes (Harun Farocki)

1983
Ein Bild (An Image)
West Germany, 25 minutes

Director, scriptwriter: Harun Farocki
Cinematographer: Ingo Kratisch
Editor: Rosa Mercedes (Harun Farocki)

1984
Peter Lorre—Das Doppelte Gesicht (The Double Face of Peter Lorre)
West Germany, 59 minutes
Directors, scriptwriters, and commentary: Harun Farocki and Felix Hofmann
Cinematographers: Wolf-Dieter Fallert and Ingo Kratisch

1985
Filmtip: Tee im Harem des Archimedes (Filmtip: Tea in the Harem)
West Germany, 7 minutes
Director, scriptwriter, commentary: Harun Farocki

1985
Betrogen (Betrayed)
West Germany, 99 minutes
Director, scriptwriter: Harun Farocki
Assistant director: Ronny Tanner
Cinematographer: Axel Block
Editor: Renate Merck

1986
Filmbücher (Filmbooks)
West Germany, 15 minutes
Director, scriptwriter, commentary: Harun Farocki

1986
Filmtip: Kuhle Wampe
West Germany, 6 minutes
Director, scriptwriter, commentary: Harun Farocki

1986
Schlagworte-Schlagbilder: Ein Gespräch mit Vilém Flusser (Catch Phrases-Catch Images: A Conversation with Vilém Flusser)
West Germany, 13 minutes
Director, scriptwriter, interviewer, and commentary: Harun Farocki

1986
Wie man sieht (As You See)
West Germany, 72 minutes
Director, scriptwriter, interviewer, and commentary: Harun Farocki
Assistant director: Michael Pehlke

Cinematographers: Ingo Kratisch and Michael Tanner
Editor: Rosa Mercedes (Harun Farocki)

1987
Bilderkrieg (Images-War)
West Germany, 44 minutes
Director, scriptwriter: Harun Farocki
Assistant director: Michael Trabitzsch
Cinematographer: Ingo Kratisch
Editor: Rosa Mercedes (Harun Farocki)

1987
Die Menschen stehen vorwärts in den Straßen (The People Stand Forward in the Streets)
West Germany, 8 minutes
Director, editor: Harun Farocki
Scriptwriters: Harun Farocki and Michael Trabitzsch
Cinematographer: Ingo Kratisch

1987
Filmtip: Der Tod des Empedokles (Filmtip: Death of Empedocles)
West Germany, 7 minutes
Director, scriptwriter, editor, and commentary: Harun Farocki
Cinematographer: Ingo Kratisch

1987
Die Schulung (Indoctrination)
West Germany, 44 minutes
Director, scriptwriter: Harun Farocki
Cinematographer: Simon Kleebauer
Editor: Roswitha Gnädig

1988
Kinostadt Paris (Cine City Paris)
West Germany, 60 minutes
Directors, scriptwriters, and commentary: Manfred Blank and Harun Farocki
Cinematographer: Helmut Handschel
Editor: Edith Perlaky

1988
Bilder der Welt und Inschrift des Krieges (Images of the World and the Inscription of War)
West Germany, 75 minutes
Director, scriptwriter: Harun Farocki
Assistant director: Michael Trabitzsch
Cinematographer: Ingo Kratisch
Editor: Rosa Mercedes (Harun Farocki)

1988
Georg K. Glaser—Schriftsteller und Schmied (Georg K. Glaser—Writer and Smith)
West Germany, 44 minutes
Director, scriptwriter, interviewer, and commentary: Harun Farocki
Cinematographer: Ingo Kratisch
Editors: Rosa Mercedes (Harun Farocki) and Klaus Klingler

1989
Image und Umsatz oder: Wie kann man einen Schuh darstellen (Image and Sales or: How to Depict a Shoe)
West Germany, 52 minutes
Director, scriptwriter: Harun Farocki
Cinematographer: Ingo Kratisch
Editors: Egon Bunne and Rosa Mercedes (Harun Farocki)

1990
Leben—BRD (How to Live in the FRG)
West Germany, 83 minutes
Director, scriptwriter: Harun Farocki
Assistant director: Michael Trabitzsch
Cinematographer: Ingo Kratisch
Editors: Rosa Mercedes (Harun Farocki) and Irina Hoppe

1991
Was ist los? (What's Up?)
Germany, 60 minutes
Director, scriptwriter, interviewer: Harun Farocki
Cinematographer: Ingo Kratisch
Editors: Rosa Mercedes (Harun Farocki) and Irina Hoppe

1992
Videogramme einer Revolution (Videograms of a Revolution)
Germany, 106 minutes
Directors, scriptwriters, and commentary: Harun Farocki and Andrei Ujica

1992
Kamera und Wirklichkeit (Camera and Reality)
Germany, 120 minutes
Directors, scriptwriters, and commentary: Harun Farocki and Andrei Ujica
Editor: Egon Bunne

1993
Ein Tag im Leben der Endverbraucher (A Day in the Life of a Consumer)
Germany, 44 minutes
Director, scriptwriter: Harun Farocki

1994
Die führende Rolle (The Leading Role)
Germany, 35 minutes
Director, scriptwriter, and commentary: Harun Farocki
Editor: Max Reimann

1994
Die Umschulung (Retraining)
Germany, 44 minutes
Director, scriptwriter: Harun Farocki
Assistant director: Ronny Tanner
Cinematographers: Ingo Kratisch and Thomas Arslan
Editor: Max Reimann

1995
Arbeiter verlassen die Fabrik (Workers Leaving the Factory)
Germany, 36 minutes
Director, scriptwriter, and commentary: Harun Farocki
Editor: Max Reimann

1996
Der Auftritt (The Appearance)
Germany, 40 minutes
Director, scriptwriter: Harun Farocki
Cinematographer: Ingo Kratisch
Editor: Max Reimann

1996
Der Werbemensch (The Ad Guy)
Germany, 3 minutes
Director, scriptwriter: Harun Farocki
Cinematographer: Ingo Kratisch
Editor: Max Reimann

1996
Theater der Umschulung (The Theater of the Retraining)
Germany, 4 minutes
Director, scriptwriter: Harun Farocki
Assistant director: Ronny Tanner
Cinematographers: Ingo Kratisch and Thomas Arslan

1996
Die Küchenhilfen (Kitchen Helpers)
Germany, 60 minutes
Director, scriptwriter, interviewer: Harun Farocki

Cinematographer: Ingo Kratisch
Editors: Rosa Mercedes (Harun Farocki) and Irina Hoppe

1997
Die Werbebotschaft (The Advertisement Info)
Germany, 3 minutes
Director, scriptwriter: Harun Farocki
Cinematographer: Ingo Kratisch
Editor: Max Reimann

1997
Der Ausdruck der Hände (The Expression of Hands)
Germany, 30 minutes
Director: Harun Farocki
Scriptwriters: Harun Farocki and Jörg Becker
Cinematographer: Ingo Kratisch
Editor: Max Reimann

1997
Stilleben (Still Life)
Germany, 56 minutes
Director, scriptwriter: Harun Farocki
Cinematographer: Ingo Kratisch
Editors: Irina Hoppe, Rosa Mercedes (Harun Farocki), and Jan Ralske

1997
Die Bewerbung (The Interview)
Germany, 58 minutes
Director, scriptwriter: Harun Farocki
Cinematographer: Ingo Kratisch
Editor: Max Reimann

1998
Worte und Spiele (Words and Games)
Germany, 68 minutes
Director, scriptwriter: Harun Farocki
Cinematographers: Ingo Kratisch, Rosa Mercedes (Harun Farocki), and Ludger Blanke
Editor: Max Reimann

1998
Der Finanzchef (The Chief Executive Officer)
Germany, 7 minutes
Director, scriptwriter: Harun Farocki
Cinematographer: Ingo Kratisch
Editor: Max Reimann

2000
Gefängnisbilder (Prison Images)
Germany, 60 minutes
Director, scriptwriter: Harun Farocki
Cinematographers: Cathy Lee Crane and Ingo Kratisch
Editor: Max Reimann

2001
Die Schöpfer der Einkaufswelten (The Creators of Shopping Worlds)
Germany, 72 minutes
Director, scriptwriter: Harun Farocki
Cinematographers: Ingo Kratisch and Rosa Mercedes (Harun Farocki)
Editor: Max Reimann

2003
Erkennen und Verfolgen (War at a Distance)
Germany, 58 minutes
Director, scriptwriter: Harun Farocki
Cinematographers: Ingo Kratisch and Rosa Mercedes (Harun Farocki)
Editor: Max Reimann

2004
Nicht ohne Risiko (Nothing Ventured)
Germany, 50 minutes
Scriptwriters: Harun Farocki and Matthias Rajmann
Director: Harun Farocki
Cinematographer: Ingo Kratisch
Editor: Max Reimann

2007
Aufschub (Respite)
Germany, 40 minutes
Scriptwriter: Harun Farocki

2009
Zum Vergleich (In Comparison)
Germany, 61 minutes
Director: Harun Farocki
Scriptwriters: Harun Farocki and Matthias Rajmann
Cinematographer: Ingo Kratisch
Editor: Meggie Schneider

2012
Ein neues Produkt (A New Product)
Germany, 37 Minutes

Director, editor: Harun Farocki
Cinematographer: Ingo Kratisch

2013
Sauerbruch Hutton Architekten (Sauerbruch Hutton Architects)
Germany, 73 minutes
Director, editor: Harun Farocki
Cinematographer: Ingo Kratisch

Installations by Harun Farocki

1995
Schnittstelle (Interface)
Germany, 23 min (loop)
Lille Métropole Musée Moderne d'art, Villeneuve d'Ascq, France
Director, scriptwriter, and commentary: Harun Farocki
Cinematographer: Ingo Kratisch
Editor: Max Reimann
Format: Betacam SP, col., sound
Double channel, 2 videos

2000
Ich glaubte Gefangene zu sehen (I Thought I was Seeing Convicts)
Germany, 23 min (loop)
Generali Foundation, Vienna
Director, scriptwriter: Harun Farocki
Cinematographer: Cathy Lee Crane
Editor: Max Reimann
Format: Betacam SP, col. and b/w, sound
Double channel, 2 videos

2000
Musikvideo (Music-Video)
Germany, 50 min and 20 sec (loop)
Media City, Seoul
Director, scriptwriter: Harun Farocki
Cinematographers: Harun Farocki and Antje Ehmann
Editor: Harun Farocki
Format: Mini-DV, col., silent

2000
Auge/Maschine (Eye/Machine)

Germany, 23 min (loop)
Galerie Greene Naftali, New York, and ZKM (Zentrum für Kunst und Medien), Karlsruhe, Germany
Directors, scriptwriters: Harun Farocki, Matthias Rajmann, Ingo Kratisch, and Rosa Mercedes (Harun Farocki)
Editor: Max Reimann
Format: Betacam SP, col., sound
Double channel, 2 videos

2001
Auge/Maschine II (Eye/Machine II)
Germany, 15 min (loop)
Galerie Greene Naftali, New York, and Brugge 2002, European Capital of Culture/desire productions, Bruges, Belgium
Directors, scriptwriters: Harun Farocki, Matthias Rajmann, Ingo Kratisch, and Kilian Hirt
Editor: Max Reimann
Format: Digital Betacam, col. and b/w, sound
Double channel, 2 videos

2003
Auge/Maschine III (Eye/Machine III)
Germany, 25 min (loop)
Coproduction with Institute of Contemporary Arts, ICA, London, with support from ZDF/3sat, Mainz, Germany, and Galerie Greene Naftali, New York
Directors, scriptwriters: Harun Farocki, Matthias Rajmann, Ingo Kratisch, and Rosa Mercedes (Harun Farocki)
Format: digital Betacam, col., sound
Double channel, 2 videos

2004
Gegen-Musik (Counter-Music)
Germany, France; 23 min (loop)
Lille 2004, Lille, France, Fonds Image/Mouvement Centre National de la Cinèmatographie, Fonds DICREAM
Director, scriptwriter: Harun Farocki
Cinematographer: Ingo Kratisch
Editor: Max Reimann
Format: digital Betacam, col. and b/w, sound

2005
Drei Montagen (Three Assemblies)
Germany; *Drei Frauen*, 13 min; *Ulrike Meinhof*, 11 min; *Tatort: Mordkommando*, 5 min (loop)
Idea, realization, and montage: Harun Farocki
Format: video, col. and b/w, sound
Installation for three screens

Installations by Harun Farocki 237

2005
Aufstellung (In-Formation)
Germany, 16 min (loop)
TRANSIT MIGRATION, Kulturstiftung des Bundes, Halle an der Saale, Germany
Director, scriptwriter: Harun Farocki
Format: DV, col. and b/w, silent
Single channel

2005
Ausweg (A Way)
Germany, 14 min (loop)
Director, scriptwriter: Harun Farocki
Format: DV, col. and b/w, sound
Single channel

2006
Hörstationen (Listening Stations)
Germany, 1 min each (loop)
Generali Foundation, Vienna
Idea and realization: Antje Ehmann and Harun Farocki
Format: 7 sound loops
Installation for 7 phones

2006
Zur Bauweise des Films bei Griffith (On Construction of Griffth's Films)
Germany, 9 min (loop)
Generali Foundation, Vienna
Idea: Antje Ehmann and Harun Farocki
Realization: Harun Farocki
Format: DV, b/w, silent
Two channels, 2 videos

2006
Arbeiter verlassen die Fabrik in elf Jahrzehnten (Workers Leaving the Factory in Eleven Decades)
Germany, 36 min (loop)
Generali Foundation, Vienna
Idea, realization: Harun Farocki
Format: DV and digital Betacam, col. and b/w, sound
Installation for 12 monitors

2006
Synchronisation (Dubbing)
Germany, 3 min (loop)
Generali Foundation, Vienna
Idea and realization: Antje Ehmann and Harun Farocki

Format: DV, col., sound
Single channel

2007
Vergleich über ein Drittes (Comparison via a Third)
Germany, 24 min (loop)
Kulturstiftung des Bundes, Halle an der Saale, Germany, and mumok (Museum Moderner Kunst Stiftung Ludwig Wien), Vienna
Scriptwriter, director: Harun Farocki
Format: 16 mm, col., sound
Double channel, double projection

2007
Deep Play
Germany, 2 hours 15 min (loop)
MA.JA.DE., Berlin
A collaboration with Antje Ehmann, Wiebke Enwaldt, Christiane Hitzemann, and Ronny Tanner, with support from DFB Kulturstiftung, Berlin, and Cine-Plus Media Service GmbH & Co. KG, Berlin
Director, scriptwriter: Harun Farocki
Editor: Bettina Blickwede
Format: DV, col., sound
Installation for 12 screens

2007
Übertragung (Transmission)
Germany, Switzerland; 43 min (loop)
Commissioned by "Kunst Öffentlichkeit Zürich" with support of Schwyzer-Winker Stiftung
Idea: Antje Ehmann
Director, scriptwriter: Harun Farocki
Editor: Meggie Schneider
Format: Mini-DV, col., sound

2008
Fressen oder Fliegen (Feasting or Flying)
Germany, 24 min (loop)
HAU (Hebbel am Ufer), Berlin, with support from Siemens Arts Programm, Haupstadtkulturfonds, Berlin
Editor, and idea: Antje Ehmann
Realization: Antje Ehmann and Harun Farocki
Format: Mini-DV, col. and b/w, sound
6 videos, 6 screens

2009
Ernste Spiele III: Immersion (Serious Games III: Immersion)
Germany, France, Belgium; 20 min (loop)

Harun Farocki Filmproduktion, Berlin, with support from Medienboard Berlin-Brandenburg GmbH; co-produced by Jeu de Paume, Paris, and STUK, Leuven, Belgium
Director, scriptwriter: Harun Farocki
Cinematographer: Ingo Kratisch
Editors: Harun Farocki and Max Reimann
Format: digital Betacam, col., sound
Double channel, 2 videos

2010
Das Silber und das Kreuz (The Silver and the Cross)
Germany, 17 min (loop)
Produced for The Potosí Principal exhibition
Concept and realization: Harun Farocki
Editor: Christine Niehoff
Format: video, col., sound
Double projection

2010
Umgießen: Variation von Opus 1 von Tomas Schmit (Re-Pouring)
Germany
Variation I and II: 20 min; variation III: 21 min (loop)
Commissioned by Osram Art Projects: Seven Screens
Concept and realization: Harun Farocki
Format: installation for 7 light steles, video, silent

2010
Serious Games I: Watson ist hin (Serious Games I: Watson Is Down)
Germany, 8 min (loop)
Harun Farocki Filmproduktion, Berlin, with support from Medienboard Berlin-Brandenburg GmbH, Bienal de Sao Paulo, and KUB (Kunsthaus Bregenz), Bregenz, Austria
Director: Harun Farocki
Cinematographer: Ingo Kratisch
Editor: Harun Farocki
Format: video (double projection), col., sound

2010
Ernste Spiele II: Drei tot (Serious Games II: Three Dead)
Germany, 8 min (loop)
Harun Farocki Filmproduktion, Berlin, with support from Medienboard Berlin-Brandenburg GmbH, Bienal de Sao Paulo, and KUB (Kunsthaus Bregenz), Bregenz, Austria
Director: Harun Farocki
Cinematographer: Ingo Kratisch
Editor: Harun Farocki
Scriptwriters: Harun Farocki and Matthias Rajmann
Format: video, col., sound

2010
Sonne ohne Schatten (Serious Games IV: A Sun without Shadow)
Germany, 8 min (loop)
Harun Farocki Filmproduktion, Berlin, with support from Medienboard Berlin-Brandenburg GmbH, Bienal de Sao Paulo, and KUB (Kunsthaus Bregenz), Bregenz, Austria
Director: Harun Farocki
Cinematographer: Ingo Kratisch
Editor: Harun Farocki
Scriptwriters: Harun Farocki and Matthias Rajmann
Format: video (double projection), col., sound

2011
War Tropes
Germany, 35 min (loop)
Harun Farocki Filmproduktion, Berlin, commissioned by Kleist Festival, Maxim Gorki Theater, Berlin, funded by Kulturstiftung des Bundes, Halle an der Saale, Germany
Concept and realization: Antje Ehmann and Harun Farocki
Format: 6 videos, b/w and col.

2012
Parallel
Germany, 16 min (loop)
Director: Harun Farocki
Format: video, col., sound

2014
Parallel II
Germany, 9 min (loop)
Director: Harun Farocki
Format: video, col., sound

2014
Parallel III
Germany, 7 min (loop)
Director: Harun Farocki
Format: video, col., sound

2014
Parallel IV
Germany, 11 min (loop)
Director: Harun Farocki
Format: video, col., sound

Critical Bibliography

Adorno, Theodor W. *Aesthetic Theory* [1969]. Ed. Gretel Adorno and Rolf Tiedeman, trans. Robert Hullot-Kentor. Minneapolis: University of Minnesota Press, 1997.
—. "The Essay as Form" [1958]. In *Essays on the Essay Film*, ed. Nora M. Alter and Timothy Corrigan, 60-81. New York: Columbia University Press, 2017.
—. *Minima Moralia: Reflections from Damaged Life* [1951]. Trans. E. F. N. Jephcott. London: Verso, 1987.
—. "Transparencies on Film" [1966]. Trans. Thomas Y. Levin. *New German Critique*, no. 24/25 (Autumn 1981-Winter 1982): 199-205.
Alter, Nora M. "Dead Silence." In *Harun Farocki: Against What? Against Whom?*, ed. Antje Ehmann and Kodwo Eshun, 171-178. London: Koenig Books, 2009.
—. *The Essay Film After Fact and Fiction*. New York: Columbia University Press, 2018.
—. "The Political Im/perceptible: Farocki's 'Images of the World and the Inscription of War.'" *New German Critique*, no. 68 (Spring-Summer 1996): 165-192.
—. *Projecting History: German Nonfictional Cinema, 1967–2000*. Ann Arbor: University of Michigan, 2002.
—. "Two or Three Things I Know about Harun Farocki." *October*, no. 151 (Winter 2015), 151-158.
—. *Vietnam Protest Theatre: The Television War on Stage*. Bloomington: Indiana University Press, 1996.
Alter, Nora M., and Timothy Corrigan, eds. *Essays on the Essay Film*. New York: Columbia University Press, 2017.
Althen, Michael. "Kino wie noch nie: Das große Aufräumen." *FAZ*, March 25th, 2008.
Arnold, Dagmar. "Offensichtlichkeit und 'Art des Sehens': Harun Farockis Film Wie man sieht." In *Versuche über den Essayfilm*, ed. Hanno Möbius, 76-83. Marburg, Germany: Inst. für Neuere Dt. Literatur, 1991.
Aurich, Rolf, and Ulrich Kriest, eds. *Der Ärger mit den Bildern: Die Filme von Harun Farocki Close up no 10*. Konstanz, Germany: UVK Medien, 1998.
Balsom, Erika. "Moving Bodies: Captured Life in the Late Works of Harun Farocki." *Journal of Visual Culture* 18, no. 3 (December 2019): 358-377.
Barthes, Roland. *Mythologies* [1957]. London: Vintage Books, 1993.

Baumgärtel, Tilmann. *Vom Guerillakino zum Essayfilm: Harun Farocki Werkmonographie eines Autorenfilmers*. Berlin: b_books, 1998.

Baute, Michael. "The Quarter-Dollar Scene." In *Harun Farocki: Against What? Against Whom?*, ed. Antje Ehmann and Kodwo Eshun, trans. Benjamin Carter, 194-197. London: Koenig Books, 2009.

Becker, Jörg. "Images and Thoughts, People and Things, Materials and Methods." In *Harun Farocki: Working on the Sight-Lines*, ed. Thomas Elsaesser, trans. Neil Christian Pages, 55-60. Amsterdam: Amsterdam University Press, 2004.

—. "In Film Denken." *RAY*, February 2004, 32-34.

Bellenbaum, Rainer, and Sabeth Buchmann. "Between the Faces." In *Harun Farocki: Against What? Against Whom?*, ed. Antje Ehmann and Kodwo Eshun, trans. Antje Ehmann and Michael Turnbull, 110-115. London: Koenig Books, 2009.

Bellour, Raymond. "The Photo-Diagram." In *Harun Farocki: Against What? Against Whom?*, ed. Antje Ehmann and Kodwo Eshun, trans. Benjamin Carter, 143-151. London: Koenig Books, 2009.

—. "Pourquoi Harun nous était si précieux." *Trafic* 93 (Spring 2015): 66-73.

Benjamin, Walter. "Hardware." In *One Way Street* [1928], ed. Michael Jennings, 84. Cambridge, MA: Harvard University Press, 2016.

Benning, James. "May 19, 1944 and the Summer of '53." In *Harun Farocki: Against What? Against Whom?*, ed. Antje Ehmann and Kodwo Eshun, 36-37. London: Koenig Books, 2009.

Berg, Ronald. "Harun Farocki, Hamburger Bahnhof—Museum für Gegenwart." *Frieze*, no. 15 (June-August 2014).

Bird, Daniel. "Source: An Exhibition of Media Art Installations." *Fuse Magazine* 26, no. 3 (2003): 49-51.

Blumenthal-Barby, Martin. "Counter-Music: Harun Farocki's Theory of a New Image Type." *October*, no. 151 (Winter 2015).

Blümlinger, Christa. "De la lente elaboration des pensées dans le travail des images." *Trafic* 13 (1995).

—. "Harun Farocki, circuits d'image." *Trafic* 21 (1997): 44-49.

—. "Harun Farocki: Critical Strategies." In *Harun Farocki: Working on the Sight-Lines*, ed. Thomas Elsaesser, trans. Sally Laruelle, 315-322. Amsterdam: Amsterdam University Press, 2004.

—. *Harun Farocki: Du Cinéma au Musée*. Paris: P.O.L., 2022.

—. "Incisive Divides and Revolving Images: On the Installation Schnittstelle." In *Harun Farocki: Working on the Sight-Lines*, ed. Thomas Elsaesser, trans. Roger Hillman and Timothy Mathieson, revised by Thomas Elsaesser, 61-66. Amsterdam: Amsterdam University Press, 2004.

—. "La question de la visibilité selon Harun Farocki." In *Archives au présent*, ed. Patrick Nardin, Catherine Perret, Soko Phay, and Anna Seiderer. Paris: PUV, 2017.

—. "Les parallèles de Farocki: ce que le jeu met en jeu." *Trafic* 93 (Spring 2015): 85-93.

—. "Memory and Montage: On the Installation *Counter-Music*." In *Harun Farocki: Against What? Against Whom?*, ed. Antje Ehmann and Kodwo Eshun, trans. Michael Turnbull, 101-109. London: Koenig Books, 2009.

—. "Slowly Forming a Thought While Working on Images." In *Harun Farocki: Working on the Sight-Lines*, ed. Thomas Elsaesser, trans. Robin Curtis, 163-175. Amsterdam: Amsterdam University Press, 2004.

———. "Travail de la mémoire et mémoire du travail—Vertov/Farocki: A propos de Contre-Chant." *Intermédialités/Intermediality*, no. 11 (Spring 2008).

———. "Über das allmähliche Verfertigen der Gedanken beim Filmemachen (Gespräch mit Harun Farocki)." *Falter*, no. 21 (1991): 26-27.

———. "Visibility, as Harun Farocki Sees It." In *Montages: Assembling as a Form and Symptom in Contemporary Arts*, ed. Cristina Baldacci and Marco Bertozzi, 203-220. N.p.: Mimesis International, 2018.

———. "What's at Play in Farocki's *Parallel*." In *Berlin Documentary Forum 3 Catalog*, ed. Hilda Peleg and Erika Balsom, 182-189. Berlin: Berlin Documentary Forum, 2014. Program catalog.

Brecht, Bertolt. *Brecht on Theater*. Ed. and trans. John Willet. New York: Hill and Wang, 1964.

Brenez, Nicole. "Harun Farocki and the Romantic Genesis of the Principle of Visual Critique." In *Harun Farocki: Against What? Against Whom?*, ed. Antje Ehmann and Kodwo Eshun, trans. Benjamin Carter, 128-142. London: Koenig Books, 2009.

César, Filipa. "Joint Leopard Dot." *e-flux*, no. 59 (November 2014), https://www.e-flux.com/journal/59/61115/joint-leopard-dot/.

Creischer, Alice, and Andreas Siekmann. "No Cars, Shoot-outs and Smart Clothes." In *Harun Farocki: Against What? Against Whom?*, ed. Antje Ehmann and Kodwo Eshun, trans. Antje Ehmann and Michael Turnbull, 116-121. London: Koenig Books, 2009.

Deleuze, Gilles. "Postscript on Control Societies" [1990]. *October* 59 (Winter 1992): 3-7.

de Ruyter, Thibaut. "Tout doit disparaître! Jusqu'à épuisement des stocks disponibles." *artpress+* (May 2005): 66-69.

Didi-Huberman, Georges. "How to Open Your Eyes." In *Harun Farocki: Against What? Against Whom?*, ed. Antje Ehmann and Kodwo Eshun, trans. Patrick Kremer, 38-50. London: Koenig Books, 2009.

———. "Remonter, Refendre, Restituer." In *L'Image-Document, Entre Realité et Fiction*, ed. Jean-Pierre Criqui, 68-92. Paris: Images en Manoeuvres Éditions, 2010.

Diederichsen, Diedrich. "Harun Farocki (1944-2014)." *Trafic* 93 (Spring 2015): 74-77.

———. "Napalm Death." In *Harun Farocki: Against What? Against Whom?*, ed. Antje Ehmann and Kodwo Eshun, trans. Karl Hoffman, 51-56. London: Koenig Books, 2009.

Dziewior, Yilmaz, ed. *Harun Farocki: Weiche Montagen/Soft Montages*. Bregenz, Austria: Kunsthaus Bregenz, 2011.

Ehmann, Antje. "Megaphone, Chocolate Kisses, and Spray Cans: Harun Farocki's Guerilla Tactics." In *The Physiognomy of Power: Harun Farocki/Florentina Pakosta*, ed. Thorsten Sadowsky, 166-168. Salzburg: Verlag für moderne Kunst, 2021.

———. "What Ought to Be Done?" In *Harun Farocki, What Ought to Be Done? Works and Life*, ed. Kim Eunhee and Antje Ehmann, 35-38. Seoul: National Museum of Modern and Contemporary Art, Seoul, 2018.

Ehmann, Antje, and Kodwo Eshun. "A to Z of HF or: 26 Introductions to HF." In *Harun Farocki: Against What? Against Whom?*, ed. Antje Ehmann and Kodwo Eshun, 204-219. London: Koenig Books, 2009.

Ehmann, Antje, and Kodwo Eshun, eds. *Harun Farocki: Against What? Against Whom?* London: Koenig Books, 2010.

Ehmann, Antje, and Carles Guerra, eds. *Harun Farocki: Another Kind of Empathy*. London: Koenig Books, 2016.

Ehmann, Antje, and Artur Liebhart, eds. *Harun Farocki: Pierwszy raz w Warszawie/First Time in Warsaw*. Warsaw: Centrum Sztuki Współczesnej Zamek Ujazdowski, 2012.

Elsaesser, Thomas. "El ojo de Farocki Desconfió." *Otra Parte*, no. 2 (Autumn 2001): 31–49.

—. "The Future of 'Art' and 'Work' in the Age of Vision Machines: Harun Farocki." In *After the Avant-Garde Contemporary German and Austrian Experimental Film*, ed. Randall Halle and Reinhild Steingröver, 31–49. Rochester, NY: Camden House, 2008.

—. "Harun Farocki: Filmmaker, Artist, Media Theorist." In *Harun Farocki: Working on the Sight-Lines*, ed. Thomas Elsaesser, 11–40. Amsterdam: Amsterdam University Press, 2004.

—, ed. *Harun Farocki: Working on the Sight-Lines*. Amsterdam: Amsterdam University Press, 2004.

—. "Holocaust Memory as the Epistemology of Forgetting? Re-wind and Postponement in *Respite*." In *Harun Farocki: Against What? Against Whom?*, ed. Antje Ehmann and Kodwo Eshun, trans. Karl Hoffman, 57–68. London: Koenig Books, 2009.

—. "'It Started with These Images': Some Notes on Political Filmmaking After Brecht in Germany; Helke Sander and Harun Farocki." *Discourse* 7 (1985).

—. "Making the World Superfluous: An Interview with Harun Farocki." *Harun Farocki: Working on the Sight-Lines*, ed. Thomas Elsaesser, 177–189. Amsterdam: Amsterdam University Press, 2004.

—. "Political Filmmaking After Brecht: Farocki, for Example." In *Harun Farocki: Working on the Sight-Lines*, ed. Thomas Elsaesser, 133–153. Amsterdam: Amsterdam University Press, 2004.

—. "Simulation and the Labour of Invisibility: Harun Farocki's Life Manuals." In "Life Remade: Critical Animation in the Digital Age," ed. Esther Leslie and Joel McKim. Special issue, *Animation* 12, no. 3 (November 2017): 214–229.

—. "Working at the Margins: Film as a Form of Intelligence." In *Harun Farocki: Working on the Sight-Lines*, ed. Thomas Elsaesser, 95–108. Amsterdam: Amsterdam University Press, 2004.

—. "Working at the Margins: Two or Three Things About Harun Farocki." *Monthly Film Bulletin* 50, no. 597 (October 1983), 269–270.

Eshun, Kodwo. "A Question They Never Stop Asking." *e-flux*, no. 59 (November 2014). https://www.e-flux.com/journal/59/61076/a-question-they-never-stop-asking/.

Eunhee, Kim. "Harun Farocki: Chasing the Invisible Powers Governing Our Lives." In *Harun Farocki, What Ought to Be Done? Works and Life*, ed. Kim Eunhee and Antje Ehmann, 23–27. Seoul: National Museum of Modern and Contemporary Art, Seoul, 2018.

Färber, Helmut. "De près, de loin—'Quelque chose deviant visible'." *Trafic* 93 (2015): 102–110.

Fernández H., Diego, ed. *Sobre Harun Farocki*. Santiago: Metales Pesados, 2014.

Fiduccia, Joanna, ed. *Cahier #2: A Magical Imitation of Reality*. Milan: Kaleidoscope Press, 2011.

Flusser, Vilém. *Into the Universe of Technical Images*. Minneapolis: University of Minnesota Press, 2011.

—. *Towards a Philosophy and Photography*. London: Reaktion Books, 2000.

—. *Gestures*. Minneapolis: University of Minnesota Press, 2014.

Fore, Devin. "The Operative Word in Soviet Factography," *October* 118 (Fall 2006): 95–131.

Foster, Hal. "Vision Quest: The Cinema of Harun Farocki." *Artforum* (November 2004): 157–161.

Foucault, Michel. "The Confession of the Flesh: A Conversation with Alain Grosrichard, et al." In *Power/Knowledge: Selected Interviews & Other Writings, 1972–1977*, ed. Colin Gordon, 194-228. New York: Pantheon Books, 1980.

Gianetti, Claudia. *Harun Farocki: Playing the Game, Spiel und Spielregeln*. Oldenburg, Germany: Edith Russ Haus für Medienkunst, 2013.

Gradoni, Martine. "Notes sur 'Une vie RFA' de Harun Farocki." *Documentaires*, no. 12 (Autumn 1996): 27-30.

Grafe, Frieda. "Blutig ernst: Harun Farockis Film 'Etwas wird sichtbar'." *Süddeutsche Zeitung*, July 16th, 1982.

Griffin, Tim. "Tim Griffin in Conversation with Harun Farocki." *Artforum* 43, no. 3 (November 2004): 162-163.

Grundmann, Roy, Peter Schwartz, and Gregory Williams, eds. *Labour in a Single Shot: Critical Perspectives on Antje Ehmann and Harun Farocki's Global Video Project*. Amsterdam: Amsterdam University Press, 2022.

Hamers, Jeremy. "Videogramme einer Revolution: Le dispositif farockien retourné." *Cahiers Louis-Lumière* 4 (Spring 2007): 118-125.

Holert, Tom. *Politics of Learning, Politics of Space: Architecture and the Education Shock of the 1960s and 1970s*. Berlin: De Gruyter, 2011.

———. "Tabular Images: On *The Division of All Days* (1970) and *Something Self-Explanatory* (15x) (1971)." In *Harun Farocki: Against What? Against Whom?*, ed. Antje Ehmann and Kodwo Eshun, 75-92. London: Koenig Books, 2009.

Holl, Ute. "Construction Sites and Image Walls: Harun Farocki's *In Comparison*." In *Harun Farocki: Against What? Against Whom?*, ed. Antje Ehmann and Kodwo Eshun, trans. Antje Ehmann and Michael Turnbull, 160-162. London: Koenig Books, 2009.

Hüser, Rembert. "Nine Minutes in the Yard: A Conversation with Harun Farocki." In *Harun Farocki: Working on the Sight-Lines*, ed. Thomas Elsaesser, 297-314. Amsterdam: Amsterdam University Press, 2004.

———. "Wo fängt das an, wo hört das auf? Laudatio zum Peter-Weiss-Preis 2002 für Harun Farocki." In *Peter Weiss Jahrbuch*, 21-31. Röhrig Universitätsverlag, 2003.

Hyun-Suk, Seo. "Notes for *What Farocki Taught*, Remake." In *Harun Farocki, What Ought to Be Done? Works and Life*, ed. Kim Eunhee and Antje Ehmann, 125-184. Seoul: National Museum of Modern and Contemporary Art, Seoul, 2018.

Jihoon, Kim. "Notes on Harun Farocki's Video Installations: Working with the Paradox of the Post-cinematic Conditions." In *Harun Farocki, What Ought to Be Done? Works and Life*, ed. Kim Eunhee and Antje Ehmann, 811-846. Seoul: National Museum of Modern and Contemporary Art, Seoul, 2018.

Joshi, Ruchir. "Harun and the Sea of Arguments." In *Harun Farocki: Against What? Against Whom?*, ed. Antje Ehmann and Kodwo Eshun, 198-203. London: Koenig Books, 2009.

Keenan, Thomas. "Light Weapons." *Documents*, no. 1-2 (Fall–Winter 1992): 136-146.

Knepperges, Rainer, ed. "The Green of the Grass: Harun Farocki in *Filmkritik*." In *Harun Farocki: Working on the Sight-Lines*, ed. Thomas Elsaesser, trans. Roger Hillman and Timothy Mathieson, 77-82. Amsterdam: Amsterdam University Press, 2004.

Kreimeier, Klaus. "Die Arbeiter verlassen die Fabrik." *epd Film*, no. 7 (July 1995): 2-3.

——. "Enlargement of the Field of View: About *Videograms of a Revolution*." In *Harun Farocki: Against What? Against Whom?*, ed. Antje Ehmann and Kodwo Eshun, trans. Antje Ehmann and Michael Turnbull, 179-185. London: Koenig Books, 2009.

——. "Wenn der Film möglich ist, ist auch Geschichte möglich: Harun Farockis und Andrei Ujicas Filmschleife 'Videogramme einer Revolution'." *Frankfurter Rundschau*, February 20th, 1993.

——. "Wie man sieht, was man sieht: Über einen Film von Harun Farocki." *epd Film*, no. 8 (1987): 22-25.

Krolczyk, Radek. "Work in Progress: Arbeit ist ein zentrales Thema des kürzlich verstorbenen Filmemachers Harun Farocki." *Konkret* 9 (2014): 51-53.

Lee, Kevin B. *Interface 2.0*. For *Frames Cinema Journal*. https://vimeo.com/199578794.

——. *Learning Farocki: A Video Essay in Three Parts*. Goethe Institute, 2019.

Lindeperg, Sylvie. "Suspended Lives, Revenant Images: On Harun Farocki's Film *Respite*." *Trafic* 70, 2009.

Maier, Birgit. "Kriegsinschriften: Harun Farockis Arbeit am Bild." *Frankfurter Zeitung*, April 18th, 2000.

Martin, Thomas. "Wie man sieht: Der Filmemacher als Sammler." *Freitag* 11, March 5th, 2004.

Melo, Adrián. "Acerca de la filmografia de Harun Farocki." *Kane* 1, Buenos Aires (2004): 16-31.

Möller, Olaf. "Passage along the Shadow-Line: Feeling One's Way Towards the *Filmkritik*-Style." In *Harun Farocki: Working on the Sight-Lines*, ed. Thomas Elsaesser, trans. Roger Hillman, 69-75. Amsterdam: Amsterdam University Press, 2004.

Möntmann, Nina. *Brave New Work: A Reader on Harun Farocki's Film "A New Product."* Cologne: Verlag der Buchhandlung Walther König, 2014.

MUAC, Museo Universitario Arte Contemporaneo, UNAM, editor. *Harun Farocki: Visión, Producción, Opresión*. Mexico City, 2014.

Mühling, Matthias. "Gefängisbilder: Harun Farocki." In *40 Years Video Art.de Digital Heritage*, Part 1, 302-305. Ostfildern, Germany: 2006.

Müller, Heiner. "Mich interessiert die Verarbeitung von Realität: Ein Gespräch mit Harun Farocki über Kulturgrenzen und Film, über Godard und Walt Disney (1981)." In *Heiner Müller: Gesammelte Irrtümer; Interviews und Gespräche*, 61-68. Frankfurt: a. M., 1996.

Farocki, Harun, Matthias Michalka, and Museum Moderner Kunst (Austria). *Harun Farocki: Nebeneinander*. Cologne: Verlag der Buchhandlung Walther König, 2007.

Nara, Lee. "Atlas of Gestures, Essay of Hand Signals: Image Thesauri and Image Thought." In *Harun Farocki, What Ought to Be Done? Works and Life*, ed. Kim Eunhee and Antje Ehmann, trans. Chung Doo Hee and Aaron Cumberledge, 675-716. Seoul: National Museum of Modern and Contemporary Art, Seoul, 2018.

Nau, Peter. *Zwischen zwei Kriegen (Nacherzählung und Protokoll)*. Munich, 1978.

Nicklas, Jens. "Etwas wird sichtbar: Filmemacher Harun Farocki im Gespräch." 20er. *Die Tiroler Straßenzeitung*, no. 67/05: 22-23.

Niels van Tomme, ed. *Visibility Machines: Harun Farocki and Trevor Paglen*. Issues in Cultural Theory, UMBC, 2014.

Pantenburg, Volker, *Farocki/Godard: Film as Theory*. Trans. Michael Turnbull. Amsterdam: Amsterdam University Press, 2015.

———. *Film als Theorie: Bildforschung bei Harun Farocki und Jean-Luc Godard*. Bielefeld, Germany: Transcript, 2006.
———. "Manual: Harun Farocki's Instructional Work." In *Harun Farocki: Against What? Against Whom?*, ed. Antje Ehmann and Kodwo Eshun, 93-100. London: Koenig Books, 2009.
———. "'Now that's Brecht at Last!': Harun Farocki's Observational Films." In *Documentary Across Disciplines*, ed. Erika Balsom and Hila Peleg, 142-163. Cambridge, MA: The MIT Press, 2016.
———. "Working Images: Harun Farocki and the Operational Image," In *Image Operations: Visual Media and Political Conflict*, ed. Jens Eder and Charlotte Klunk, 49-61. Manchester: Manchester University Press, 2017.
———. "The Labor of Authorship: Harun Farocki's Early Writing." *Grey Room*, no. 79 (2020): 78-89.
———. "TV essay Dossier, 1: The case of Westdeutscher Rundfunk (WDR)." *Critical Studies in Television* 14, no. 1 (2019): 106-138.
Parrika, Jussi. *Operational Images from the Visual to the Invisual*. Minneapolis: University of Minnesota Press, 2023.
Pascher, Stephan, ed. "Images of the World: A Brief Introduction." *Merge* 16 (2005): 12-18.
Peleshyan, Artavazd. "Distance Montage, or the Theory of Distance" [1971/72]. In *Documentary Films of the Armenian Soviet Republic*, ed. Hans Joachim Schlegel, 79-100. Constance: UVK, 1999.
Pontbriand, Chantal/Jeu de Paume, ed. *HF / RG*. Paris: Black Jack éditions, 2009.
Rancière, Jacques. "Les incertitudes de la dialectique." *Trafic* 93 (2015): 94-102.
Raqs Media Collective. "Harun Farocki in Dehli." *art* 21 (2009).
Rebhandl, Bert. "Enemy at the Gate: Harun Farocki's Work on the Industrial Disputes of Film History." In *Harun Farocki: Against What? Against Whom?*, ed. Antje Ehmann and Kodwo Eshun, 122-127. London: Koenig Books, 2009.
Reichenbach, Benedikt, ed. *Harun Farocki Diagrams: Images from Ten Films*. Cologne: Verlag der Buchhandlung Walther König, 2014.
Robinson, Denise. "HARUN FAROCKI: Serious Games." *Artlink*, no. 35:1 (March 2015): 62-65.
Rodowick, D. N. "Eye Machines: The Art of Harun Farocki." *Artforum* (February 2015).
Rosen, Philip. *Change Mummified: Cinema, Historicity, and Theory*. Minneapolis: University of Minnesota Press, 2001.
Rosenbaum, Jonathan. "The Road Not Taken: Films by Harun Farocki." In *Harun Farocki: Working on the Sight-Lines*, ed. Thomas Elsaesser, 157-161. Amsterdam: Amsterdam University Press, 2004.
Scherer, Christina. "Bilder kommentieren Bilder: Die Analyse von Film im Film; Schnittstellen zwischen Harun Farocki und Jean-Luc Godard." *AugenBlick* 34 (December 2003): 73-85.
Schmidt, Wolfgang. "Learning with Harun." In *Harun Farocki: Against What? Against Whom?*, ed. Antje Ehmann and Kodwo Eshun, trans. Michael Turnbull, 166-170. London: Koenig Books, 2009.
Schmitt, Uwe. "Harun Farockis erstaunlicher Filmessay 'Leben BRD.' *Frankfurter Allgemeine Zeitung*, September 22nd, 1990.
Siebel, Volker. "Painting Pavements." In *Harun Farocki: Working on the Sight-Lines*, ed. Thomas Elsaesser, trans. Roger Hillman, 43-54. Amsterdam: Amsterdam University Press, 2004.

Siekmann, Andreas. "A Diagrammatic Analysis of *In Comparison*." In *Harun Farocki: Against What? Against Whom?*, ed. Antje Ehmann and Kodwo Eshun, 155-159. London: Koenig Books, 2009.

Skorecki, Louis. "Qui est Farocki?" *Cahiers du cinéma*, no. 329 (November 1981).

Soo-Young, Nam. "All Images Are Right." In *Harun Farocki: What Ought to Be Done? Works and Life*, ed. Kim Eunhee and Antje Ehmann, trans. Chung Doo Hee and Aaron Cumberledge, 567-592. Seoul: National Museum of Modern and Contemporary Art, Seoul, 2018.

Steyerl, Hito. "Beginnings." *e-flux*, no. 59 (November 2014). https://www.e-flux.com/journal/59/61140/beginnings/.

Theriault, Michèle, ed. *Harun Farocki: One Image Doesn't Take the Place of the Previous One.* Montreal, 2008.

Tomme, Niels van. *Visibility Machines: Harun Farocki and Trevor Paglen.* Baltimore, MD: Center for Art, Design and Visual Culture, 2014.

Vahland, Kia. "Spiel mit dem Tod." *Süddeutsche Zeitung*, February 14th, 2014.

Verwoert, Jan. "Production Pattern Associations: On the Work of Harun Farocki." *Afterall: A Journal of Art, Context and Enquiry* 11 (Spring/Summer 2005): 65-79.

Virilio, Paul. *War and Cinema: The Logistics of Perception.* Trans. Patrick Camiller. London: Verso, 1989.

Voltzenlogel, Thomas. *Harun Farocki: Une Hantologie du Cinéma.* Grenoble, France: Université Grenoble Alpes, 2021.

Young, Benjamin. "On Media and Democratic Politics: Videograms of a Revolution." *Harun Farocki: Working on the Sight-Lines*, ed. Thomas Elsaesser, 245-260. Amsterdam: Amsterdam University Press, 2004.

Zeyfang, Florian. "Inscriptions vidéographiques." *Art* 21 (2009).

—. "Video Inscriptions." In *Harun Farocki: Against What? Against Whom?*, ed. Antje Ehmann and Kodwo Eshun, trans. Michael Turnbull, 186-193. London: Koenig Books, 2009.

Index

About Narration (Erzählen), 52, 68-72, 225
About: "Part-time Work of a Slave" (Über 'Gelegensarbeit einer Sklavin'), 113
About Song of Ceylon by Basil Wright (Über "Song of Ceylon" von Basil Wright), 46, 114-118, 225
Adams, Eddie, 152
Adorno, Theodor, 20, 37, 159, 172; on the essay, 9, 52, 66, 86
Aesthetic Theory, 20
Aesthetics of Resistance, The (Die Ästhetik des Widerstands), 122-123
agit-prop, 5, 17, 21, 161
agitation, 16, 57-58, 62-63, 205n8. *See also* agitational skits; "making agitation scientific and politicizing science"
agitational skits, 149
alienation, 173; techniques, 77. *See also* Brecht, Bertolt; *Verfremdungstheorie* (alienation effect)
American Direct Cinema, 146
American Forces Network (AFN), 66-67, 169
An Image (Ein Bild), 26, 53, 84-85, 130, 227
Anders, Günther, 160
Anleitung, Polizisten den Helm abzurissen (How to Remove a Police Helmet), 6, 222
apparatus, 40, 144; cinematic, 45; *dispositif*, 144; filmic, 34
Arbeit mit den Bildern: Eine Telekritik von Harun Farocki, Die (The Struggle with Images: A Critique of Television), 28, 38, 42, 224

Arbeiter verlassen die Fabrik (Workers Leaving the Factory), 21, 52, 101-102, 186, 231
Arbeiter verlassen die Fabrik in elf Jahrzehnten (Workers Leaving the Factory in Eleven Decades), 5, 21, 56, 101, 237
archive, 46, 86, 155, 177; of Harun Farocki, 112, 129, 130; image, 150; library for moving images, 102, 186-187; virtual, 166, 184, 195
Arendt, Hannah, 90
Ärger mit den Bildern: Eine Telekritik von Harun Farocki, Die (The Trouble with Images: A Critique of Television), 28-39, 86, 114, 179, 187, 223
Arslan, Thomas, 18, 97
art, 85-86, 122-124, 166-167, 177-178; contemporary, 3, 10-11; exhibition, 25, 49, 55, 165; fine, 18, 44, 157; gallery, 12, 52, 110, 191; installation, 10-11, 21-22, 103, 108-109, 116, 171
As You See (Wie man Sieht), 86-92, 101, 119, 139, 168, 207n48, 228
Ästhetik des Widerstands, Die (The Aesthetics of Resistance), 122-123
atomic bomb, 147, 170, 173
Aufschub (Respite), 74, 163-164, 233
Auge/Maschine I–III (Eye/Machine I-III), 10, 15, 167-176, 235
Auschwitz, 43, 158-160, 163-164, 212n8; photographs, 157, 159; trials, 122

Ausdruck der Hände, Der (The Expression of Hands), 5, 102, 119, 186–190, 232
autobiography, 3, 16, 134
avantgarde, 135; cinema, 138, 206n28

Bao, Lin, 6
Barbara, 19, 31
Barthes, Roland, 14–15, 25, 62, 180, 192; "third meaning," 43. See also *Mythologies*
Battle: Scenes from Germany, The (Die Schlacht), 22, 121, 225
Baudelaire, Charles, 127
Bayrische Rundfunk, 130
Beatt, Cynthia, 19, 109, 160, 172
Becher, Bernd and Hilla, 81, 207n41
Before Your Eyes—Vietnam (Etwas wird Sichtbar), 72, 130, 149–156, 226
Bellour, Raymond, 4
Benjamin, Walter, 25, 70, 109, 154, 195
Bense, Max, 167
Berlin Wall, 72; fall of, 165, 198n8
Berlin–Die Sinfonie der Großstadt (Berlin-Symphony of a Great City), 116–117
Berlin–Symphony of a Great City (Berlin-Die Sinfonie der Großstadt), 116–117
Berrio, Gaspar Miguel de, 20, 108
Betrayed (Betrogen), 2, 127–139, 228; Brechtian influence, 136–138
Betrogen (Betrayed), 2, 127–139, 228; Brechtian influence, 136–138
Between Two Wars (Zwischen zwei Kriegen), 23, 52–53, 72–84, 136, 225
Bild Zeitung, 124, 143
Bild, Ein (An Image), 26, 53, 84–85, 130, 227
Bilder der Welt und Inschrift des Krieges (Images of the World and the Inscription of War), 9–10, 19, 53, 109, 156–164, 229. See also *Bilderkrieg* (Images-War)
Bilderkrieg (Images-War), 43, 74, 157, 163, 229
Bildungsroman, 71, 194
Bitomsky, Hartmut, 5, 49, 60, 64
Bonheur, Le (Happiness), 131
Boot, Das, 139
Brady, Matthew, 88

Brecht, Bertolt, 13–17, 61, 120, 127; on class struggle, 26, 56, 59, 78, 126; exile, 120–122; on radio, 42; on war, 177. See also epic theater; gestus; *Lehrstücke* (learning plays); *Umfunktionierung* (refunctioning)
Breslauer, Rudolf, 163
Bresson, Robert, 22, 114
bricolage, 154
Brock, Bazon, 48
Brook, Peter, 147
Brunner ist dran (Brunner Is Next), 127, 224
Brunner Is Next (Brunner ist dran), 127, 224
Büchner, Georg, 181
Buildings 1–2 (Häuser 1–2), 47, 225
Buñuel, Luis, 187

Caillois, Roger, 135
Camp Westerbork, 163
Campaign Volunteer, The (Der Wahlhelfer), 5, 140, 221
Casablanca, 120
Castro, Fidel, 13, 57, 181
Catch Phrases–Catch Images: A Conversation with Vilém Flusser, 7, 13, 121, 124–127, 228
Cavalcanti, Alberto, 114, 117
CGI, 192–193, 195
Chaplin, Charlie, 103
Chernobyl nuclear disaster, 161
Clash by Night, 102
Class Relations, 85, 136
coding, 53, 160, 161
Cold War, 120, 141, 157, 164
collage, 44, 45, 48, 147
colonialism, 3, 44, 108–109, 114, 156
commodity culture, 26–27, 74, 95, 134
Comparison via a Third (Vergleich über ein Drittes), 103–107, 238
compilation film, 42, 98, 101, 157
Conrad, Tony, 83
consumer society, 27, 57, 67, 87, 138
Cooley, Michael, 90
Crane, Cathy Lee, 18
Creischer, Alice, 108, 177

Crime and Punishment, 119
critical theory, 14, 36. *See also* Adorno, Theodor; Frankfurt School; Horkheimer, Max
criticism, 25, 62, 100, 127; film, 1, 9, 112–113
Crosby, Bing, 141
cultural profit, 12
Curtiz, Michael, 120
Cutterin (editor), 41, 53

D'Antonio, Emile, 45
Dahn, Thai Bihn, 146
Dalí, Salvador, 187
Danton's Death (Danton's Tod), 181
Danton's Tod (Danton's Death), 181
Day in the Life of a Consumer, A (Ein Tag im Leben der Endverbraucher, Ein), 26, 98, 226
Death of Empedocles, 114
Debray, Regis, 13, 57
Deep Play, 70, 134, 238
défilement, 11, 114, 160
Deleuze, Gilles, 119
Denkbilder (thought images), 37
Descripción del Cerro Rico e Imperial Villa de Potosí, 20, 108
Deutsche Demokratische Republik (DDR), 184–185
Deutsche Film- und Fernsehakademie Berlin (DFFB), 5, 18, 21, 34, 68, 97, 140
didactic film, 59, 61
digital media, 22, 192; archives, 46, 195; editing, 50–52; shift from analog, 10, 164–167, 188
direct cinema, 21, 34, 95, 100, 174
distance montage, 11, 42, 157–158
Division of All Days, The (Die Teilung aller Tage), 17, 59–64, 144, 180, 222
documentary, 29–30, 62, 95, 146, 172, 187; and fiction, 32, 38, 177; film, 123, 127, 146; footage, 52, 61, 103, 141, 147, 186; observational, 95, 99; television, 8, 29, 37, 42; theater, 121. *See also* essay film
Dörrie, Dorris, 139

Double Face of Peter Lorre, The (Peter Lorre: Das Doppelte Gesicht), 7, 118–121, 228
double-screen projection, 107, 109, 171
Dow Chemical Company, 146–147. *See also Nicht löschbares Feuer* (Inextinguishable Fire)
Duc, Thich Quang, 146
Dudow, Slatan, 76, 114
Dütsch, Werner, 8, 199n28
Dutschke, Rudi, 181

editing, 18, 32, 39–43, 53, 81, 187; analog, 51; as art production, 44; digital, 11, 50, 52; style, 86, 137, 153. *See also Ausdruck der Hände, Der* (The Expression of Hands)
education, 16, 55, 57–58, 61, 65, 115. *See also Lehrstücke* (learning plays)
Ehmann, Antje, 18, 21, 55, 110, 149, 177, 199n28
Eine Einstellung zur Arbeit (Labour in a Single Shot), 55, 110, 149
Eine Sache, die sich versteht (15x) (Something Self-Explanatory [15x]), 49, 59, 65–68, 136, 180, 223
Einmal wirst auch Du mich lieben: Über die Bedeutung von Heftromanen (Someday You Will Love Me Too: About the Meaning of Dime Store Novels), 67, 223
Eisenstein, Sergei, 11, 59, 115
Elsaesser, Thomas, 13, 73
Engström, Ingemo, 18, 68
epic theater, 120. *See also* Bertolt Brecht
Epstein, Jean, 186
Erkennen und Verfolgen (War at a Distance), 167, 171–173, 233
Ermittlung, Die (The Investigation), 121–122
Ernst, Wolfgang, 183
Ernste Spiele (Serious Games), 134, 174, 176–177, 238
Erzählen (About Narration), 52, 68–72, 225
essay film, 9, 73, 80, 86, 114, 139
Etwas wird Sichtbar (Before Your Eyes—Vietnam), 72, 130, 149–156, 227

Everyone a Berliner Kindl (Jeder ein Berliner Kindl), 25-26, 221
exile, 118-122
Expression of Hands, The (Der Ausdruck der Hände), 5, 102, 119, 186-190, 232
Eye/Machine I, 167-171, 235
Eye/Machine II, 170-171, 236
Eye/Machine III, 170-171, 236

Fanon, Frantz, 141
fascism, 73-74, 77, 121. *See also* National Socialism
Fassbinder, Rainer Werner, 112
Feature (Fernsehfeatures), 8, 46
feature film, 73, 127-128, 136, 139.
Fernsehfeatures (Feature), 8, 46
Film Subsidy Laws, 7
Filmbücher (Filmbooks), 112-113
Filmkritik, 13, 15-16, 111, 114, 128, 137
Fire in the Lake, 153-154
Fitzgerald, Frances, 153-154
flow, 32, 42, 81; of film, 57; and realism, 116. *See also* sequence
Flusser, Vilém, 5, 46, 124, 156, 184, 186. *See also Catch Phrases–Catch Images: A Conversation with Vilém Flusser*
forensic method, 158, 163-164
Fort White, 175
Foster, Norman, 119
Foucault, Michel, 119, 144
found footage, 29, 42, 52, 142, 154, 182. *See also Umfunktionierung* (refunctioning); *Verbundsystem* (integrated system)
Frankfurt School, 14, 36
Frecot, Janos, 47
FSK Kino, 129
führende Rolle, Die (The Leading Role), 184-185, 231
Fuller, Sam, 186
Funke, Jaromír, 81
Für eine Philosophie der Fotografie (Towards a Philosophy of Photography), 124

Garanger, Marc, 158
Gardner, Alexander, 88
Geheimnis und Gewalt, 92
gemordete Stadt, Die (The Murdered City), 48
Georg K. Glaser—Schriftsteller und Schmied (George K. Glaser–Writer and Smith), 22, 92-94, 230
George K. Glaser—Writer and Smith (Georg K. Glaser–Schriftsteller und Schmied), 22, 92-94, 230
German romantic tradition, 25
Germany Year Zero, 47
Geschmack des Leben, Der (The Taste of Life), 84, 123, 226
gestus, 120, 136, 187, 195; gestic thinking, 120, 187. *See also* epic theater
Ghosts, 31
Giant, The (Der Riese), 119
glitch, 70, 133, 192
Glomb, Ronald, 138
Godard, Jean-Luc, 22, 34, 65, 85, 115
Goll, Philip, 6
graffiti, 72, 153-154
Griffith, D. W., 103
Grundrisse, 65
Guevara, Ernesto "Che," 57
Gulf War, 165, 166, 172; installations, 164, 173

Happiness (Le Bonheur), 131
Häuser 1–2 (Buildings 1-2), 47, 225
Heidegger, Martin, 5
Heimat, 73, 139
Herbst, Helmut, 130
Here and Elsewhere, 49, 65
Hinderer, Max Jorge, 108
Hiroshima, 147, 212n8
Holert, Tom, 74, 200n43, 212n12
Hollywood, 67, 118-119, 146, 150, 190, 193
Holocaust, 73, 160, 163
Horkheimer, Max, 36, 90
How to Live in the FRG (Leben BRD), 21, 34, 95, 134, 175, 230
How to Remove a Police Helmet (Anleitung, Polizisten den Helm abzurissen), 6, 222
HUAC. *See* U.S. House Un-American Activities Committee

Hüser, Rembert, 50
Huston, John, 120

Ich glaubte Gefangene zu sehen (I Thought I Was Seeing Convicts), 10, 70, 101, 119, 235
ideology, 20, 65, 68, 96, 136; critiques of, 25; Marxist, 57; and media, 159, 185, 193; and myth, 14
Ihre Zeitungen (Their Newspapers), 13, 124, 141-145, 222
Images of the World and the Inscription of War (Bilder der Welt und Inschrift des Krieges), 9-10, 19, 53, 109, 156-164, 229. See also Images–War (Bilderkrieg)
Images–War (Bilderkrieg), 43, 74, 157, 163, 229
I Married a Dead Man, 131
In Comparison (Zum Vergleich), 93, 103-108, 233
independent film production, 5, 7, 18, 139
indexicality, 37, 188, 193; of photography, 46, 126
Indoctrination (Die Schulung), 94, 96-99, 139, 229
Industrial Reserve Army, The (Die industrielle Reservearmee), 34-36
industrialization, 40, 90, 101; "the industrialization of thought," 21
Industrie und Fotographie (Industry and Photography), 8, 81-84, 226
industrielle Reservearmee, Die (The Industrial Reserve Army), 24-36
Industry and Photography (Industrie and Fotographie), 8, 81-84, 226
Inextinguishable Fire (Nicht löschbares Feuer), 6, 15-18, 136, 146-150, 170-176, 181, 222
Ins Universum der technischen Bilder (Into the Universe of Technical Images), 124
Interface(Schnittstelle), 10, 50-53, 137, 161, 171, 235
intertitles, 29, 45, 103, 164, 171
interview, 15, 32, 96, 121-124, 126
Interview: Heiner Müller, 121, 227
Into the Universe of Technical Images (Ins Universum der technischen Bilder), 124

Intolerance, 20, 101, 103
Investigation, The (Die Ermittlung), 121-122
Irish, William, 131
I Thought I Was Seeing Convicts (Ich glaubte Gefangene zu sehen), 10, 70, 101, 119, 235

Jackson, Jesse, 181-183
Jean–Marie Straub and Danièle Huillet at Work on a Film Based on Franz Kafka's "Amerika" (Jean-Marie Straub und Danièle Huillet bei der Arbeit an einem Film nach Franz Kafkas Romanfragment "Amerika"), 84, 85, 130, 136, 227
Jean–Marie Straub und Danièle Huillet bei der Arbeit an einem Film nach Franz Kafkas Romanfragment "Amerika" (Jean-Marie Straub and Danièle Huillet at Work on a Film Based on Franz Kafka's "Amerika"), 84, 85, 130, 136, 227
Jeder ein Berliner Kindl (Everyone a Berliner Kindl), 25-26, 221
Jenzeits der Grenzen: Betrachtungen eine Querkopfs, 92

Kael, Pauline, 112
Kantor, Alfred, 158
Kapital, Das, 59
Kings of the Road, 112
Kittler, Friedrich, 5, 156
Klier, Michael, 74, 119
Klingler, Klaus, 19
Kluge, Alexander, 36, 114
Kohl, Helmut, 150
Kracauer, Siegfried, 25
Kratisch, Ingo, 19, 97, 130
Krenz, Egon, 184
Kuhle Wampe, oder wem gehört die Welt (Kuhle Wampe, or Who Owns the World), 76-78, 114
Kuhle Wampe, or Who Owns the World (Kuhle Wampe, oder wem gehört die Welt), 76-78, 114
Kuleshov, Lev, 158
Kurzfilme von Peter Weiss, 114

Labour in a Single Shot (Eine Einstellung zur Arbeit), 55, 110, 149
Lang, Fritz, 118
Language of Revolution, The (Die Sprache der Revolution), 62, 180-185, 223
Leacock, Richard, 34
Leading Role, The (Die führende Rolle), 184-185, 231
Leben BRD (How to Live in the FRG), 21, 34, 95, 134, 175, 230
Lefkes, Ursula, 5, 188
Lehrstücke (learning plays), 63, 115. See also Bertolt Brecht
Leigh, Walter, 114, 117
Lenin, Vladimir, 181
liberation politics, 57
Lili Marleen, 138
Lorre, Peter (László Löwenstein), 7, 118-119
Lost One, The (Der Verlorene), 121
Lutens, Serge, 84, 158

Mad Love, 119
Mahler, Gustav, 74
Make-Up, 84, 158
"making agitation scientific and politicizing science," 57, 62
Malcolm X. See X, Malcolm
Maltese Falcon, The, 120
Man Is Man (Mann ist Mann), 120
Mann ist Mann (Man is Man), 120
Marat/Sade, 121
Marker, Chris, 43, 165, 214n50
marketing, 13, 27, 153
Marx, Karl, 36, 59, 180
mass media, 36, 44, 147, 157, 185
mass production, 94
Mayakovsky, Vladimir, 27
Meins, Holger, 5-6
memory, 122, 158; constructed, 40, 173; historical, 80, 93; and nostalgia, 82
Mercedes, Rosa (Harun Farocki), 15, 154, 201n59, 226-233
Miéville, Ann-Marie, 49
Minima Moralia: Reflections from Damaged Life, 20

mise-en-scène, 28, 45, 103
Mississippi Mermaid, 131
Mitscherlich, Thomas, 5
Moderatoren im Fernsehen (Moderators), 7, 42, 224
Moderators (Moderatoren im Fernsehen), 7, 42, 224
Modern Times, 103
modernity, 109, 116-117
Monroe, Marilyn, 102
montage, 11-12, 36, 52, 115-118, 162, 172; dialectical, 48; distance, 42, 88, 157-158; of ideas, 81; 86; soft, 22, 65, 171, 177; Soviet, 78. See also Eisenstein, Sergei; Peleshyan, Artavazd
Morris, Norman, 147
Muenzenberg, Willi, 122
Müller, Heiner, 22
Müller, Katrin, 137
multi-screen installation, 21-22
Murdered City, The (Die gemordete Stadt), 48
myth, 14-15, 20, 180, 185, 192-193. See also Barthes, Roland
Mythologies, 14, 25, 62, 180

narrative, 7, 38, 40, 68-71
National Socialism, 77, 119, 126
New German Cinema (NGC), 138
Newman, Paul, 134
Nicht löschbares Feuer (Inextinguishable Fire), 6, 15-18, 136, 146-150, 170-176, 181, 222
Nicht ohne Risiko (Nothing Ventured), 8, 99, 108, 233
Nicolae Ceauscescu, 184
Niggemeyer, Elisabeth, 48
Night and Fog, 83
Norman, Skip, 18, 141
Nothing Ventured (Nicht ohne Risiko), 8, 99, 108, 233
NTCE, 99
Numéro Deux, 49

Oberhausen Manifesto, 139
On Construction in Griffith's Films (Zur Bauweise des Films bei Griffith), 20, 237

On Display: Peter Weiss (Zur Ansicht: Peter Weiss), 7, 114, 121-124, 226
On Literature (Über Literatur), 70
One + One, 85, 154
One-Way Street, 154
operational images, 43, 61, 162-163, 169, 173
operational language, 92, 131, 205n18; and meta-language, 14-15; and revolutionary language, 62, 180
operative images, 14-15, 98, 162, 167-168
optical unconscious, 20, 43, 100, 195. See also Benjamin, Walter
oral history, 70-71
Oskar Langenfeld, 7

pacing, 28, 32, 37
Painters Painting, 45
Pantenburg, Volker, 8
Parallel I-IV, 21-22, 66, 102, 116, 190-195
Paris Commune, 102
Pasolini, Pier Paolo, 154
Paveway, 170-172
Peck, Raoul, 18
pedagogy, 12, 15-16, 57-58
Peleshyan, Artavazd, 11, 42, 157-158, 160, 200n44. See also distance montage
performance, 134-135, 138, 180-181
Peter Lorre: Das Doppelte Gesicht (The Double Face of Peter Lorre), 7, 118-121, 228
Peter Weiss, 7, 114. See also *Zur Ansicht: Peter Weiss* (On Display: Peter Weiss)
Petersen, Wolfgang, 5, 139
Petzold, Christian, 4, 18-19, 31, 130, 139, 201n69, 210n30
photography, 9, 81, 124; and history, 158-159; and painting, 44-46
Pickup on South Street, 186-187
picture puzzle (*Vexierbild*), 37, 87, 148
Pilotinnen, 139
Pressey, Sidney L., 58
propaganda, 169, 183, 187-188, 114
protest, 5-6, 140-141, 143; anti-war, 146, 150-151, 177

Querelle, 112

Rajmann, Matthias, 19
Ralske, Jan, 19
Red Army Faction (RAF), 6
Reichsautobahn, 88
Reichstag, 47
Reifenschneider und seine Frau, Der (The Tirecutter and His Wife), 33, 95
Reimann, Max, 19
Reina Sofia Museum, 108
Reissner, Larissa, 68, 70
Reitz, Edgar, 73, 139
Remember Tomorrow Is the First Day of the Rest of Your Life, 66, 142, 223
Renoir, Jean, 135
Renov, Michael, 95
repetition, 17, 30, 42, 67, 86, 196. See also gestus; *Verfremdungseffekt* (alienation effect)
Resnais, Alain, 83, 211n2
Respite (Aufschub), 74, 163-164, 233
Retour de Martin Guerre, Le (The Return of Martin Guerre), 131
Retraining (Die Umschulung), 61, 97-99, 231
Return of Martin Guerre, The (Le Retour de Martin Guerre), 131
reunification, 3, 98, 184
revolution, 62, 71, 165, 185; and language, 62, 180-184; industrial, 89; in Latin America, 13, 156. See also *Sprache der Revolution, Die* (The Language of Revolution); *Videogramme einer Revolution* (Videograms of a Revolution)
Richter, Gerhard, 37
Riese, Der (The Giant), 119
Rosler, Martha, 147, 177
Rossellini, Roberto, 47
Rudenski, Dyk, 187-188
ruin value, 47
Ruttmann, Walter, 116

Saeger, Willi, 47
Sanders, Helke, 5
Sanders, Helma, 34-35

Sarah Schumann malt ein Bild (Sarah Schumann Paints an Image), 22, 44-46, 225
Sarah Schumann Paints an Image (Sarah Schumann malt ein Bild), 22, 44-46, 225
Sauerbruch Hutton Architects (Sauerbruch Hutton Architekten), 26, 94, 100, 234
Sauerbruch Hutton Architekten (Sauerbruch Hutton Architects), 26, 94, 100, 234
Saussure, Ferdinand de 62
Scaruffi, Piero, 130
Schlacht, Die (The Battle: Scenes from Germany), 22, 121, 225
Schluckebier, 92
Schmitt, Carl, 154; "Theory of the Partisan," 156
Schnittstelle (Interface), 10, 50-53, 137, 161, 171, 235
Schulung, Die (Indoctrination), 94, 96-99, 139, 229
Schütz, Klaus, 114
Seidenstücker, Friedrich, 47
Sekula, Allan, 20, 177
self-reflexivity, 42, 69, 80, 96, 126, 135
Serious Games (Ernste Spiele), 134, 174, 176-177, 238
Siedler, Wolf Jobst, 48
Siekmann, Andreas, 104, 177
Siemens, 102
Silber und das Kreuz, Das (The Silver and the Cross), 20, 24-25, 108-109, 239
silence, 31, 45, 164
silent film, 164, 187
Silver and the Cross, The (Das Silber und das Kreuz), 20, 24-25, 108-109, 239
Silverman, Kaja, 15, 44, 65
Simmel, Georg, 25
Simonoviescz, Andre, 138
simulation, 164, 169, 173, 177, 194
single-channel production, 22
Single: A Record is Being Produced (Single: Ein Schallplatte wird produziert), 84, 226
Single: Ein Schallplatte wird produziert (Single: A Record is Being Produced), 84, 226
16 mm film, 20, 23, 103, 163
Socialist Film Cooperative, 6
Sohn-Rethel, Alfred, 74
solidarity, 78-79, 98, 141, 145
Someday You Will Love Me Too: About the Meaning of Dime Store Novels (Einmal wirst auch Du mich lieben: Über die Bedeutung von Heftromanen), 67, 223
Something Self-Explanatory [15x] (Eine Sache, die sich versteht [15x]), 49, 59, 65-68, 136, 180, 223
Song of Ceylon, 114-118
Sontag, Susan, 154
Spandauer Volksblatt, 13
Speaking about Godard, 16
spectatorship, 32, 120, 146, 166, 171; and shift from analog to digital technology, 15, 177
Speer, Albert, 47. *See also* ruin value
split-screen, 49, 65
Sprache der Revolution, Die (The Language of Revolution), 62, 180-185, 223
Springer, Axel, 6, 124; company, 13
Springer Publishing Company, 13
Stadtbild (View of the City), 46-48, 81, 226
State I Am In, The, 31
Sternberg, Josef von, 119
Still Life (Stilleben), 26, 44, 232
Stilleben (Still Life), 26, 44, 232
Stroheim, Erich von, 112
Struggle with Images: A Critique of Television, The (Die Arbeit mit den Bildern: Eine Telekritik von Harun Farocki), 28, 38, 42, 224
Suhrkamp, 27, 39, 91
super 8 film, 2, 5
surveillance, 62, 90, 101, 119, 156

tabloid, 13, 125, 143
Tag im Leben der Endverbraucher, Ein (A Day in the Life of a Consumer), 26, 98, 226
Tanner, Ronny, 154
Taste of Life, The (Der Geschmack des Leben), 84, 123, 226
technology, 42, 88-90, 126, 184, 192; and education, 149; and the real, 46, 165; therapeutic, 176; of war, 87, 91, 140, 170-174

Teilung aller Tage, Die (The Division of All Days), 17, 59-64, 144, 180, 222
Tel Quel, 65
Their Newspapers (Ihre Zeitungen), 13, 124, 141-145, 222
Third Reich, 3, 47, 88, 183
Tirecutter and His Wife, The (Der Reifenschneider und seine Frau), 33, 95
Towards a Philosophy of Photography (Für eine Philosophie der Fotografie), 124
Trafic, 1, 16
Transit, 139
trauma, 32, 89, 174-175
Tretyakov, Sergei, 62
Trip to Hanoi, 154
Trouble with Images: A Critique of Television, The (Die Ärger mit den Bildern: Eine Telekritik von Harun Farocki), 28-31, 33-34, 36-39, 86, 114, 223
Truffaut, François 131
truth, 36-38, 126, 157; *Kinopravda* (film truth), 107
Turing, Alan, 53
Two Paths (Zwei Wege) 23-25, 221

Über 'Gelegensarbeit einer Sklavin' (About: "Part-time Work of a Slave"), 113
Über Literature (On Literature), 70
Über "Song of Ceylon" von Basil Wright (About Song of Ceylon by Basil Wright), 46, 114-118, 225
Ujica, Andrei, 18, 21, 50, 165, 184
Umfunktionierung (refunctioning), 10, 38
Umschulung, Die (Retraining), 61, 97-99, 231
U.S. House Un-American Activities Committee (HUAC), 120

"Vacuum Cleaners or Machine Guns: A Travelling Cinema for Technologists," 149. See also *Nicht löschbares Feuer* (Inextinguishable Fire)
Varda, Agnés,131, 211n2
Verbundsystem (integrated system), 9-10, 69, 72, 79, 154

Verfremdungstheorie (alienation effect), 17, 52, 120, 136, 138. See also Bertolt Brecht
Vergangenheitsbewältigung, 73
Vergleich über ein Drittes (Comparison via a Third), 103-107, 238
Verlorene, Der (The Lost One), 121
Vertov, Dziga, 107; Academy, 5; the interval, 11, 157-158
Vexerbild (picture puzzle), 20, 37, 56, 87, 148, 159
video games, 52, 175-176, 190-193, 195
Videogramme einer Revolution (Videograms of a Revolution), 21, 50, 165, 181, 184-185, 230
Videograms of a Revolution (Videogramme einer Revolution), 21, 50, 165, 181, 184-185, 230
Vietnam Discourse (Vietnam Diskurs), 121
Vietnam Diskurs (Vietnam Discourse), 121
Vietnam War, 6, 124, 143, 146, 149-150, 153
View of the City (Stadtbild), 46-48, 81, 226
Vigne, Daniel, 131
Virilio, Paul, 5, 156
virtual reality (VR), 21, 162, 172, 175, 193
voice-over, 38, 75, 103, 114, 143, 157
Vrba, Rudolf, 162

Wahlhelfer, Der (The Campaign Volunteer), 5, 140, 221
War and Cinema: The Logistics of Perception, 156
War at a Distance (Erkennen und Verfolgen), 167, 171-173, 223
War Tropes, 21, 177, 240
Warhol, Andy, 45
waste, 54, 79, 106; industrial, 78
Wehner, Herbert, 122
Weimar Republic, 76, 140
Welles, Orson, 112, 135
Wenders, Wim, 112
West Berlin, 54, 98, 140, 143-144, 185
West Deutsche Rundfunk (WDR), 7-8, 28, 41, 149
West Germany, 31, 35, 56, 138-139, 140, 185
Wetzel, Kraft, 127
Wetzler, Alfred, 162

White Christmas, 6, 141-144, 222
Wie man Sieht (As You See), 86-92, 101, 119, 139, 168, 207n48, 228
Wietz, Helmut, 130
Wildenhahn, Klaus, 33, 95
Words of the Chairman, The (Die Worte des Vorsitzer), 6, 140, 145, 221
Workers Leaving the Factory (Arbeiter verlassen die Fabrik) [1995], 21, 52, 101-102, 186, 231
Workers Leaving the Factory [1895], 55, 101-102, 185
Workers Leaving the Factory in Eleven Decades (Arbeiter verlassen die Fabrik in elf Jahrzehnten), 5, 21, 56, 101, 237
World War I, 88, 150
World War II, 71, 121, 124, 152, 162; aftermath, 3, 47, 185-186
Worte des Vorsitzer, Die (The Words of the Chairman), 6, 140, 145, 221
Wretched of the Earth, The, 141

Wright, Basil, 46, 115. See also *Song of Ceylon*; *Über "Song of Ceylon" von Basil Wright* (About *Song of Ceylon* by Basil Wright)
"Written Trailers," 3, 22, 94

X, Malcolm, 181-182

Yella, 31, 99

Zeit, Die 57
Zischler, Hanns, 68
Zum Vergleich (In Comparison), 93, 103-108, 233
Zur Ansicht: Peter Weiss (On Display: Peter Weiss), 7, 114, 121-124, 226
Zur Bauweise des Films bei Griffith (On Construction in Griffith's Films), 20, 237
Zwei Wege (Two Paths), 23-25, 221
Zweites Deutsches Fernsehen (ZDF), 100
Zwischen zwei Kriegen (Between Two Wars), 23, 52-53, 72-84, 136, 225

GPSR Authorized Representative: Easy Access System Europe, Mustamäe tee 50, 10621 Tallinn, Estonia, gpsr.requests@easproject.com

www.ingramcontent.com/pod-product-compliance
Lightning Source LLC
Chambersburg PA
CBHW031238290426
44109CB00012B/352